THE BAD TIMES BIBLE

Dear Tammy,
Welcome to the club!!
I hope you get something out
of this mess of a book!
It sucks that you are going through
this but I know you are one
scrappy lady/health, love and
I wish you that will be just fine.
lotsa power. You aren't alone
darlin.
Lots of Love
Pete

PETER MACKENZIE HAMMOND

ISBN: 1497575680
ISBN 13: 9781497575684

The Legal Stuff.

The author of this book does not dispense medical advice or prescribe the use of any technique as a form of treatment for physical, emotional, or medical problems without the advice of a physician, either directly or indirectly. The intent of the author is only to offer information of a general nature to help you in your quest for emotional and spiritual well - being. In the event you use any of the information in this book for yourself, which is your constitutional right, the author assumes no responsibility for your actions. Now, that being said, if this book changes your life for the better, the author takes full credit and you should tell him so.

We kid, we kid!

To those who have *been* there, those who *are* there and for those who just want to *be* there...

This book is dedicated to you.

Foreword

THIS BOOK WILL change lives.

This book will save lives.

This book will reach those who have never been reached by books.
It will be read by those who don't normally read.
It will touch those who aren't normally touched.

This book should be left in motel rooms, in bar wash-rooms and in hospital waiting rooms.
It should be given away by doctors, therapists and counselors.
It should be broadcast on public television.
It should have its own emergency number. This is 911 in a book.

This book will wash through the streets and cities of pain and distress, cleansing and comforting as it goes.

This book will act like a warm embrace for the scared and suffering, with its powerful messages, one of them being 'You Are Not Alone'.

This book should be read by those enjoying good times, as an act of gratitude, and as an insurance policy if and when the bad times happen (and happen they surely do).
And this book is the one insurance policy that guarantees to pay out when times get tough.

Pete wrote this book as an act of service.

And we must now play our part in this service to others:

By spreading the word in any way we can, by singing its praises to everyone who can no longer sing, to everyone who only feels like crying, to anyone facing difficulty and crisis.

This truly is a Bible for Bad Times. And the time for this bible is now.

John C. Parkin, author of the F**k It books.

Introduction to the BTB

Welcome, you brave reader, you!

Why is it that so many self-help people come off as so damn flaky? Don't raise that eyebrow at me... this is a field manual and I'm just a regular dude.

Why is it that a lot of these "gurus" seem like such fakes? Some of them seem about as sincere as a kiss on the cheek after a kick to the nuts. All right—that may be a *little* harsh—there are lots of *really* great people out there sincerely trying to help others, but you get what I am saying. Or maybe you don't.

What I mean is, where is the book from the regular guy? The one who isn't a multimillionaire in a suit with a big watch and a smile to match on the cover? Where is the book that isn't written by a doctor or some other well-to-do "expert"?

Where is the book written by a regular, nobody like you and me?

Okay, I know you aren't a nobody, don't be too sensitive now. I suppose you could argue that no one wants to read a book written by a nobody, but I'm betting on you readers being real savvy people who know a good tale when you read one.

So speaking as a nobody, I hope this book takes flight. Next thing you know, I'm a best selling, self-published success story, and *then* my friends, *then* I become a *somebody.*

That's when I start acting like a flake, or a giant asshole... I kid, I kid. Speaking of nobody's. The fact of the matter is, we are all going to become *no-bodies* one day, and this scrappy little book is gonna help you get there in awesome style! Wait, that came out all wrong...

So all kidding aside, why did I write this horrible book?

Well, horrible situations call for horrible books...

As a young man I had a nervous breakdown, fell into a deep, terrifying depression and in the midst of that crisis was diagnosed with Hodgkin's disease, a form of cancer. During this period I searched high and low but never found a book that was as raw and insane as the experiences I was having, written by someone who I felt was really coming from ground zero. Someone I could *relate* to.

As a frustrated, scared and angry young man, I just wanted to pick up a book that screamed the truth in a language that spoke to *me.* The books I was seeing were all so... *nice.* If I was feeling like this, surely others were too. Cancer is not polite. Depression is a living nightmare. It's hard to be "spiritual" when you are shitting your pants in fear. Crisis is like having your insides torn to pieces over and over again; most of the time I felt like there was nowhere to turn. So I took notes, wrote a lot and tried to make sense of the craziness I was experiencing.

I wrote this book in the spirit of the angry young man I once was. I would go over my journals and notes and put myself "back there" to fully feel what I had gone through. Even all these years later, it wasn't hard to do. The experiences in this book are so ingrained in me that once I started writing, the crazy kept coming. It was almost like the 21 year old version of me took over and the current version of me disappeared. Freaky.

I wrote this book for that scared, lonely kid I used to be and for those people going through similar experiences right now. I closed my eyes, opened my heart and let that crazy fucker speak to me. That being said, it is important to note that I wrote this book for the young person going through very intense stuff *for the first time*. This is an intro to crisis if you will. The person I was then is very different from the person I am now. I do use a lot of the same exercises and techniques in my life today that are written here, but I am most definitely a different person now. Still crazy, but a different kinda crazy.

You will find that this book has repeating themes. I mention certain things over and over again because I want to drill them into your hearts. In the midst of crisis we don't often think clearly, so please understand that *I know* I repeat certain concepts but that I do this for the benefit of the reader who is in the place *I once was*, and who comes to this book with a less than clear mind.

When I started this project, my goal was to be brutally honest and to be as truthful as I could; I made myself blush more than once writing it. That being said, my primitive attempt at communicating these intimate experiences will at times come off as crass, juvenile, and insulting to some people. For this I do not apologize. I've done what I felt was needed to drive my points home, even if that meant using strong language, rude humor or disturbing images. I hope that people will take the time to look *beyond* the language and into the *heart* of this book.

Besides, if you want to be offended by something in this world, be offended by things that have more weight than swearing. Be offended by things like oppression, violence, starvation, poverty, rape, murder, brutality of all sorts and giant corporations that are destroying our world, *not* by some guy who used curse words while trying to write a book to help people.

Make sense? Right on.

Even though I wrote this book primarily for young men in crisis, please don't be fooled into thinking this material is *only* for the young bucks. I truly believe that this book is for anyone who has an interest in human behavior and in life's struggles, but I sincerely hope this book finds the people who really *need* to read it. It just so happens that I wrote it with the group that I feel is the most vulnerable in mind when it comes to all this emotional touchy feely shit, *the young adult male*, more on that later.

This book isn't just for those people in crisis either.

I have written it for "both sides of the hospital bed." Much of the information in this book is applicable to many people in many different circumstances, male, female, old and young. This is a book about life, something we are all a part of, and I believe there is something for everyone here. If you have a heart beating in your chest, I am sure that something in this book will resonate with you. At least I *hope* something does!

I called this book *The Bad Times Bible* because that is the title I immediately heard in my head when I had an inspired moment in my car (brought on by yet another rough experience in my life) that spurred me to write it. Some may be offended by the use of the word *bible* for obvious reasons but in reality this *is* a holy text of sorts *to me*. I am passionate about my life and the tools and techniques, personal philosophies and ideas that have gotten me this far. What I discuss in this book are things that worked for me that I want to share in the hopes that others may benefit from my experience. I hope that is understood.

It concerns me that our technology is surpassing our humanity. It concerns me that we are so plugged into technology but so tuned out of ourselves. It scares me that so much of our culture exists online and that everywhere you look there is someone glued to a device of some sort.

People go to clubs and then text each other while there. Watch people in the cities. We are literally living with our heads down!

I want to see us get round the campfire again. I want us to share our stories and knowledge like our elders did. Okay, maybe *our* elders shared them over beers in the bar, but you know what I mean.

We gather around big screen TVs and social media sites and that's fine. But let's also do something else. Lets connect with each other the way we used to, *many* moons ago.

In my early twenties I lived on an old farm property and used to have people over for bonfires. We would bullshit each other, tell stories and it was some of the best times ever. There is something primal and very peaceful about getting around a fire. It's even better with friends. What are we here to do anyway? The same as our ancestors—we are here to eat, sleep, procreate and keep repeating the process. I also believe we are also here to share our stories, explore what it is to be human and light the path for others with our experiences.

Simple right?

It can be, but sometimes our lives get sidetracked and/or enhanced by things like sickness and disease. This book is going to act as the proverbial fire for us to get around. I hope it also lights a fire under your ass and in your heart.

Sometimes we get knocked off the path by crisis. When that happens, we are left scrambling, trying to get back on the path again. Sometimes the path gets washed away or *completely* bombed to shit. We then need to build new roads for ourselves. Or build a raft, boat or airplane. Sometimes we just need to sit in the wreckage for a while.

This is not a book about being perfect or having a perfect life. In my opinion there is no such thing. Sometimes when you think you are being knocked *off* of your path you are actually getting knocked back *on* to it. Life can be like that sometimes.

This is a book about being human and about taking an honest look at my own life experiences in the hopes that I could learn from them, grow from the challenges I have experienced, and pass on some things that I feel are helpful. To put it simply, this book is a tool that may help you help yourself, a friend, or a loved one navigate the stormy waters of crisis.

Besides, there is no guarantee that *anything* in this book will help you. There are no guarantees in life aside from the fact we are *all* destined for a dirt nap. I'm simply a human being trying to give back, to do something positive before my light gets put out. If this book suits you, fantastic, if you hate it, leave it on a park bench or in a bathroom stall (like John mentioned in his awesome foreword,) for someone who may benefit from its contents.

I hope the following tale will be worth your valuable time. I also hope this book makes you think, makes you laugh and brings some light into the darkness that may be surrounding you or someone in your life right now. If this book accomplishes that, I will die a happier man for all the craziness I have lived through.

In giving you this book, I give you my heart ladies and gentleman.

Enjoy.

Now let's get to it.

1

AND SO IT BEGINS...

*"The world breaks everyone, and afterward, some
are strong at the broken places."*
ERNEST HEMINGWAY

WELCOME TO YOUR fucking nightmare friend.

I guarantee that no self-help book in the world has ever started with this line. That's why this is a field manual and not a self-help book, right?

Close your eyes for just a second and picture me welcoming you with love in my heart, and a big *knowing* and *understanding* smile on my face. Oh yeah, I'm also giving you a powerful, loving, crushing bear hug. Got it? Good. Sorry if I crushed your smokes. I really wish you'd quit.

Anyway, welcome my friend, to *whatever* crazy experience you are currently going through that brought you to this book. I want to thank you for joining me here to enjoy this tale o' craziness, loss and redemption. Were going to have a *gooood* time!

Sort of...

Even though I have just greeted you with a loving, crushing embrace, (cause that's how I roll,) lets make one thing crystal-clear.

There will be *no* sugar coating here, my good friends. I'm gonna give it to you straight and honest. Cool? All right, lets go.

My name is Pete. I'm not some super successful guy in terms of being cash wealthy, famous or successful in any given profession. I don't have a medical background, a university degree or 500,000 followers on Twitter. *Yet.*

I'm a regular person living a regular life. My last job was driving a side load recycling truck, picking up trash all day—real glamorous, right? I'm just another schmo trying to make his way in the world. I also have a burning desire to help people out, and this just happens to be the shit I know best. It sucks to be me. Continuing on...!

Crisis...what is it? Crisis can be defined as anything that knocks you into the realm of uncertainty and chaos. A cancer diagnosis, a car accident, a divorce, and the time you tried to kiss your roommate in college when you were drunk and confused and he punched you out, the insensitive *bastard*. All of these things can make you feel like you are losing your mind, body and perhaps your life.

Anyone experiencing the white knuckle hell ride known as crisis knows it's no walk in the park. It isn't easy or fun and sure as hell doesn't feel very "spiritual" at first. Before we go any further into this book lets just take a minute to address the "S" word for a second shall we? I'll give you my two cents on the topic so you will understand where a brother is coming from and then we will move on.

The mere mention of spirituality to some people brings rolling eyes, crossed arms and shaking heads, *especially* from men. Some think that spirituality consists of naval gazing and browsing new age bookstores filled with books on magical concepts and all kinds of "nonsense". Well, sometimes it is I suppose, but lets go deeper into this.

Dropping the "S" word may bring images to mind of tortured souls travelling to India to "find themselves" or perhaps visions of monks dressed in robes, meditating, chanting, and burning incense on top of a mountain in Tibet. Maybe they think of Oprah dressed in white, surrounded by flowers interviewing the latest bestselling "guru" who's book is going to change your life. Insert your own image and/or definition here.

To *me*, being spiritual is what we do by default, as I believe we are spiritual beings having a human experience here on earth. To *me*, it's not so much the case that we are trying to *learn* how to be "spiritual" or how to become enlightened, as much as it is that we are trying to *remember* that we are spiritual beings trapped in these lower vibrational meat suits, wandering the earth trying to find our way home or *back* to the source of the energy that runs our bodies that we have all seemingly been separated from, forgetting that the portal that connects us to that source and to each other is thumping away in our chests, *if we could only close our eyes and sit still for a damn minute.*

Sorry, went a little deep a little there, I'll warn you next time.

To *me*, enlightenment means you are just trying to drop the big bag of heavy, scary shit you may be carrying, or to simply stop being a slave to your own mind. Which is *far* from being a simple task right?

To *me*, doing spiritual work means that you are trying to understand or perhaps un-burden yourself from that which troubles you in your heart. It means trying to light up the world and *lighten the hell up!*

Spirituality or having a spiritual practice to me is not so much about "achieving" anything as it is *experiencing* a sense of peace, gratitude and perhaps feelings of happiness, contentment and compassion in the *present* moment. It is about recognizing that the nasty, disturbing things in us have as much value as the good vibes we chase, and it is about showing up every day willing to be slaughtered once more. I have come to learn that the path of healing or enlightenment is a journey, not a destination. You are *never* finished. It is work and it is sometimes *very* hard and it is an absolute worthwhile use of your time in my opinion. How you get "there" is up to you, should you want or need to even go "there". Here's a hint, if it makes your heart swell, it's a path out of hell!

Finally, in my world, being a "spiritual" person means you pay attention to the inner life. You nurture that thing that some people call your *spirit*. Hell, anything you do coming from your heart is spiritual! But that is just how this kid sees it.

Now that we got *that* out of the way, we can move on!

When crisis hits, it is terrifying, shocking, unnerving and we are typically unprepared for it. If we're lucky, we have good friends, family and resources around to help us navigate the shit storm. Now if you are a miserable bastard, this is a *great* chance at a new beginning. Funny thing is, assholes usually don't get sick—they live forever and end up looking like an angry piece of human beef jerky that just radiates misery and cynicism. Truth be told, those people do at least get their anger out. They bleed the poison. But we will get back to that later.

Even if friends and family surround you when crisis hits, it doesn't mean the ride is going to be any smoother. Sometimes it actually makes things worse. All the unwanted attention, questions, uncomfortable moments and general annoying bullshit that go along with being the poor bastard in trouble can be quite unsettling. Nobody likes being the center of attention and honored guest at the pity party. Well, *some* do, okay, *many* do, but that ain't you I hope. That being said, it's important to remember that when it comes to the stress and emotional impact a cancer diagnosis brings, you could say the whole family gets cancer. Not just the patient. You are all in this together. It could be argued that being alone in stressful times might make it easier. But what *can't* be argued in this world is the fact that kittens are cute as hell, but this isn't a book about kittens, so let's continue.

The absolute *best* thing about being in crisis is that it presents a fantastic opportunity to start over. The Chinese characters for crisis mean *danger* and *opportunity*. Stop rolling your eyes at me and read on before you judge. I don't think this is unreasonably optimistic, nor something I'm saying just to keep myself from climbing a tower with a high-powered rifle. It is a cold hard fact and I stand by it. There is *no better time* to completely examine your life than when it is on fire. If your life was a house, crisis is like a house fire. My suggestion is grab the shit that really means something to you and let that house burn. Enjoy the pretty flames and start thinking about pouring the next foundation. To push the house fire analogy even further, this book is going to help you become the firefighter, the investigator, *and* the contractor who will all deal with that burning house that is currently your life. But let's start with the first steps. Life has just punched you in the face. *Hard*. What do you do?

Well, first we need to take stock. We need to gather information about the truck that just ran us over. Did we get the plate number? Are there any witnesses who can tell us what happened? Was it our fault? Did anyone else get hurt? Are you gonna eat that burrito?

When you get terrible news, the first thing most people feel is shock. You simply can't process the information. You just sit there like an idiot and try to make sense of what just happened. The next thing you realize is that your life is never going to be the same again.

Let me stop you right there and save you many hours of wasted time. *Your life is never going to be the same again.* Go to a mirror and say it to yourself in a matter of fact tone:

"My life is never going to be the same again."

You could also add, "*And that's okay*" at the end of it. Now we move on.

When we receive terrible news, it is human nature to try and "undo" it somehow. We struggle with it in our minds. Accept that things are going to be different and that you are going to have a huge hand in it. That is step one. Unless you have an actual time machine, shit isn't going to change. If you did have a time machine, you might go back in time and screw something up that messes your life up even worse in the future, so there's *that* danger. Your life can only change moving forward. Okay, it can also change while sitting quite *still* for all you members of the meditation nation.

But you get what I mean.

I know it feels next to impossible to avoid this but, *try* not to torture yourself with "what ifs" and all that business. You may go through all sorts of scenarios of how things could have been different leading up to the moment you received the news that has rocked you. That is a totally normal reaction to have. But just stay in *this* moment and with what is happening *right now*. You have a brain tumor? Okay, what now? You get it.

Easy? No. There will be a time to grieve the death of your old life and way of living and thinking, but for now, let's take some *action*. Deep inside you is a reserve of strength and resolve you didn't know existed. Trust me, its there. Dig into it and lets keep going.

When you receive earth-shattering news of any sort, it is in this lunatic's opinion that you have got to get to work dealing with the situation right away *before* the situation starts to deal with you, if you catch my drift.

My background is in having had cancer and mental illness in the form of depression and anxiety disorder. I have experienced both of

these situations as a patient and I have been the caregiver in such scenarios as well. I have also been in car wrecks, had shit jobs and some bad
relationships, but for the purposes of this book I'll be drawing upon my
cancer and mental illness experiences. The information and suggested
exercises in this book can apply to pretty much *any* stressful situation in
life, but I will be talking primarily about cancer and how to deal with that
party of a situation. Come to think of it, the relationships weren't *that*
bad, I have dated fine women, but that's another book.

So let's start with the cancer diagnosis. You look up and see that the
truck that just hit you is being driven by a tumor that's now driving away,
laughing at you and grabbing at its crotch, telling you to *"suck it!"*

Take a DEEP breath.

Now take 10 more. Get used to doing this, friend.

Before you get the cancer diagnosis, you might already be feeling
some ill effects, although this is not always the case. Sometimes the disease gets discovered through an injury, a blood test or routine examina-
tion. My cancer was found by accident, but we will get to that later.
It goes without saying that whatever the case may be, this part of the
experience can be especially stressful and terrifying. The initial discovery
of cancer leads to a battery of tests where they do strange, alien autopsy-
type shit to your body. The medical teams will use different tests and
procedures to rule out where the cancer is and isn't.

Some of these procedures are surgical and invasive. Some are non-
invasive but just as stressful, so during this initial period it is good to have
two things.

First, you need a really good friend or family member who will be
the information gatherer, driver, and the person you can ask, *"I know I'm
a pain in the ass but can you please go get me a drink of water?"* I suggest that
you avoid asking your girlfriend, wife or partner unless they can be rock

solid and not all grabby and scared and more stressful than helpful. I'm not picking on the loved ones or the ladies. Women are fierce; they push babies out of their vaginas and did that in fields and caves without pain meds. I truly love and respect women. I am just making a point that I'll go into more deeply later in the chapter called, "How to be a Kick Ass Friend". However, should you happen to be blessed with a partner who can handle being the rock for you, you should immediately fall to your knees, kiss them squarely on their ass and thank them from the bottom of your heart. 'Nuff said.

When I was going through the testing phase, I was lucky enough to have both of my parents involved. I know I'm lucky to have both parents in my life *period*. My mother, a former nurse, was great during the meetings with the doctors, but in waiting rooms she was so stressed out that I could feel it radiating off of her. I spent my time worrying about her and how she was feeling. It only increased my stress and reminded me of how terrible I felt for putting my parents through this insanity.

Believe me, I am grateful to have the type of mother who would do that for me, don't get me wrong. If you have *any* sort of positive relationship with your mother, good luck keeping her away at a time like this. What I am saying is that it is crucial to have a person who is going to go with you to your appointments and gather intel on what is happening. It is also way better if that person is calm. If that person is too close to you, it may be harder for them to stay objective and clear-headed.

If you don't have someone to go with you, take a little tape recorder or take notes. It's a good idea for two reasons. First off, this will allow you to stay focused and in the moment without worrying about missing or forgetting any potentially crucial information. The second reason to record these sessions is that this action is a means of asserting control over yourself and what's happening to you. Today's cell phones have recording capability; so take advantage of that feature to keep all the important information on file.

Being drugged and fucked with surgically makes it hard to remain on top of your game, so having someone there to drive your ass around and take notes will help the most. You, my friend, should be busy spending that time learning how to control your breath and your emotions. It is imperative that you stay as calm and relaxed as possible during this time. Focusing on what is going on in the present and not projecting your thoughts too far into the future is extremely important. I know that seems impossible, but there is no need to freak yourself out anymore than you already might be. Again, if you don't have someone to drive you around or be with you, don't panic.

During treatment, the only period I had someone with me was during the exploratory surgery and testing phase. When treatment started, I needed to be alone. As much as it sucked to be alone in some ways, I found it harder to deal with the emotions of those around me during treatment. I was messed up enough inside and didn't need any more stress. I have always felt people's energy and emotion very deeply and during treatment I found it was simply too overwhelming to be around those who were concerned or worried for me. If you have to, you can do this alone. I promise you.

There may be times however, when you are feeling the side effects of treatment, or are physically incapable of driving after a surgery that you will need a driver. Make sure you have someone at the ready. See if there are services in your area that can help you out. There is always the Facebook shout out too I suppose.

When I was diagnosed with cancer, the first thing I did was call a family meeting. Before I talk about the meeting, let me give you the background of how the wheels came off my happy wagon.

I was back living at home then, because I had experienced a nervous breakdown at my warehouse job. The breakdown happened after treating my body and mind like shit with drugs, alcohol and angry thoughts and not being able to handle it. So lets stop right there.

This next part is for the eyebrow raising douche bag that is thinking right now, "Nervous breakdown? Fucking pussy."

Sigh… for the non-ignorant reader, skip down a few paragraphs to the one so eloquently and tastefully titled "Enter the Shit Storm," while I make things clear to our ignorant friend. Consider the following to be an open letter to meatheads and insensitive bastards everywhere. Or maybe to the part of *you* that on some level feels this way towards yourself. Its cool, I've been there too.

I have encountered this tough guy attitude many times and have always tried to set their owners straight. These attitudes really need to be addressed. Oh, and all you tough guys please remember, I'm doing this because I love you and want to see you shine like the beautiful little sun I know you can be.

Dear Tough Guy,

First of all, what the fuck are you doing reading this book? If you are such a badass, you shouldn't need this book right? Save your judgment for jury duty.

Mental illness has very little to do with toughness or will. When your chemicals are fucked, they are fucked. You can be a tough guy and "handle your business" any way you want, but to face that shit head on when you don't feel you have a "head" at all is a tall order for anyone.

I have worked with, and met some really tough, solid dudes in my life, especially during my time working as a doorman. Getting to know some of these guys made me realize that no one is safe from pain and suffering in this world. No one is bulletproof. The myth of the heroic superman is just that, a myth. After spending time talking with and getting to know these guys, I realized that a lot of them were sensitive, big-hearted people. In my opinion, this is the exact quality that made them so powerful. Yes, there are real psychos out there, but most times they have very little if any really close relationships and you can spot them a mile away and avoid them.

The "tough guys" I met working as a doorman gave a shit about people, especially the ones they loved, and god help you if you did anything to jeopardize that. There were many guys who thought they were ten feet tall and bulletproof who had their asses handed to them and left the bar in shame or in a crumpled heap after being exposed for the morons they were. Their mouths wrote checks their bodies couldn't cash and some paid dearly.

It doesn't shock me that so many young men these days use weapons or fight in packs. Even though I don't think fighting is the answer most times, (there are times when violence is unavoidable) when words and diplomacy fail, I do have more respect for those who have enough honor to stand alone and handle their business with their hands and know when the other guy has had enough. A coward uses a knife or a gun. A coward needs ten of his friends to help him handle his business with one person. A bar fight used to be a relatively harmless right of passage for the young male, now people are getting killed for no reason. It is pathetic and sad to read about people getting killed or seriously injured because of these circumstances. It really is.

Some of my buddies are professional mixed martial artists who could literally beat people to death if they wanted to, with their bare hands. They are all incredibly intelligent, dedicated, passionate and humble dudes. They don't walk around in TAPOUT gear and talk shit. They are the real deal. The "tough guys" who roll into our gym usually last about a class or two because their ego can't handle the fact they are getting smashed and controlled by people half their size and weight.

The true "tough" guys are men with love in their hearts for their friends, teammates and have a passion for life in general. I will talk later about the power of love but for an easy demonstration of said power, go and grab a cute little bear cub away from its mother. See what happens. Man I'm sensitive, must be the diaper rash. That's called self-deprecating humor. Google that shit.

You have got to lose the tough guy attitude. That attitude tells me and everyone else around you that:

A: You are afraid on some level of being exposed or hurt. Or you are just afraid of the situation you are in. Which is cool. Shit happens. You'll get over it.

B: You are ignorant, which means you are probably not that smart, or maybe you're the product of a shitty environment. Not really your fault and you can change. Hit the books; expand your mind as much as you hit the weights or the bottle and see how your life changes.

C: You are insecure. 'Nuff said.

In my experience, without heart and soul and a healthy dose of humility, you can't successfully navigate the deep waters of life. You'll eventually drown in your own ignorance, ego and ultimately your own loneliness, grasping for a clue and wondering what the fuck just happened.

If it isn't you in the meat grinder, it's gonna be someone you love, and being a tough guy only matters in fights or if you are actually a straight male ballet dancer or figure skater. So spare me the "I can handle anything" bullshit because brother I promise you some day—especially if you are a soulless douche bag, bottom feeder, waste of human flesh with a faux hawk—life will eventually bring you to your knees.

Then, and only then, will you know what it is to be in dire need of compassion and grace. I'm not talking about what you say before you stuff your cakehole before dinner at grandma's house, either. So if you are going to be a wise ass, put this book down, better yet, read on and learn something. Maybe I can help.

Back to the point. See! Told you I loved you and want the best for you! I honestly really do, but you *know* I had to take a little poke at you.

Enter The Shit Storm.
So losing my mind at work wasn't pretty.

I had a psychotic break that had me run from the warehouse, through the offices, and ended with me locked in the boardroom, curled into the fetal position on top of the table with the lights out and speaking in tongues. Yes, that happened. I snapped. My cheese had finally slipped off the cracker.

An understanding supervisor who is still a good friend and a *beautiful* human being who's name starts with a K and rhymes with "scary", signed me off on "sick leave." Feeling like I was well out of my goddamn mind, I called my mom and asked if I could come home to figure out what was wrong. My family was kind enough to let me bring my big bag of crazy into their house to try and get better.

Things didn't get better. I was a complete basket case. The doctors I saw all had different ideas as to what was wrong. I couldn't sleep; I was losing weight and was really paranoid, anxious and depressed. I couldn't leave the house. It was a big deal when I walked around the block by myself without feeling like I was going to die.

Clinical depression isn't feeling sad and eating chocolate ice cream on the couch like a teenage girl. It's not a self-esteem problem. I have always had good self-esteem. For me, clinical depression was like being possessed by demons. It was terrifying. I have had cancer, been a doorman in the Yukon facing off against coked-up miners, I've dated Irish Italian girls, been in horrible car crashes and have worked in a daycare. As scary as those experiences were, they don't come close to the terror and bleakness I felt dealing with depression. The only thing scarier than mental illness is stand-up comedy, and we all know those motherfuckers are all *nuts* right?

The point is, I would gladly go through cancer again rather than deal with the mental illness. I know all you hard-core cancer patients are freaking out right now. Take a breath. I'll elaborate further later on, for now just take my word for it and remember this is *my* experience I'm talking about, not yours.

To make matters worse, I developed severe chickenpox. Go ahead and laugh asshole, I'll find you and turn you into a hand puppet, and I have big hands. I was 21 and it sucked horribly. I was pretty far out of my mind, spending most of my days hiding in the furnace room in the basement of my parent's house. That was where I could be upset and no one would find me. When I wasn't hiding in the basement or in my room, I was in the depression day program in the hospital psych ward. THAT was a lot of fun.

It was seriously like being in an alternate universe where your worst fears have come true. I was in a room with people who were as sick as, or worse than, I was. The worst part was the staff made us all walk together to the lunchroom and people would stare at the drooling gaggle of us. We were an interesting bunch, for sure. It was humiliating to be in that program and I always worried that I would run into someone I knew.

That being said, I also learned a great deal about how mental illness has torn people, families and lives apart while in that program. There were people from all stages, ethnicities, and all walks of life in that room. Rich people, poor people, men and women alike. I was humbled by the strength and resilience I witnessed while listening to all their stories. These were some *very* brave, *very* tough people to be able to wake up everyday to the nightmare that their lives had become, and *still keep trying to make themselves better.*

These were powerful teachers who didn't even know it.

Things continued to worsen. At one point, I seriously thought malevolent forces were trying to kill me or I was cursed. I'm not even religious but I went so far as to call a friend of the family who was a priest and got a purification ritual performed on me. That's one step down from an exorcism, you should know.... Yeah, I was bat-shit crazy, baby. Crazy and *desperate.*

So the chickenpox was kicking my ass and making me even crazier than I was already feeling. I developed a fever and ended up going to the hospital burning up with a *raging* temperature. I was starting to see things that weren't there. When I finally saw a doctor, they told me that I had chicken pox and to go home. Pissed off, I started to leave when some old doctor came out, stopped me and asked the intake nurse if I had chickenpox, and then asked how old I was.

Apparently, for adults with chickenpox, there is a high risk of viral damage to the organs or something like that. He then sent me right up to get an X-ray, which revealed a mass in my chest--this led to more tests and the eventual cancer diagnosis. Chickenpox saved my sorry ass. Correction, chickenpox and one wise and wily old doctor who actually gave a shit.

That story is weird on so many levels. For that doctor to come out at that exact time was weird. For him to single me out in that room was even weirder. The fact that he disappeared in a blaze of pure white light, leaving all of us in that waiting room, crying and filled with a sense of love and peace is even crazier. Okay, so the last thing didn't happen but even if it did, you wouldn't have believed me anyway, you cynical bastards!

Shock and Awe

So what was it like to receive the news that I had cancer? My honest answer is that I felt a sense of relief. Yes folks, I felt relief at first. You see; I was suffering from depression, anxiety and panic attacks. I spent my days drowning in anxiety and fighting off horrific thoughts and feelings. I had begun to think that I was *never* going to get better and that I had somehow lost my mind for good. I really felt my mind was broken and that my soul was dirty and tainted forever.

People close to me were scared for me and some were scared *of* me. I spent my time trying to figure out what was wrong with me and thinking about blowing my head off. I couldn't see a way out. I felt like I had dishonored my family, my friends and myself. I felt like I had let *everyone* down. I was convinced that I had ruined my life and that the best solution was to jump off a bridge or crash my car. I really didn't believe I could get better. There was no light or hope and yet I was too much of a coward to kill myself. Yes, I think it takes as much guts to kill yourself as it does to live when you are sick in the head. Do I think it is right? No. You hurt all those around you and nothing has changed. Except for you are no longer a meat suit owner/operator.

I thought about suicide to get some relief.

When the cancer diagnosis came I was relieved—I now had a way out that was *honorable* in my mind. If I killed myself, I felt that I would shame and hurt my family and friends. But if cancer took me out, while sad, it would be much more socially acceptable and in my mind, *easier* on my family to deal with. This made me feel better and it also made me decide to try even harder to get my life together.

On a side note, if you talk badly about someone who has committed suicide, even though it is probably your anger or pain talking, I *really* hope you did as much talking and more importantly as much *listening* to that person while they were still alive. I also hope you tried to convince them to get help. It's pretty easy to judge and condemn from afar; it isn't so easy to stay close to someone and be there with that person while they try to find their way through the mess of mental illness. I'm just sayin'.

Back to the family meeting.

My family was gathered around the kitchen table. I didn't really know what to do or say but I said something like this:

"Okay guys, this is a really weird, surreal and difficult situation for all of us, but all I ask is that you respect what I have to say. If I say I don't want to talk, that truly means I don't want to talk. If I am upset and ask to be left alone that is what I want. Please respect my choices."

So that was step one.

I just wanted to regain a sense of control, seeing as how I had lost my job, my apartment, my mental health and now my physical health, too. I wanted to control what I could, and I wanted to let everyone know that I was going to call the shots.

So call a family meeting and let them know what you want and don't want. Let them know the limits and the boundaries you are comfortable with. If you are on your own, tell whoever is closest to you, *even if it is just the cat*. You know how pushy they get around feeding time.

Family and friends often feel powerless in these situations and try hard to be helpful. Sometimes they try a little too hard and this can be suffocating and tough when all you want to do is rest and spend some quiet time alone. So tell them what they can do. The same applies to friends. Tell them what you need and don't need. This is not a time to fuck about and pussyfoot around peoples' feelings. You need to take control of your life and your situation immediately. Speak plainly and they will understand. If you have never put yourself first in your life, *now* is the time to do so.

Taking control starts with your environment—your family and friends are a big part of that. Don't be an asshole about it. Always be respectful. The people that love you are going to be hurting too, and you will at different times need to be the rock for them.

People will appreciate the guidance from you because trust me, it gets weird when you get sick. It was terrible when I had the nervous breakdown; it was like I was dead. Mental illness is scary to others, they run from it like the plague. I understood and quite frankly, I was so messed up, I felt I was better off alone.

When I had cancer I would see friends sometimes and they would not know what to do or say. I had to constantly be the one opening up the lines of communication and showing them the way. It sucks, but it goes with the territory of taking control. I know it is *really* hard to do when you are out of your mind and stressed out or sick as a dog from treatment, but you have sometimes got to tell people what you do and don't need.

Got it? Great, lets move on. *"Wait!"* you are screaming:

"You assume that I can even talk to my friends and family?"

Good point. Wait a minute! What's that behind you there? Oh look! It is a giant neon flashing sign shaped like an arrow pointing at another giant neon flashing sign that says:

"THERE IS AN OPPORTUNITY FOR HEALING FOR ALL OF YOU HERE!!! PLEASE TAKE ADVANTAGE OF IT!"

Sickness and being in crisis offers a powerful opportunity for everyone involved to drop all the games and all the bullshit and get right down to the business of living and being truly alive. It takes courage to be honest with people when talking about how you feel or how they make you feel, but it is a necessary step to take in my opinion. It also takes a lot of energy to play those games with yourself and with the people in your life. You may find yourself lacking in the energy department while going through treatment so don't waste it on games and bullshit.

It's simply not worth it. Ever.

Now is the perfect time to start being honest with yourselves and the ones you love. Hell, with *everyone* in your life, period!

Stop pointing fingers. There is a great Native American saying that says when you point a finger at someone, three point back at you. Think about that for a minute.... Stop laying blame and start talking to each other. Trust me, you don't want to be the person at the funeral that says they wished they could have said (insert whatever you want here) but now Jimmy, Dad, Mom, Uncle Frankie, etc. is dead and I now am left with all this pain!!

Conversely, if it's you who is on the way out, you don't want to exit the meat cage with unfinished business, things left unspoken and feelings unexpressed. Maybe *you* do, but I personally think that would suck.

Not only will it make your physical death more unpleasant and trying than it has to be, but you run the risk of coming back as a ghost on some reality TV program with some asshole trying to connect you to your loved one to do *what you guys should have done while still living on the earth plane!* No offense to those shows, I have enjoyed them myself quite a few times. In my world, asshole can be and is oftentimes, a term of endearment.

That's just embarrassing for all of us. Again, no offense to those people, but it *is* awkward, right? Avoid all that, be the person who drops it all and opens the lines of communication. At the very least, write a letter to those people you want to connect with.

Make a video that expresses how you feel—maybe one day you will be able to sit and do it in person. Easier said than done? Not really. The beautiful thing about serious illness is the powerful feeling of *"Well fuck it, I'm gonna say what I gotta say because I might not be around to say it!"* that comes with it. I find being sick is kind of like being really drunk, you turn into an asshole or you tell everyone you love them.

When your life is threatened by sickness, things become much more clear. The ridiculousness of our ego and its battles with our hearts and minds become exposed as the frauds and the waste of precious time that they are in the face of a life threatening illness.

If you are lucky, or if you decide to embrace this opportunity to change your life and magic happens, your eyes and heart get ripped open and the truth comes marching into your heart like drunk Irishmen into a pub on St. Paddy's day, loud, messy and unruly.

But ultimately good intentioned, right boys?

So take another *biiiiiig* breath and let it out. Keep repeating this, and let's move on.

———— ∞ ————

2

TOOLS FOR THE TRIP

*"Give me six hours to chop down a tree and I will
spend the first four sharpening the axe."*
ABRAHAM LINCOLN

GET A BACKPACK, man-satchel, ex Special Forces duffel bag, whatever. You are going to need tools and other things for this little adventure you're going on. Make sure it's something you can take everywhere, because it is going to be with you everywhere you go. Once you have selected your backpack, school bag, etc., get a notebook too.

Get a really nice pen, because you are going to be doing a lot of writing. No excuses—you will write if you *really* want to dig in and gain from this experience, in a really deep and meaningful way, no less. Don't worry that you aren't a "writer." I am not asking for *War and Peace* here, just an effort made to jot some shit down. That notebook is going into your backpack and that backpack is going to go with you everywhere, just to remind you once more of course.

I will be making suggestions as to what to write about we go along, but for now it is essential to get a notebook and a pen and get ready to write your ass off. The best part of crisis is the whole "getting to know yourself" thing. The best way to start *that* process is to write. I don't care if it is just gibberish, but you must write. No hands? Write with your feet. Can't write? Use a tape recorder to get your crazy monkeys back into their cages. This part is non-negotiable. You will be downloading your shit old school into that (those) notebook(s) every day, many times a day. Why? Because writing helps give us...wait for it... *a sense of control!*

From the minute the shit hits the fan, thou shalt be writing. I don't want to hear:

"I can't, I'm too stressed out to write right now."

That's like saying you are too thirsty to drink. The best time to sit and write stuff down is when you feel like you are going to lose it. I don't want to hear,

"I have a learning disability."

Too bad. I don't care if it looks like a three-year-old howler monkey did the writing. This isn't a test and no one is ever going to see this. You will write.

Oh yeah, before we continue, know that when I say notebook, I mean a real notebook. I don't mean a laptop or any electronic bullshit. I am talking pen and paper. Why? Let me count the reasons:

1. You don't need a lot of money to buy a notebook or a pen. They're also easier to steal.
2. They are portable and don't need a power source.
3. They don't catch viruses and then refuse to work.

4. Occasionally I am going to get you to do exercises that require you to write things down and then burn them. You want to do that with a laptop? Be my guest.

5. You won't be distracted by clown porn and never get to writing. Use the porn as a reward for writing.

6. There is something intimate, immediate and sacred about writing with a pen into a notebook.

Spend time getting to know those words; they won't be seen in Guns 'N Ammo or Fight! Magazine, but they are as powerful as anything you will find there. Don't kid yourself pal. Writing allows us to get closer to ourselves more quickly. When I say closer I mean it is easier to get clearer about "the situation." I don't mean that douche bag from that show on the idiot box, either.

You are going to figure out who you are and who you aren't at this time in your life and what in the hell is happening to you. It is going to make the chaos a little easier to endure, because clarity brings a sense of calm, and understanding. Whether you are writing about learning a submission at the dojo, or writing about the madness in your head, clarity makes you feel better, and this in turn makes your situation easier to understand and experience. Capiche?

Besides, this may be the first time you even *think* about this stuff. Writing is awesome and good for you. That's a fact.

START THE DAY OFF…. WRITE!!

Begin every day with a big glass of fresh water and with three pages in the notebook. I don't care if it is gibberish. I don't care if it is the same line over and over. (*Pete is a dipshit, this is stupid. Pete is a dipshit, this is stupid….*) Just write for three pages—it gets all the random, annoying mental clutter out of the way. Occasionally, you will hit a vein of insight and powerful stuff will just come *ripping* out of you. Write and you will feel better. Writing is also a good way to start the day because you are:

A. Telling your brain what to do.

B. Directing your focus and energy and not waiting for anxiety to direct you.

C. Taking control of yourself and dictating the course and feel of the day.

For those of you that need a little more direction or structure, you can include these topics in your daily journaling:

Daily Goals: What are your goals for the day? Is it to not give in to fear or anxiety and run screaming down the street or jump off a bridge? Is it to make someone feel better? Is it to laugh even though you feel like screaming? Write down some daily goals and then try to accomplish them. *Try* is the operative word here. I get that you are under enough stress as it is.

Yesterdays Victories: What happened yesterday that you felt was a "win?" Did you accomplish any of the previous day's goals? Put them down and feel good about them you bastards!

The Gratitude List: I know you may be too freaked out to start thinking of this and there is an entire chapter dedicated to it, BUT make a simple entry in your journal everyday listing the things, people, feelings and thoughts you are grateful for. Whatever you feel grateful for. Start making a list. Trust me, it helps.

If you feel you need to go into detail, do it. Writing lots about what you are grateful for is good medicine for the soul. It takes us out of ourselves and that alone is a way to relieve pressure. Want to take it further?

Write a letter to the people you feel gratitude towards and send it to them. Imagine receiving a letter in the mail from a friend telling you how grateful they are to have you in their lives. Yeah, pure awesomeness. So do it yourself!

You are mining for energy when you write; at the same time, you are releasing energy. It is great exercise for your brain and your soul.

So when you wake up, get your brain onto the treadmill and take out the trash. What other exercise lets you clean up your head and gain insight at the same time? Well, I guess real exercise and yoga. Like you guys are going to do yoga.... Truth is, yoga is good for you and you meet beautiful women there, but hey, *don't do it*.

I like to go to Brazilian Jiu-Jitsu, that's my happy place; to each their own. No comments needed about rolling around with dudes either, please and thank you. It's too easy. Moving on....

There is something else about the journaling thing. There are no mistakes; it is all about clearing the memory banks. Forget the years of programming about being nice, polite, coloring inside the lines and all that shit. Write from the heart and let it flow. Be wild, be fearless, and be *honest*, even if it feels bad or wrong or embarrassing at first. Just don't judge it, don't correct it and above all, don't write thinking about how it "looks" to anyone else. If you are really paranoid about someone reading your innermost thoughts, write them out, read them out loud and then burn them. Writing out our fears, reading them out loud and then burning them is a nice little ritual to get into. It feels good to do it. Be careful though. Don't burn down the house.

Burning things in order to create new life is a part of nature. Fires are the reason forests are continually regenerated. Fires burn up all the decaying, dead vegetation on the forest floor, clearing the way for new growth. Some species, such as the jack pine, even rely on fire to spread their seeds. The jack pine produces resin-filled cones that are very durable. The cones remain dormant until a fire occurs and melts the resin.

Then the cones pop open and the seeds fall or blow out. Maybe we aren't so different from those jack pine cones. Writing down and burning all the things that may be "decaying" our spirits clear the way for new energy, and maybe a fresh perspective. Maybe we need a little fire (crisis) to burn off the things that are keeping us from growing. But again, when burning anything, please take the necessary precautions to stay safe. Be careful you little bastards!

I remember writing about how I felt like a coward because of the fear I was feeling. It made me feel terrible to read it at first. But after writing about it in depth, I began to see many things that helped me realize I wasn't a coward, but a person completely out of their element. It helped to get it out and get it on the page, and yes, it felt *great* to burn what I wrote sometimes.

So get it out and get it down on paper. It doesn't have to make sense. It just has to be done. Period. Writing is an incredible tool and a fantastic habit for all of us. It is the poor man's shrink and the wise man's best friend. Write, you bastards! Write!! Then have another big glass of water and smile because you have started the day off…. wait for it, WRITE! Yeah, yeah I can hear you.

Remember to get a good hiding place for your notebook if you are leaving it out of the backpack. This is a sacred text that is for you and you only. Do not lose it because you will feel even worse than you already do when your idiot friends find it. Hide that little bastard. Well, I suppose you could leave it for your lady to find and she might think you are a real sensitive sweetheart and all of a sudden it's on like Donkey Kong, swinging from the vines and all that….

Now that I have put all that pressure on you to write I must also add that it is always good to take in the moment too. I like a combo of both. Sitting there, looking around and taking things in as they come, and also making time to write. I like capturing insights about my life and working things out on paper, but don't rob yourself of simple moments either.

Find the balance that works for you. You will see that "who you are" can change quickly and often in life.

When you write, you capture your journey on paper and it's interesting to look back on further down the road. Emotions and feelings are like ghosts, you may feel them but you can't see them and they aren't really tangible. You make them real by using words to express them and bring them into the "real" world. Some say that *all* words are lies, but we won't go into that just yet.

I suppose that it could be argued that chasing our feelings is a little like chasing a ghost, but in the crisis experience, especially if you are young and just starting to figure out the world, I feel writing is a powerful habit to develop, if even to just be used as a coping tool or a way to get your head clear of the clutter while you go through this shit. You could even say that writing is a way to get those emotional "ghosts" to stop haunting you. Exorcise their asses!

So now you've got your backpack, your first journal and your pen(s). You are suiting up for the journey.

Speaking about suiting up—this may be funny to some people, but I am a big believer in crisis clothing. What is this crisis clothing I speak of? Well, gather up a chair and I will tell you my sweet, messed-up friend.

When I was sick, my grandmother sent me a jacket. It was a crazy multi-colored coat and I decided to wear it to treatment. It became my treatment coat. It was my suit of armor. When I put it on, I was safe.

When we were children some of us had snugglies, maybe a special blanket... something that made us feel safe. This is the same idea. Get a piece of clothing that is to be used in this way. Maybe it's a favorite hat or a hoodie or a lucky pair of sneakers, the point is, we are developing a sense of control:

"When I put on this shirt I am powerful."

Right? We are building *ritual*. We are dictating the action here with our intentions:

"This is my ass- kicking power outfit. When I wear this I am in charge, I am focused and I am a powerful beast. Watch me fucking roar."

Get it? When I go to Jiu-Jitsu and put on my Gi, my mindset changes. I feel different. I know that I am going to do Jiu-Jitsu. I feel strong in my Gi. My Jiu-Jitsu surrounds me. I become it. You are creating an energy field around you. You are creating a vibe based on what that clothing means to you. When you wear it, you build on it. You build it up. By the way—if you don't train in a martial art, go find a good dojo and train. You will thank me.

So we have our power outfit, our backpack with our notebook and our pens. Now we need a pocket rock. It sounds silly, but just find a rock or something that you can slip into your pocket to squeeze or rub when you are feeling less than grounded or scared.

You WILL feel shit-your-pants scared at times, friend. I say that to the dudes who are like,

"Bro, yo, I got dis...."

I say this with love, shut the fuck up and drop the tough guy act. We went over this. You will get scared. It's okay to be scared. Waiting for tests or treatment is nerve-wracking stuff sometimes. Also, if you get really angry, you can hurl that sucker and smash something.

That rock is going to symbolize the strength and calm you need—and have—deep down. It is going to let you know that you are still here. I had a smooth one that I would rub and squeeze. When you are finished laughing at the idea of me rubbing something hard and smooth in my pocket, we will continue. Sick bastards.

Now we need a theme song. Yes! A theme song! You need music to set the pace. When you wake up, you put on your music and you know that in listening to it, you are going to imagine wrapping yourself in light (*this is "woo-hoo" energy work stuff,*) and power and set the tone for an epic day of taking care of yourself and your business, rebuilding your body and your life.

Drive by a job site where guys are framing a house or doing construction and most times you will hear music blasting. Get the music to build your house. Pick something that inspires and empowers you. Every mission needs a theme song. Music is powerful and most definitely a tool. Pick yours. Pick many songs and crank 'em.

So now we are suited up, pumped from the music and armed with some tools. How can we lose? Well, it really isn't about losing come to think of it. The idea of winning and losing is really stupid to me. Sit down and let Uncle Petey drop some wisdom on ya.

I played high school rugby and we sucked, but we had heart and will and never quit. Other teams racked up points, but never broke us—we ate their shit and came back for seconds. Our team spirit was monstrous, and *that* was worth a whole lot more than frigging points. When we did *finally* win a game, it was like we won the championship. It really is how you live and play the game. Let's talk about our headspace for a bit here.

Although crisis doesn't feel like a game, having a sense of humor will help you in more ways than it will hurt. So develop that sense, please. Try to laugh everyday if you can. I know that in the throes of a clinical depression, cancer treatment or any bad time, it is a near-impossible task to do, but if you can, laugh. It feels good and your body loves it. It also puts those around you at ease.

Here's a true story: I once woke up in the middle of the night in a lot of pain because my armpits had blistered from radiation treatment. It looked as if someone had taken a belt sander to them. Being the quick-thinking little bastard that I am, I found some of my mom's pads and no; I'm not talking the football kind here. They were in the bathroom. I didn't have them with me for comfort and they weren't in my backpack. I took the pads and jammed them into my armpits and tried to go back to sleep.

Lying in bed with blown-out armpits and my mother's pads...see? You are smiling! That is FUNNY! I had a chuckle because it was so weird and gross and hilarious. I improvised like a champ and came up with a great solution.

When I told the nurses what I did the next morning at the cancer clinic, they cried laughing. It helps everyone when you laugh at yourself and aren't afraid to make fun of your situation a bit. So laugh when you can.

At the very least try to smile. I know that you *totally* want to punch me in the face right now for saying that, but trust me it helps.

In 1984, an article in the journal *Science* showed that when people mimic different emotional expressions, their bodies produce physiological changes that reflect the emotion, too, such as changes in heart and breathing rate. Another German study found that people felt happy just by holding a small pen clenched in their teeth, imitating a smile. So try it out and see if it helps. Don't know about that pen thing but hey, give it a shot!

I know that when I smile at someone they usually smile back and that feels pretty good. My mom's best friend told me once to "fake it till you make it" and it always stuck with me. She had been through all the crap life can throw at you and knew what she was talking about.

I took her words to heart and still use this technique to this day. It is simple. Smile. That's it. You might look and feel like a lunatic but on some level, it helps. One day you won't be faking it anymore. Simple and beautiful, but not easy, I know.

There was a point during my nervous breakdown/pre-cancer days when I was so medicated, I would try to read and simply couldn't. I would look at one page and an hour would go by. One fine day, my mother told me that I had an appointment with a doctor to get my medication sorted out and she would be by to pick me up at eleven.

"Please be cleaned up and ready to go when I arrive," she asked. This was early in the morning, at about 6:30am. She left for work and I sat down in a chair to take on the grand task of reading a magazine. I was still sitting there hours later, unshaven, not dressed and only six pages into the magazine when she came to pick me up.

In a huff, my mother frantically hustled me into some clothes and into the car, all the while frustrated by my inability to be ready and "cleaned up" to see the doctor. As we neared his office, the traffic snarled up and I had to get out and run the rest of the way.

There I was, running down the street like an idiot in a fog, pill bottle in hand, trying not to be late for my appointment. I remember laughing at the irony—I was a complete disaster, on the verge of suicide from my complete inability to function and my mom wanted me to shave and *look good for the doctor.* That's like putting on your best outfit to be on the radio.

The point I *didn't* get was that my mother wanted me to try, despite the fact that I was a drooling mess, to at least *appear* to have some of my shit together.

My mother understood the principle of "fake it till you make it" and was trying hard to implement it. Or maybe she was trying to make it all better in the only way she knew how. Regardless, I made it to my appointment on time, and for the record, my mother, at least in *my* mind, is a saint.

She could have easily told me I was on my own when all of this started and I really don't know what I would have done. I am grateful beyond words for my family's love and support. I will never point a finger their way. I made my choices in life and they were there to help me deal with the consequences when it all went bad. They showed me what unconditional love is.

There, that statement makes up for all the hell I've put my parents through right?

Sigh.

So lets get back to it. We have our clothes, some tools, and a theme song. Now we need to pick our team.

The legendary rap group Cypress Hill once said:

"When the shit goes down, you better be ready."

Part of being ready is to have people around you that you trust and love. We will discuss this more in the "How to be a Kick Ass Friend" chapter, but lets touch on it a bit now.

Here is the awful truth: a lot of your friends are going to suck at this. Your own family may be terrible at being a support system. Worse case scenario, you are alone and have no one to be your support system.

Well, the good news is, if you have an Internet connection you will definitely find people online who will support you. Here is the thing though, there is a big difference between someone being there to fully support you and someone being there to listen to you for a bit, (but not *really* listen) and then lay *their* shit on you. When looking for support online, take the time to find groups that are legit. Check out www. stupidcancer.org. This is a *great* place to start. Don't just troll random chat rooms looking for help. It's creepy and sad. There are some great resources out there, but nothing is as helpful as a real flesh-and-blood friend.

In the old days, people used to hang out together a lot more. Friendships were developed in real time, with real people doing real things in the real world. You may have 800 friends on Facebook but how many of them will help you bury a body and not tell? If you are lucky enough to have one good friend, that is often all you need.

In a crisis, you need people you can trust. You need people who are going to be there for you, no matter what. You need people who understand what is going on or are willing to try to figure it out with you. The easiest way to decide who one of these people might be is to picture yourself lying in a hospital bed, sick as a dog. Who is with you? Visualize your funeral. Who is carrying your casket? *That* is a good indication of who your solid friends are going to be. Harsh and perhaps a tad bit morbid, *but* it clears things up a bit.

When the testing phase is over, you are going to be given a treatment plan. Again, it's going to be a good idea to decide whether or not you want someone with you. If you decide you are going to do treatment, (because not everyone is going to choose to do traditional treatments,) remember to have plans to get *to* treatment. If you have a car, decide whether or not you want to drive yourself to treatment all the time. You might be too sick to drive and may need a friend to drive you there and back. There are also services that can provide rides to treatment for people without other options (the Red Cross is one). Check your area for resources or organizations that can help you.

These are the basic tools for the ride. I know it seems like a pain in the ass, but I promise you that if you try to incorporate some of these aspects into your treatment/crisis experience, you will benefit from them.

I hope that, armed with these simple tools, you are now feeling more and more ready to take this crisis experience head-on. I hope you are gearing up to *really* get into this.

There is a place you can put some of these new tools to work, a place where you will want to be in control and focused. This is a place that you will be spending quite a bit of your time. This place is called....

3

THE WEIGHTING ROOM

An invulnerable armor is patience.
GAUTAMA BUDDHA, *THE GOSPEL OF BUDDHA*

OH THEY SUCK so bad don't they?

These dreaded places where we sit and wait for news that will change our lives *forever.*

Those often-soulless rooms with old, donated magazines reminding us of the warm, safe, *dreamlike* past, a past now contrasting *harshly* with how terrifying and foreign the present seems to be. Rooms with nervous people, sitting beside terrified people trying to look cool and brave. Fake smiles stretched over exhausted faces, fiddling, twitching hands and wiggling feet. The smell of sweat. The low murmur of polite conversation between patients, family members and friends, all of them waiting in tortured silence for their name to be called by the nurse or volunteer and all of them *dreading* it at the same time.

This is the waiting room. Where the weight of the world sits on your shoulders.

Back before we had cell phones, tablets, iPads and gaming devices, we had the old-school staples of distraction—magazines, books, conversation, pensive silence and fidgeting. For some, the waiting room is a horrible place because you have to just *sit* there. We all know what happens when you are forced to sit and wait. We think. We *think and think and think* some more. Usually we are thinking about whatever we are in that waiting room for. Unless you are already an accomplished meditator, or have a natural ability to just let go, you may find it takes superhuman focus to not get caught in that think-trap.

Superhuman focus takes concentration and nothing robs you of that like anxiety and fear. The drugs you may be on at the time can make it hard to focus as well. Sometimes that's a good thing, though. I fell asleep many times in the waiting room, down in the basement of the cancer clinic where the radiation rooms were. I would take too many anti-anxiety pills or anti-puke drugs and pass out in my chair. That was great—the nurse would come wake me up and then I'd groggily walk into the treatment room and get blasted while half asleep.

The waiting room is a place where, unless you're napping, you may be assaulted by thoughts and feelings that are not always helpful. This makes it the *perfect* environment to practice the breathing and mental ninja techniques you will read about in this book.

The mind is like an elementary school bully sometimes. It can at times seem uncaring, insensitive, unrelenting and *just plain mean*. Thoughts will come at you like thugs in a dark alley. Be prepared for this. Have your journal ready to go. They say the pen is mightier than the sword, I say the pen IS your sword. You will slay the thoughts that relentlessly attack you with your words. At the very least, like dealing with annoying children, you will acknowledge their existence—by writing them down. You will start to see patterns in your writing and you will see the same messages over and over. The mind is like an angry little child sometimes, screaming to be heard and demanding attention. Not unlike a child we need to pay attention and listen to our minds, teaching and training it as we go.

Sometimes our minds need a time out too.

Children will say the craziest shit to get your attention. Like a child in a tantrum, your mind will mess with you and start sending fearful thoughts demanding your attention.

Don't buy into the fear and believe what you are "hearing" and feeling. Fear is to be learned from, not ignored or run away from. Acknowledge the feelings and thoughts by writing them down, stay with the moment for a minute, and then let them go. Walk the razor's edge, as the Buddhists say. When you walk the edge of a razor, you are in the moment, completely focused on the task at hand. One slip and you fall off the edge. That is a great mental image to focus on, walking a razors edge, step by step, all focus and control. In the meantime, keep writing.

If you are too sick to write, focus on your breathing. Like in meditation, let the thoughts dissolve and go away. Sit and breathe in and out until the nurse calls your name. By the time you finish this book you will never want to hear about breathing or meditating again. The beautiful thing about meditation is that it allows you to start exploring your inner space, the *inner* world.

Meditation doesn't have to be complicated and means a lot of different things to a lot of people. The waiting room is an excellent place to do it. Sitting calmly breathing in and out and letting your mind's struggles dissolve is a great way to spend your time.

Meditating allows you access to a very calm, stable place inside of your self. Regardless of your *outer* circumstances, developing a practice that allows you to reset, refresh and *let go* of the struggles the ego sets in motion on a daily basis is a powerful choice to make, and a fantastic habit to develop. In a world where the "solution" to what ails us is often-times prescribed in pill form, meditation is a powerful, natural, ancient and *free* solution to many of our stress based issues. My girlfriend Terri said it best when talking about meditation. Terri said, "Take your meds." Meaning, take the time to meditate. It is at the very least a powerful com-pliment to any prescribed solution. I love it; we are taking the term back.

"Take your meds!"

It has been said that we have a natural predisposition to having good mental health and that it is our *thinking* that messes everything up. I would have to agree. The waiting room is an *excellent* place to start honing your mental skills, so get off your goddamn phone, tablet, ipad, what-ever and practice this shit!

When you are getting treatment, the same applies. Focus on your breathing. I have been woken up many times on the radiation machine because I had fallen asleep from breathing exercises. Pretty impressive considering that I felt like a coiled spring wrapped in a suit of sheer terror for the first few treatments. The body follows the breath so give it a shot.

The other thing you can do in the waiting room is to practice being a good listener. Being a good, active listener is simply bearing witness to someone else's experience. Don't jump in or try to fix them or one-up them. Just let them talk. Let them just get all the crazy out and be fully present. Hear them. No matter how fucked up and scared you feel, I can guarantee you there is someone in that room who feels worse. Look for opportunities to be of assistance.

If you see someone who looks scared and alone, their eyes darting around the room, meet them with a smile. If they are close to you, say hello. I have had many conversations with people in waiting rooms that made me feel better to have been of service, even in that small way. Being sick and fucked-up gives you an opportunity to be bigger than your "self".

Being a good listener gives you the opportunity to be a rock for someone else, a sounding board. Believe me, it feels great to listen to someone and hear similar fears coming out of their mouths at 1000 miles an hour. It makes you feel less alone. It makes you feel a connection and less like that dude out on a raft lost at sea in the dead of night. It has been said that suffering, or being around suffering *activates* our compassion. So it makes sense that we connect through that suffering and resulting compassion. Speaking of compassion, there is a simple and powerful way to develop your compassion, which is *perfect* for when you are in the waiting room people watching.

I truly *love* this exercise and try to use it daily wherever I am, whatever I am doing. I have read many different versions of this exercise in many books and it can be done by anyone, anywhere regardless of race, color, creed, religion or belief. Its easy, all you do is look at someone and think that they were once your own mother.

Don't freak out and think you have to believe in reincarnation to make this work. Don't complicate it or overthink it, put all that aside. Get out of your head and into your heart. Its super easy! Male, female, young or old, *simply try to see them as if they were your own mother at one time*. It flips a switch in me that makes me love that person or feel compassion towards them. I feel a certain gentleness or softness in my heart that is beautiful to experience. My heart reacts to this every time. It is very powerful in its simplicity.

Now, if you hate your mother, or have issues with her, try a different relative instead. Maybe see that person as a child you once had. Do whatever gets that feeling of compassion going; whatever wakes your heart up.

If you do hate your mom, see her as a small, hurt child and work from there. Like I just said, see her as *your* child or a child *you once had*. This simple exercise can shift your energy quickly. I use this exercise when I *allow* people to piss me off. It isn't fool proof or perfect, but if you start to do it when you are calm and then do it when you are angry, you will see the results. Do it everywhere. Sitting on a bus or at a stop-light in your car.

Simple and powerful. The best stuff in life is. In my experience, doing this exercise has saved people from my wrath and from me doing dumb shit I would regret later. Use it with the difficult people in your life and see if it helps.

So get turned on my friends. You really feel your humanity and com-passion when you give yourself to others. Even when all you give is your attention, your *full* presence and have a willingness to listen, you are giv-ing someone a huge gift. It is a rewarding habit to get into and is a pretty good thing to do in general I believe.

I will never forget the kindness I was shown in those days. I remem-ber early in my cancer journey, sitting next to an old guy in the waiting room. I was really nervous. He just leaned over and asked me how I was doing. I lied and said I was okay. I asked him how he was and he told me the same, he was fine.
Two big lying bastards.

Anyway he smiles and asks me if I've seen the vampires yet. This was waaay before Twilight. He was talking about the blood lab people. I laughed for real. For a split second, I laughed for real. Sometimes a split second of relief makes a huge difference. I remember how the man felt to me. He was a veteran. Calm, been-there-done-that, but without any cockiness. When he said I would be all right, I believed him. If you can take a moment to help somebody get out of themselves even for a second, *do it*. They may remember you years later and put it in a book.

The other inhabitants of the waiting room are the nurses and office staff. I used to always mess with them and go out of my way to ask how they were doing and try to make them smile or get a laugh out of them. These people work really hard and see awful shit everyday; so don't take your anger or sadness out on them. I used to want to strangle patients that gave nurses and staff a hard time, like they were the only sick people in the room.

I remember being in the emergency room with a friend who was in the last 72 hours of his life. He was loaded with tumors and very sick. I had been visiting him at his apartment when his temperature shot way up so I raced him to the hospital. We were in a small room with a couple of beds divided by a curtain. Behind the curtain in the bed next to him was a *very* old man. He was angry and probably scared, but was taking it out on the staff, going out of his way to be belligerent. After ten or fifteen minutes of him complaining loudly and incessantly, my buddy finally yelled out at him:

"You are not the only sick person here sir, so please keep it down!"

The old man really ramped it up then, demanding to know who had said that. Again, my friend reminded the old boy that he wasn't alone in the room and the old man then turned his verbal assault on us, calling us whippersnappers and other insults from the 1920's. We found out from the nurse later that he was 94 years old and a former judge. He was used to being the one in charge. Afraid and frustrated by his position of vulnerability and grasping for control, he took his frustrations out on those around him.

Sickness does not give you an asshole pass. It does give you an opportunity to be honest though, and that is a gift in itself. Yes, sometimes you are going to blow up and tell someone to fuck right off. Or maybe you might try to run someone off the road with your station wagon on the way to treatment because he pretended to shoot you when you passed him on the inside lane because he was dragging his ass in the fast lane. You, being a little sensitive, might then give chase and make the old motorcycle he was on pull for all its worth, making that guy's asshole pull the vinyl seat up into itself in terror. I guarantee that prick will think twice before doing a stupid hand gesture like that again though. For the record, the fast lane is for going fast, not what *you* think is fast. You wanna cruise 20 under the speed limit? Do it in another lane friend.

So don't be an asshole, period. If someone is deserving of a verbal beat down, let them know how you feel, but chances are they are dealing with something and are expressing it the only way they know how. I suppose that argument goes both ways. I have also seen cranky nurses and staff. I know you get calloused working in those environments, but please try hard to keep your shit together and be kind. Everyone is stressed and wants to be home. We all want the same thing! So let's all take a breath and make that happen and get through the day without all the bullshit and unnecessary drama.

The waiting room is a place where lots can happen. The bottom line is, it's an environment where you can really freak yourself out, so be prepared. Bring a journal, bring a book, and bring music. If you are better off alone, come alone. If you need someone, ask someone to come with you. Don't be too proud to ask for help boys. Whatever it takes to make the experience at least *tolerable*, do it. You will spend a lot of time waiting for things, so be prepared. If you aren't feeling it, wear a hoodie and put the hood up, close your eyes and visualize, or do deep breathing exercises. Take big breaths and let the world fall away. Listen to music, do all this at once! Whatever feels right at the time.

Remember to *try* to be aware of those around you, and help when and how, you can. Always remember *you* can be the person to change someone's day. A smile and a kind word can make a huge impact on a person in crisis, and that feels a lot better than just sitting there feeling like a victim.

Take control, walk the razor and keep breathing and writing. Don't be pushed around by your thoughts, they are yours to control, and let go of. Smile and laugh when you can, or make someone else laugh. Now get to treatment, you are going to be late and end up with a shitty parking spot.

4

BELIEFS AND FEELINGS

"The mind that opens to a new idea never returns to its original size."
ALBERT EINSTEIN

IT IS INEVITABLE that at some point in your life, you are going to have your beliefs challenged. Like I said at the end of the last chapter, the waiting room is often the place where you will find yourself rappelling into the deep, dark crevasses of your psyche.

Or in this day and age, updating your goddamn status on Facebook.

When this happens, you might find out that your physical health isn't the only thing being threatened. When faced with a long health crisis, you may find yourself really examining and perhaps challenging the beliefs you hold about yourself and life in general. You may struggle with, or feel confused by the challenges to the "absolute truths" that you had previously felt so sure of.

As scary as that may be, questioning your beliefs is totally normal and absolutely a part of this process. Remember, we are getting torn down and rebuilt. Is it essential to examine every part of ourselves? No, but this is a great opportunity to examine ourselves to see what works well and what can be changed or let go of.

It is no different when you tear an engine down in a car. You look at the engine as a whole and replace the parts that are worn or need to be replaced or upgraded. You gotta get your hands dirty. The whole point I believe is to become a healthy, complete, organic and spiritual machine again. Our belief systems are part of that rebuilding or shedding process.

I'm all about diving into the scary stuff. I like to do the worst first, so let's look at the dark side of our belief systems. For some of us, the beliefs that we hold about ourselves can be anything but flowery and lovey-dovey. Sometimes our beliefs may make us feel ugly or like bad people. They may cause uncomfortable feelings regarding how we feel about our lives and the people in them that we must now face and deal with.

The beliefs we possess are not there to harm us, but to give us the opportunity to be released from suffering. They are there to be re-examined and perhaps re-defined. You may even drop them entirely. When you take the time to do this, no matter how tough it is I can promise that you, on some level, will feel better.

This is a fantastic time to ask yourself what exactly it is that you believe anyway. Do your current beliefs even serve you? Are they helping you or hurting you? This is the perfect time to decide what you want to believe in, if anything at all. Here is a list of possible things to ponder and scribble about in your journal:

What kind of life do you want to build?

Do your current belief systems support that life or hinder it?

What if you woke up and didn't know your past?

What if you didn't know the culture you were raised in, your personal history or even how you felt about yourself?

What appeals to you or repulses you when looking at other cultures or people? What kind of person would you want to be?

How far away or different from that kind of person are you now, and what is in the way of becoming that person?

Who would your role models be and why choose them for that role?

What beliefs do you base your reactions to events in your life on?

I know this is a lot of shit to think about, but again, you might have more time to think these days if you will put that cell phone, tablet, or laptop down. Why not do something progressive with that time?

Personal beliefs are based on many things. For instance, if you come from a religious family, your cancer experience may be seen as a test from God. Many believe that through suffering, we gain wisdom about our-selves and our lives. Others may view the cancer as being the result of a karmic debt we need to pay. The examples are endless.

Although the previously mentioned concepts may help some people deal with their current predicaments, I also feel that they can confuse, frighten and add a whole new level of stress to the situation. These kinds of beliefs don't seem really helpful at all to me. Before you begin scream-ing about faith and God and all that, hear me out.

We seem to need explanations from outside of ourselves to feel bet-ter about things and to make sense of events in our lives. We might go to psychics for insight, we may search and scream and look up at the sky, shaking our fists at whatever entity we feel is responsible for screwing our lives up. It is great to be a seeker. It is great to go on a wonderful path of self-discovery. Perhaps it's even better when you aren't *forced* to do it by crisis.

Or is it? When are you going to do it anyway? Sometimes crisis forces that path upon you. But don't ever give away your power and hope to be *saved*. There is a lot you can do for yourself to take control of your life. Taking action and having an *active* role in your recovery feels a whole lot better than just *waiting*. I think it is a huge mistake to sit back and not take an active role in your own healing. There is a difference between trusting that you are going to be fine and having blind faith and hoping for the best. I also know that it is *very* hard to trust our-selves and our bodies, even the course of our lives, when the shit hits the fan and our lives blow through the guardrail and over the cliff.

Here is another concept: sometimes shit just happens. I think stress; our environment and the genetics we inherit play a huge role in our mental and physical health. I also believe the thousands of messages we send to ourselves in the form of thoughts and feelings have a *huge* impact on our bodies and on the results we see in our lives, probably more so than any other factors at play. Belief systems are a huge part of what those messages are going to be and how we are going to "receive" them. Or *re-conceive* them. Yeah, fancy stuff, I know. Come to think of it, maybe shit doesn't just *happen* after all.

These are big concepts but well worth the headaches and the time spent on thinking about them. Men will spend hours upon hours rebuilding cars and shit like that, but run like hell from thinking about, and working on, themselves. *That* is being a pussy. The beauty of being sick and messed up is that you are too burnt out to run away from yourself. Being in crisis presents a unique opportunity where you can really benefit from spending time with your sorry ass playing "get to know ya."

When crisis hits in your life you may find yourself questioning everything. If you aren't, well maybe you are rock-solid in your beliefs or perhaps you are a Zen master, or maybe you are just really stubborn. Maybe you don't give a shit! However, as a young adult, you may start asking the big questions about the existence of God or Gods, the meaning of life and the possibility of an afterlife.

Do yourself a favor and try to take it easy with those questions. You can get yourself all freaked out in a hurry with the big questions. Raging on and screaming to an invisible god may make for a great scene in a movie, but in real life it can be very frustrating and leave you feeling like an idiot and completely drained. Just my two cents...

If you need me, I'll be reading hate mail from the fanatics and the religious right. And just to address the fanatics and the religious finger-pointers who are fuming right now, please hear this.

If you believe your god is so mighty and powerful, show them a *little* respect and know they can stand up for themselves. Okay? Your god does not need help defending him or herself or itself for that matter. If they are *all* knowing and *all* seeing and *all that*, they can take care of themselves. To me, the concept of defending a God is like an infant trying to defend its parent. It seems silly and unnecessary.

Focus on yourself, on this moment, on being compassionate. Be concerned with helping your fellow fucking man. And while I'm on this soapbox, if a single almighty God exists, He or She or It doesn't need salespeople. You know who I am talking about, you doorknockers. God does not need salespeople, period. And to finish off, I want to quote my dad. When asked by a high-ranking member of the church why he didn't go to church, my father grinned and coolly replied, "I'm a businessman. I cut out the middleman."

OOOOOH!!!! THAT is some gangster shit right there. 'Nuff said pops. I love that guy.

Back to the whole illness thing...

Illness can seem to reduce us in all aspects of our lives. Illness can boil us down; break us down to the basics of being alive. Illness can reduce us to functioning with only the essential working or *not* working parts of our lives. We sometimes become base and reactionary. Part of that breaking down process involves going through our internal make up. When we get run down and tired we get to see what lies within us. *Or the lies within us, right? Right?* Sorry. Couldn't help myself, it was right there for the taking.

I now want you to hear Morgan Freeman's voice reading the following dramatic, over- descriptive, poorly written paragraphs slowly and with *great feeling* in your head.

An old man lies dying in his bed.

He looks out the window, his gaze fixed upon a child playing alone outside. The old man purses his dry, cracked lips with practiced bitterness as his hands gather up the worn sheets into tight fists, the ancient, scarred knuckles turning white and shaking with the resolute effort of one who is desperately trying to hold on to life. A life that to most who knew him would argue was never worth living for all the vitriol he spewed while living it. These powerful hands with their crushing, unrelenting grip on the old sheets, a physical demonstration of an angry soul's unwillingness even now, to yield to the tender mercies of life.

This last, desperate act of strangling these linens have become the sad equivalent of a last stand taken by an angry old man, a physical protest against an unavoidable fate, a final testament to a life of hard labor in mind, body and spirit.

The old man stares hard at this child, who is laughing and squealing with the delight, joy and abandon that only the very young and unaffected possess.

His failing heart aches with a profound longing for redemption, a cursed feeling possessed and only truly understood by the unfortunate few whose time has come and who now face a bitter, lonesome end. Longing hopelessly, impossibly for a chance to start over, the old man feels a sudden shift inside his chest as the feelings of deep sadness, bitterness and regret which have held hostage his heart for so long, suddenly release their life-long grip on him.

The old man gasps, eyes wide and mouth agape, struck suddenly, almost violently by an insight so powerful and visceral in nature that for a fleeting second he forgets that he is dying. For these last, few, precious seconds, the hardness around his heart dissolves as he becomes awareness incarnate, this final redemptive realization seemingly surging through every cell of his being, blazing brightly through his quickly fading consciousness...

"Sometimes the mental and emotional walls we ran up against in life didn't even belong to us. Those walls were put there, brick by emotional brick by other people in our lives, accepted and allowed to be put into place because of our own low opinions of ourselves. The sad thing is, we stacked those bricks. We decided to keep them because we didn't know that we could simply discard them, or crush them and use them to make our own foundation blocks to build something we loved and could be proud of. People in our lives handed us those bricks, those opinions of us, and we kept them and built those walls around our hearts and heads. Sometimes those people wore our faces. We had the choice. We didn't know we did, but we did. We always did... And you do right now old man."

The wrinkled hands slowly relinquish their grip on the worn sheets as an old heart releases ancient pain and then beats no more... and an enlightened soul slips away.

The room is quiet now, the only movement being a curtain that stirs slowly from a gentle breeze carrying the sound of a child who is laughing and squealing with the delight, joy, and abandon that only the very young and unaffected possess...

Don't be like that old man and spend a lifetime collecting other people's bricks, other people's weight. Don't wall yourself up in negative emotion or opinion. Let those who want to bring you down keep those shitty old bricks, those thoughts and feelings and opinions that make up the walls around our hearts, walls that keep us from emotional freedom, genuine happiness and inner peace.

If anything, lets *crush* those bricks with our love and positive, forward moving, life affirming intentions and build *our own* foundation blocks made from *our own* powerful truths that are held together by the mortar called love and self-respect. You are worth it my friend. Build yourself a beautiful, powerful world. Ya feel me?

So, I ask you, *who* built the village in your head that keeps you from the truth in your heart? Okay, that was all a bit cheesy, okay *very* cheezy, but it made sense, right?

Sickness introduces us to our walls and foundations or lack thereof. A solid foundation of love, trust, compassion and self-respect will allow us to build a good life for ourselves and carry us through it. When you hit a wall inside yourself, try to feel that love, compassion and self-respect. Let that be your starting place. I know you may be thinking this is flowery shit, but we will explore this love thing later. It is *powerful* stuff.

Looking at what we believe or what we *think* we believe can give us great insights into what is serving us or working against us. Reinforcing forward moving, positive beliefs or thoughts can really empower us in a crisis situation, while buying into beliefs that don't truly serve us can make us fearful or uncomfortable. Examine that shit like a CSI. In the end, *what we think, we believe and we receive*. So choose wisely my friends!

Being sick can make us feel small and powerless, fearful and weak. We can become like scared little children, looking for guidance, but from whom do we seek this guidance? Who do we look towards for help? There may be no one around who can make you "feel" better. It is a lonesome feeling when you realize that the people around you are scared and don't know what to do. It can be both exhausting and empowering, depending on the perspective you choose, to realize that no one is responsible or truly capable of making you feel better. That's *your* job and no one is more qualified for that job than you. Okay, you might have to learn on the job but so what? Show up for "work" and learn as you go. But show up.

You may feel like that soldier in a war movie who has just stepped on a landmine that hasn't gone off yet. Horrified, the rest of the troops start to back away from him. The good news is you don't need anyone to make you feel better. Believe it or not, you have the ability to make yourself feel anything you want. Personally, I think feelings are more important than beliefs. If a belief instilled in me by others makes my guts churn, or makes me feel like shit, there's a problem with it.

Feelings are very powerful. I believe that is why some people have so much trouble with the whole law of attraction thing. They can't get the *feelings* going. Why? Because they are probably so wound up in their heads and in their beliefs, that they can't generate any good vibes. They can't get down out of their heads and into their bodies to connect to the heart. It has been written that human beings operate at a certain frequency and that we are like transmitters and receivers. Or *maybe* I thought of that while really high, regardless, I believe it to be true.

To put it in musical terms, I think that when we get too much fear or hate or negative feelings going on inside, it screws up the mix. It's like listening to a track that's too loud or with the bass turned way up. It gets distorted and it isn't clear. That one "instrument" or "feeling" overpowers the rest. For you musicians reading this, you gotta produce the track yourself. A producer in the studio tells the engineer what to do. He tells him where to set the levels. Get in touch with your inner Quincy Jones and get your tracks in order. Do the producer exercise at the end of this chapter.

Feelings, especially gut feelings, are a real-time bullshit alert system. The body seems to have an intelligence of its own and is like a SUV that has all kinds of sensors in it. I will talk about intuition more later on, but here is a little tale to whet your appetite.

I used to work at this crazy bar on the west coast back in the day. One night I was working the front door with another doorman. He was a local guy who knew everyone in town. I was the new guy and my partner was giving me the lowdown on people coming in, helping me *get a feel* for the patrons. That particular night there was a huge lineup outside the bar. Suddenly this beautiful sports car pulls into the parking lot. The doors open and a couple get out of the car. They look like movie stars.

Well dressed and beautiful, they start strolling towards us. I take one look at this guy and my guts go ice-cold. I was surprised at how immediate and visceral the reaction was. I thought, *"What the hell? Am I going to have an anxiety attack?"* The reaction was that strong—it was a physical tightening of the stomach and a rush through my whole body. It made no sense; the guy was in his early thirties, good looking and well dressed. He didn't look threatening at all. Anyway, the couple comes to the front of the line and handsome guy shakes the other doorman's hand and we let them in. Still disturbed by the reaction I'm having, I ask my partner who this guy is. He tells me that he is an enforcer/hit man type for a notorious crime syndicate that loves motorcycles who has just been released from prison. His "Welcome back, thanks for keeping your mouth shut" party was starting at our bar that night. So my guts reacted correctly to this person. He was a dangerous individual who had some heavy energy around him, which my internal radar picked up. True story.

I developed such a knack for picking out the guys who were going to start trouble that my manager used to come and ask me who to look for. It was great because I could often stop fights before they started. I would go on instinct, approach my "target" and talk to them to verify my initial reaction. I learned to really trust what I was feeling. It was good to have these feelings validated because after losing my mind and then going through cancer treatment, I had at times lost touch with that intimate part of myself. There is a certain numbness that happens when there is too much emotional stimulation. It was good to thaw out and trust my guts and my body again. It was a re-connection to my body that I needed after it put me through so much chaos. (And vice versa says my body to me.)

See, when we were kids, we looked to the adults around us to help explain the world and ourselves. When you get a little older, you may realize that most people are making it up as they go along and really this whole trip on earth is hit-or-miss! We all tend to stumble along the path. Is it nice to have someone rub your back and tell you in a soothing voice that everything is going to be okay? Sure! But it sucks when that happens while your guts are screaming something different to you. Suddenly what was once soothing becomes irritating and annoying. Of course that could be some anger surfacing too. We will get into that later. Believe it or not, dudes can have body image issues too.

Beliefs are basically the concepts or ideas that we use to guide our decisions in life. When you are in the deep shit you get in touch with yourself in a different way.

So again, take a little time in the journal and write down some thoughts on the following questions:

What are my CURRENT core belief systems?

Where did I learn them?

Who were my teachers?

Do these belief systems serve me anymore?

What do I believe now?

What do I know for sure in my life?

I know it is a lot to tear yourself apart when you are dealing with the stress and chaos of sickness but it is worth the work. I mean, there really is no better time to do this. Lets face it, you aren't going to do this when things are going great are you? So take the time to have a look at what drives you and maybe it will actually speed things along when it comes to getting your life back on track. I believe that crisis is life's way of getting you back on track more than it is an inconvenience! Again, there is no right or wrong way to do this. Just look at what makes you tick. It may seem scary or intimidating, but go for it.

Check out the landscape. If you find yourself not knowing *who you are* then go back to the *how you feel* approach. *How do I feel about this? How do I feel about that?* Then ask, *"Why do I feel like this?"* As frustrating as this may seem to be, it is a very strong exercise. It can bring up some pretty heavy emotions, or reaffirm some really good things about you and your beliefs and feelings. *It is like spring-cleaning for you're self-meaning.*

Throw the shit out you don't need or use. If it doesn't serve you, it's gone. For all you computer nerds (who rule the world now and have all the money, success and hot wives, bastards!) see this as a disc defrag or a hard drive cleanup or whatever the hell you call it. Free up that mental space and watch the organic machine run a bit better.

When life shakes you hard enough, fruit drops from the tree. But we get to decide what kind of fruit we bear. You could also say when life shakes you hard enough you shit yourself, and that would be accurate, too. Shit or peaches? It could be argued that it takes a good organic fertilizer to grow good fruit, so no doubt we need both!

Our belief systems can really help or hinder us in the crisis situation. When running up against them, we need to spend some time to figure them out and see if they are there to help us or hurt us. If you find yourself sitting in a giant bowl of shit, you have got to decide if you are in fertilizer or feces.

Taking that concept one step further, in the end, it's no secret that difficult experiences can later become the fertile soil that we grow *out of* as people. Our beliefs are the seeds we plant in our hearts garden which produce the fruits that are our lives. I know you want to punch me. I kind of want to punch me right now.

The exploration and existence of these tough emotions or difficult circumstances aren't a "waste" in the end. It's all compost baby, makes it kind of simple, no? Grow baby, GROW!

The Producer Exercise:

For all you visual musical bastards out there, this one is for you.

The point of this exercise is to "produce our tracks." Let's say our emotions can be seen as musical wave files that can be monitored and manipulated. Close your eyes and see yourself in a beautiful recording studio. Pretend this studio is inside your heart. (Just go with it, you wanker.) See your emotions up on two big flat screen monitors. Each emotion has its own visual track all laid out on those screens. So if we are looking at the computer screen, our emotions could be seen as "levels." If you have never seen a music program, Google it and find out what it looks like to help you see it in your mind's eye.

Like each instrument, each emotion has a separate track. Think about the kinds of feelings you are having right now. Are their tracks balanced with respect to each other? Is your "mix" sounding right? What is not working in the track? Too much anger? Visualize bringing that level down to where it "sounds" or feels more appropriate in your internal mix. When I am in the studio doing music, I always feel the track more than hear it. I know a mix is right when it feels right. It feels right because it is sonically correct or pleasing to me. But it always registers as a feeling in my heart or body. It is just right. Just like when you are recording, imagine that you can manipulate the way your "tracks" or emotions feel. Play around in your studio. Mix your tracks.

If you can "hear" those terrible things in your head, those voices of fear telling you all sorts of lies that produce shitty feelings inside you, just remember that you need to get back into the studio and produce that shit! See the knobs of the board in front of you. Turn down the fear, keep a bit in the mix, it's valid—but turn it way down. Hit the mute buttons on the tracks that won't shut up and don't serve you. Turn up the love and turn up the trust. Turn up all those good feelings inside until the mix feels great. Mess around with this and see what comes of it. Produce the soundtrack of your life!

Our beliefs and belief systems can be *very* interesting things to explore. When we take the time to figure what they are and what they aren't, we just might come out of these messed up situations a whole lot clearer.

As tough or challenging as it is to do this, there is a benefit to it. So go see what you are made of! Don't judge, don't be scared, just explore and see what's what. Its time to dig in and have a peek at yourself, you freak!

—∞—

5

INTO THE BREACH

"Bran thought about it. 'Can a man still be brave if he's afraid?'
'That is the only time a man can be brave,' his father told him."
GEORGE R.R. MARTIN, A GAME OF THRONES

AFTER THE INITIAL cancer diagnosis and after all the weird alien abduction type testing is completed, the doctors will give you the full diagnosis and discuss a treatment plan. The same goes for when you lose your shit and arrive in the mental hospital and they interview you to try to determine what course of action to take.

This is an interesting time, I mean it still sucks, but at least you are about to move forward with the treatment. There are a couple of things I want to talk about here and some of it is directed towards the doctors. Please remember I don't mean to be an asshole, it's just that I get a little frustrated with certain things.

Doctors, when you give patients less than awesome news regarding a diagnosis, *some* of you really might want to consider a different way of doing so. First of all let's get rid of the term terminal cancer.

I hate that term.

First of all, from the minute we get smacked on the arse and take our first breaths here on earth, we are *all* terminal, *every last one of us*. Now, that is not being morbid or dark or any of that. It is simply true. No one gets out alive. That being said, when dealing with disease you get deemed terminal when known treatment options have run out, or you have a disease that has a high rate of taking people out and it is in a certain stage in your body.

In my opinion, the only time it is okay to use the term "terminal" when talking about cancer is if you are going to use it to describe the experience of cancer as a terminal that you pass through to go somewhere completely new in your life. Not unlike a bus terminal, right? Otherwise it is just adding to the energy of despair and fear and we don't want to build that energy up.

I am not trying to be a super-naive optimist here; I am not a *complete* idiot. I *am* missing a few pieces. I understand that there are horrible diseases out there that we have not figured out yet.

I also believe that there is no such thing as false hope. To be clear, when I say hope, I don't mean an anxious, pleading energy that borders on worry and feels like you are begging either. I mean allowing yourself to believe, or to be open to the *possibility* that there is another way or another outcome that is possible. You might not know what that way is, but you know in your guts that there *is* a way. To not just accept what someone tells you *if you feel in your heart, guts and balls that there is another possible outcome.*

Are we clear? I suppose you could argue that what I am talking about is actually faith, but for a lot of people that has religious connotations. There are also people who believe hope is a negative emotion. I hope you get what the hell I'm talking about and if you don't, Skype me and we will chat it up. Moving on!

So...*Why* is it a bad thing to believe that something incredible may happen? Why is it assumed or perhaps insinuated that we have to, or should, lie down and die? Fuck that. I say let's just put the *present* information on the table.

Doctor: *"Jimmy, I'm not going to bullshit you. There is cancer here, here, here, here and here. Here is what we plan on doing. This has worked in the past for others and here is what we think your body can handle."*

If it is a mental illness situation, you may be told that you will have to be on medication for the rest of your life.

It is at this point that the statistics come into play and you receive the "facts" about that particular kind of cancer, or mental illness, and how people have done against it or dealt with it.

Well I say fuck the facts.

Or, if you are polite, thank the facts for their information and send them off with a hug and a smile. The facts are in the realm of the past anyway and we are right here, in the right now. *This* is where the power is.

I say this because I am a huge believer in the underdog, the unknown and in the last-minute miracle. I am a huge fan of the human spirit and have been humbled time and time again by its power. So to you cancer patients, I say: take whatever information you receive as *information* and not as *law*. We are not simple organisms. The human body is incredible and I believe we have just begun to explore the potential that we have for healing. Don't even get me started on energy fields or the human spirit.

I believe that in the near future, energy medicine will become more and more prevalent not only in the treatment of disease, but in the *prevention* of disease. I believe science will find ways of making these ancient healing techniques relevant and more importantly accepted by the mainstream. In many cancer clinics today Reiki is being offered as a complimentary treatment to "traditional" treatment. It makes me laugh thinking that blasting our bodies with chemicals and radiation is considered traditional treatment. I would like to see what the Shamans say about that one. When the mainstream world embraces the concept of energy medicine and a few generations start to learn, embrace and teach it, I believe the results we will see are going to be more powerful than any treatment we have today. I believe there is information that we already have within us that we just need to tap into somehow. I am excited to see how the world of energy medicine will merge with "modern" medicine.

To this day I remain fascinated by the mystery of life and in the unexpected. Who's to say you won't be the one who achieves the impossible? Come to think of it, fuck the word impossible too, unless you split the "I'm" from the "possible." Except you Buddhists, I know.

Who's to say *you* won't be the pioneer who finds a new way of evolving and dealing with sickness? Well, probably you yourself, but that's not entirely your fault. We are after all, programmed in many ways.

Unfortunately we humans tend to do as we are told. I bet there are actual statistics that will show that people have died on the date that they were "supposed" to die on. The doctor gives you three months as of August 3rd and you blow the fleshy Popsicle stand on November 3rd. So please, please, please, don't take any prognosis as certainty. Don't give all your power and hope and love and faith and whatever else you have keeping you together and moving forward away because someone said so.

Crisis is a house fire. Remember? So in the new house that you are building in your heart, include the INCREDIBLE VICTORY ROOM!!!! In this room, anything is possible, dreams can come true and no pain and suffering is allowed. In fact, when you walk through the door, the pain and suffering and fear are sucked out of you, turned into hope and love and re-absorbed into your body. No one is allowed in there except yourself and those you invite. That room is sacred, holy and divine—it is where you will go when you are doubtful and afraid. Make sure there is a super comfy chair there. Go and sit in there often. Yes, this sounds ridiculous and crazy but what's so normal about being sick with a disease that can kill you? Screw it man, go big in your imagination and in your heart!

Never let *anyone* or *anything* take your power, your hope or whatever you want to call it, *or* your love. That rule applies to all of us, in any situation. Never let anyone decide anything as important as your life and when it is going to end for you. So doctors, you could try to say:

"Jimmy, here is the deal, here is what's going on and I could give you statistics about how this has played out for other people and it is your choice to hear them or not. But all I can offer you is treatment options and the promise that I will not bullshit you. I won't hide behind any policy and try and cover my ass. I will tell you what I know, make suggestions and you are going to do what you are going to do and we will see what happens when it happens. Oh, and by the way, this is off the record but have you tried using cannabis oil?"

Yeah right.

I'm not smashing on the doctors right now. Doctors aren't magicians; they are people doing a job, with their own lives and their own problems. I want to believe that they are in it for the right reasons and they are going to try their best to do their best for you. But they have a tough and frustrating job. For the record, my oncologist was a rock star. I still think he is some kind of alien sent from a very compassionate planet to save many lives here on earth. I won't name him because he might not want to be included in this book but Dr. C you are an amazing human being and I am grateful to have had you as the man in charge during my time in treatment.

Informing people that they are in the throes of a serious health crisis ain't easy I would imagine. Some of them are afraid of being sued. They can't make promises about anything. They have to worry about all kinds of legal shit and they are stressed like you and me. I will always give the doctor the benefit of the doubt, but I won't lie down and just submit to whatever I am told. I hope you don't either.

Ask questions, seek out information, listen to your gut and stay in the moment. Before you say yes to any treatment plan, have it explained to you in detail. Make sure you are making a decision that you are comfortable with. Don't let anyone rush you or try and tell you to do anything you aren't comfortable with. Sure, there are lots of uncomfortable things to deal with, but you know what I mean.

So lets not write anyone off. People aren't stupid. They *know* when things aren't exactly going their way. I have been with people who have come to the realization that they are about to leave the party. They didn't need a doctor to tell them what they already knew deep inside. Lets let them figure it out for themselves. Let them decide when to call it a life. I can hear people saying, *"Well what's the use in giving people false hope?"*

When is hope false? Is it only real or validated *if* and *when* you regain your health? I never understood that one.

Don't lie or placate and say it's all going to be all right, but don't remove all hope for recovery either. That really makes me angry. There is always a chance until there isn't.

I believe people know when they are close to the end and they will do the things they need to do to prepare for that. I personally know someone who was given a five percent chance to live; he was so sick that he woke up more than once to find a priest giving him the last rites. He would tell the priest to get out because he wasn't going anywhere. He didn't say that out of sheer bravado or to put up a front. He said that because *he truly believed he was going to survive.* I seem to recall him telling me a story about winning a lottery of some sort after treatment, like winning your life back wasn't enough. Lucky bastard!

There have been people who have put a gun in their mouth, pulled the trigger and still lived. That is some pretty clear action taken and they still didn't get the result they were looking for! I am saying lets just do what we can in this moment to keep the positive vibes strong. We never really know how things are going to turn out. If the state of mind called "hope" keeps someone going. Let them be. It is their life after all.

Being positive is actually hard work in the beginning. Being positive isn't walking around like an idiot with glassy, vacant eyes saying "*Namaste*" and just being a flake. No, to me, being positive is completely trusting in your guts and believing in something deep inside you. Just to get to that point takes many falls, many cosmic smacks to the head and many "mistakes." Being positive to me is always looking for another way, another angle or another perspective that will help you and not hurt you too badly. To me, being positive and forward-moving is willing yourself to get up and move with a shit-eating grin on your face, hope in your heart and the full intent of achieving whatever goal you have in mind. Endeavour my friends, endeavor!

Is this easy? No. Does being a positive minded person mean you will feel no pain? *Hell*, no! You will probably feel *more* pain because you are putting your heart out there. You will feel pain, loss and many other emotions, but you will not hold onto them and use them as an excuse for the perceived failures in your life. You won't let them be branded on your soul. You will feel them; learn from whatever your heart is telling you about the situation that caused them and you will rise once more! Also, the more you are heart centered the more you are able to not take it all so damn *seriously*. You get good at seeing and feeling *past* the ego driven bullshit flying out of your own and other people's mouths. You start to feel people's vulnerability, which is what they are usually trying to protect with all the noise and fireworks. When I come at a situation from my head, it becomes a pissing contest, an ego war. It gets ugly quickly. When I come at someone from my heart, it is a totally different dynamic. I am no longer coming at them at all. I am just there, observing.

I have nothing to gain, nothing to win and no need to be right.

I say *offer your heart for slaughter* every moment of every day. That big beautiful heart of yours can take care of itself. It knows what to do. Let it get broken *open*. Never close it off. We try to protect ourselves from pain and in turn end up shutting out a lot of good stuff. Put your heart out there, those blood pumpers were *made* to be broken.

You can do it!

Approaching life in this way is a much healthier dynamic to operate out of. Believe me, I'm a stubborn bastard like many of you and still fall into the ego driven behavior. I have a lot to learn and a lot to forget too. But there are days or moments when I don't get caught up in this insanity and it is *awesome*. Just don't get a big head about it or you are at step one again!

To simplify it even more, and also to take the stress of having to go through this experience "perfectly," take the concept of being positive out of the equation. Just don't give in to fear or negativity and *buy* what the ego may be trying to sell you. Don't believe those dirty buggers. You feel me?

Shine your light baby. *Shine your light.*

Being aware and focused on what is happening inside us isn't easy. We all want easy.

There are a thousand books on "how to manifest this" and "7 easy steps to whatever" that make it seem easy to entirely change your life. These books sometimes leave you feeling like you did something wrong if you didn't get your intended result. That's shitty.

In my life, some things have come easy but the most satisfying results have come from something I have really worked for. The feelings of satisfaction come when I have worked tirelessly towards a goal, endeavored and it paid off. In fact, most times I have succeeded in life, the satisfaction I feel didn't come from attaining the goal itself, but in *knowing you didn't quit on yourself*.

Conversely, the worst pain lies in *knowing* you quit on yourself or someone else. When you know you took the lower, easy road, you feel like shit. Period. There are some moments or decisions, which can't be taken back or changed. Choose wisely when making these types of decisions and I strongly urge you to check your heart and guts when doing so. If only because some "mistakes" are more painful than others. In the end, if you are still breathing you can start all over again in any given moment so don't get too stressed out about it!

For example, writing music and performing it live in front of a huge crowd is really satisfying. This is a reality I have been fortunate enough to experience. Did making that experience happen come easy? No! I practiced my ass off, failed many times while practicing and onstage as well, but kept trying to get better. I was really hard on myself, sometimes way too hard on myself, but in the end it was worth it.

Was there doubt? Sure! Fear? *Absolutely*. But that fear often means you are really onto something important. When I feel fear now I look into it, I don't run from it. The crazy thing is, sometimes, when you just drop trying to do anything, shit falls into place. When that happens it is amazing.

For me it is more of an intuition thing. I check in with myself regarding any situation and decide what to do by how I feel inside about it. Sometimes I need to write things out. You will find your way and what works for you if you give yourself a chance to explore these avenues.

Now I hear, "*Well, Pete, that's a nice attitude to have, but let's be realistic!*"

Stop.

I suppose if you chain smoke cigarettes or make terrible decisions in life regarding your health you could argue cancer is a realistic *outcome* to expect. But few will argue that when it is happening to you or someone you love it feels pretty *unreal*. The whole thing seemed pretty surreal to me when it was happening! Save that shit. Deal with what's right in front of you, stay in the moment and stay focused on the results YOU want, not what someone thinks MAY or MAY NOT happen. To reduce the pressure *even more*, just stay in the moment. Breathe in and breathe out and stay in the moment. I know how hard this is to do when the moment absolutely *sucks*, but try.

Endeavour goddamnit! That is the attitude or mindset you want to adopt.

Speaking of attitude, your attitude is all you have. You didn't choose your parents, your skin color, your race or anything like that. You didn't choose the rental unit that is your body either. You certainly didn't choose your current crisis situation. Yes, some will argue that on some level you did choose all of these things, but for the sake of this particular point lets just say you didn't.

My friends, you choose your attitude *every second of every day*. So I choose to endeavor, I choose Hope, OR WHATEVER YOU WANT TO CALL IT! Well, these days I try for emptiness. But that's another book!

Speaking of hope, man I *really* need another word for that, *conviction* maybe? I am not asking the doctors to give patients anything! Hope or otherwise. Having hope or having conviction is something you give yourself. I like setting deep, heartfelt intentions for myself because they seem to resonate in the body as a truth and a destination.

There is a *big* difference between leaving this world on your *own* terms, having a total acceptance of *what is* and being cool with that, versus leaving wide-eyed and obedient to someone else's estimate of what may happen as per the statistics.

The truth is, NO ONE KNOWS!!

THAT is a fact. Doctors don't know, psychics don't know, no one knows what may happen. So what is the harm in trying to go for it with all the love and conviction and faith and whatever else you can name and muster?

Speaking of running the gauntlet of opinion, when you get tired of asking everyone in the world what to do or what may happen, and you are exhausted and crashed out on the couch not knowing where to turn next, turn to the *inside*.

I know it is hard to go there. Maybe you feel you don't really know "how to do it right" or you were raised to look to the outside world for answers. Just forget all that shit and turn inside and see what's up. Try it and let me know how it went.

I used to say that you should prepare for the worst but go for the best outcome you possibly can. Now I'm not so sure about preparing for the worst, *unless* that means fully accepting that you might die from this disease. If you go down that road, adopt the samurai mindset where thinking that you are *already* dead actually allows you to be *more* relaxed which makes your immune system work better thereby killing all the cancer in your body. I know that last bit sounds crazy, but read up on those samurai dudes. There's lots of great stuff there.

I personally would have had a hard time with that one back in the day, but I do think that way now. Try it out. Play with the idea. *It won't kill you!* I'm an asshole, I know…. But I got love for you my friend, *lots* of it.

If the time comes that your body is going to succumb to the cancer, I hope you will know it and start to make plans to deal with that outcome. I haven't earned the right to an opinion on this one as I haven't died from a disease in this life yet, but I believe spending your time worrying about the people you will leave behind is a waste of time. If you are in this position now, I say the following with all the love and respect I have. Here it goes...

Worrying about "letting them down" is a waste of time. Check in with what I'm saying before calling me a liar or some other nasty name. Get past your ego driven, knee jerk anger fueled reaction to that statement and *really* check in with it. When you survive your current illness and we meet, you can slap me for my perceived arrogance. After the slap I will tell you it was my love for you and my belief *in* you that was the driving force behind my opinion and not my ego. Then we will have some ice cream. I'll buy.

Yes, you may feel the overwhelming urge to give in to those feelings. It is absolutely normal and human to do so. In fact, it is *extremely* difficult to *not* think that way. But worrying about someone is not caring about, or *for* that person, whatever side of the proverbial bed you are on. We worry when we don't know what to do, or how to do it. Worrying is trying to control an outcome that hasn't manifested in reality just yet. Worrying is not having all the information.

Worry can also be the energy we produce when we don't trust ourselves and aren't comfortable with the situation we are in. Worrying is also a *choice* we make and it is a terrible one with real consequences. To make matters worse, we don't know what to do with this disturbing energy we are creating. So we get anxious about that too! This worrisome, anxious energy builds and starts to affect our lives and the cycle continues until we break it or choose not to engage those feelings in the first place.

You know this in your heart and yet keep worrying anyway, hoping it will change how you feel or the overall outcome. It won't, so don't. That's why we fall back on our breathing and journaling, to stay in the here and now. To be more present and effective or at least less *stressed.*

So instead of *worrying* about your loved ones, focus that energy on manifesting the outcome you would like to see. Harness that energy and focus on results you want. When you are not doing that, spend time with your loved ones *now*! Love them now! Feel that love! Let it nourish you! Put this book down now and go love somebody! Let yourself be loved! If you have a hard time letting people love you, start with animals. They are great teachers.

I wonder what would happen if you were really sick and had access to a steady stream of people who would hug you, hold you, and tell you they love you. Imagine a line of people so long that it goes beyond the horizon. Imagine all these people lining up, just *vibrating* with love for you, like a huge line up to get into a rock show, all these people just waiting to get their chance to hug you closely and whisper in your ear just how much they *love* you.

Imagine that you could receive this love *fully* into your heart without resistance to it, knowing you were worthy of it and deserving of it.

What would that do to you?

Honestly, visualize this and email me the results. I bet if you try this, it will feel good. Who are the people in that line? Are they people from your life? Your past lives? Are these people different versions of you that exist right now in other dimensions? Is it the entire cast of Sesame Street? It can be anyone and everyone! Just try it and see what happens.

I once imagined myself lying in a bed filled with purring kittens and nearly shit myself with excitement. What? THAT would be awesome and you know it!

Man, all that fur, purring, cuteness and happiness.

Talk about good vibrations!

Kittens are my kryptonite. Sue me.

So, don't see love as something you will miss but feel it as a beautiful gift of the highest human expression that you get to give, receive and experience now! FEED ON IT! If you come from a fucked up family, throw the past away and just freak them all out by being the warrior of love. Charge into them with all the love you can muster. If they can't handle it they will let you know, *but do it anyway.*

Now, if you want to take this further, see the love you receive from yourself and others as light that penetrates you and goes straight for the cells that have decided to mess your shit up.

See the light penetrate the cells and turn them back into good little soldiers that fall into line. I know that the whole visualization thing sounds a little crazy, but I love it. It makes me feel like I am doing something powerful and *that* makes me feel like I'm in control. There is a whole chapter on this visualization stuff and lots of different ideas throughout this book too, so try it out!

Going back to the odds thing—people have beaten the odds and have done the impossible and if one person can do it, another can. It is as simple as that. People thought it was *impossible* to run a mile in less than 4 minutes *until* Roger Bannister did it. Then many others did it too. Someone has to do it first and why can't that person be you? So whether it is the person who says you are going to be on medication for the rest of your life, or that you have *this* disease, or *that* disease you say thank you, and you continue living your life. Do not ever let *anyone* take your power, hope, love or dreams away from you. Period. And that includes *you.*

And/Or.

Just stay in the moment, breathe in and breathe out.

I'm an asshole, I know. But I love ya.

Goddamn this kid can rant!

So lets get back to the whole treatment thing.…

Starting treatment is weird because it is so new and freaky. There is a lot of fear and uncertainty around it. The first day of treatment is about as comfortable as getting a blowjob from an epileptic pit-bull with braces, too far?

Okay, it's like trying to anticipate what a tattoo is going to feel like. Until you do it, you just can't prepare for it. The first day of treatment is a pretty unique situation to say the least.

Like any other difficult situation, just breathe, get grounded and put one foot in front of the other. Be aware, be open, be present and move forward through the experience. It is only a first until you do it once— then it is going to be whatever you are going to make it.

I remember being bolted down onto the table for radiation for the first time and thinking how completely insane it was. I remember my mind racing—then I just went far away in my imagination and concentrated on my breathing. I remember smiling like an idiot because that is what I do sometimes when I am nervous and freaked out. It's the Asian in me I suppose. Well, that and the penis, but *anyway*! I remember everyone leaving the room and the door making this sealing, suction *"why do I feel like I'm on the wrong side of this door?"* type of sound, and I knew then that the shit was about to get *real*.

I was so wound up inside. I really felt I could rip myself off that table in an instant if I was startled or had to get out. Be prepared to feel emotions that you've never felt before. Being open to the experience is going to help you more than hurt you. Use your imagination. Visualize, breathe and dictate the action if you feel the need to control things, which would put you in a category with the majority of people on earth.

If you are feeling like trying something different, *if you can*, breathe and *let go*. Say, *"fuck it"* and go with the flow of the experience. Imagine using a rope swing and swinging out over a beautiful lake and letting go. Imagine what happens if you *don't* let go of that rope, you may swing back and smash into the trees.

I understand that we cling to what we know and are comfortable with in stressful situations, but hey, it's a new world for you now, so experiment with new ways to navigate it! Inside *and* out!

Remember, the body follows the breath; you make a *conscious* decision to breathe deep which causes the body to relax and slow down. If you can focus on your breathing, you can slow yourself down. If you feel the need to "do something" I suggest visualizing. I used to close my eyes and see myself surrounded by my ancestors, all of them with love and compassion in their eyes.

I would imagine the love in their hearts pouring into mine and I would see it as warm bright light pouring into my chest. I would visualize all their strength, love and courage coursing through the blood we share in my veins. I used to do this and it would sometimes move me to tears. Yeah, yeah, more visualization stuff, I know.

The good news is, you will settle into the routine of things. As hard as that is to believe, some of you will get used to all the crazy shit going on. We humans are so adaptable and resilient it is mind-blowing.

Before I forget and this is no joke, I swear, guys, you need to freeze your semen *before* any treatment. Yes, if you want kids—even if you aren't sure—make sure to freeze enough of your baby batter to make another one or two of you in case the treatment nukes your boys.

I remember coming into treatment one day and a new doctor asked me if I was ready for my sterility test. Responding to the confused look on my face, he calmly told me that this type of treatment could potentially cause me to become sterile and they wanted to see where my levels currently were. He said it as calmly and as nonchalantly as if he was talking about a chance of showers. Well the first thing I did was shit a goat.

I shit a full-sized goat. With horns and everything. I asked the man what exactly was he talking about and he pulled the *"Oh you didn't know?"* routine.

"No I didn't fucking know!" I screamed in my head, while I actually replied "no" in a nice calm voice, of course. I am Canadian after all. If I had known that I might become sterile, all those shower babies would have gone into an icemaker tray in my freezer. That would have been an uncomfortable moment at home while making drinks….*"I didn't ask for a white Russian!"*

ANYWAY!

The doctor then also told me that a team of doctors visiting from South Korea would observe the test.

A TEAM!!!!! God bless a teaching hospital….

So there I was, getting locked down onto the treatment table preparing for a fucking TEAM of doctors to come in to observe a test that would determine whether or not I was sterile. If you haven't figured it out yet, let me be the first to tell you to leave your dignity in the car and pack a lunch bag of humility for the whole treatment process. Remember how I talked about going away in the mind? Yeah, it's for moments like these.

What's worse than finding out you're sterile? Finding out you are sterile with six of your closest South Korean doctor friends. Oh, plus the doctor and the three techs in the room. It's a *party.*

But wait, it gets better.

I asked how this test is done. The doctor tells me that he will tape crystals to my penis and testicles, screw it, to my cock n' balls and then proceed with the regular radiation treatment. Afterward, they remove the crystals and test them to see how much radiation they have absorbed; this will determine whether or not I will be shooting blanks the rest of my life.

While I am digesting THAT whole concept, like a bad high school play, in comes the goddamn S.K.B.W.T. You know, the South Korean Ball Watching Team. Yeah, I should have made them shirts. Of course, they are all smiles, nervous laughter (Asians, right?) and clipboards. I can't tell you how awful that felt. I don't have a huge penis. My lady says I'm a grower, not a shower. Okay for you people laughing right now, stop. That's not nice at all. I didn't pick my penis. If I could I would have went for something a little more… ambitious.

Oh wait; *I'm having a pre-birth memory*!!

Yes! It's me up in the pre-birth world picking my body! Oh those are nice eyes, very good choice. Nice heart, very strong—excellent choice, pre-birth Pete!

Oh look! I am being brought over to the penis picking station!

Oh look! Yes!! I'm grabbing the big black one! What's that? I can't have that one? Why not? But I don't want this one! What do you mean it's all they have left in my color??? Wait! Hold on! WAAAAAAAIIIIITTTT!

Doctor: It's a Boy!

Nurse (whispers): Barely...

You get my point.

The team gathered around the table, getting ready for the big, er, average show. The doctor obviously loved the spotlight and took his sweet time with my pants. I felt like I was on the *Creepy Uncle Cozy* show. I didn't know where to look. I didn't know what to do with my hands. My pants were being slowly undone and my underwear pulled down by a stranger in front of a *team* of complete strangers from a foreign country. At least they were Asian; it could have been a team from the Congo. Is that racist? No more racist than me digging on my Asian brothers I guess. They can take it though. I love you all and you know it.

The worst part was the note taking. The S.K.B.W.T were furiously taking notes. Writing many bad jokes about my poor little friend down there. Those doctors with their knowing, sympathetic expressions... and I think I also detected a little cockiness. Really? I actually wrote "*little* cockiness???"

So I tried to salvage what dignity I had left with a feeble joke: *"If I see a camera or a ruler, someone is getting hurt."* But no one heard me as the doctor slowly taped a frigging jewelry store to me. I just tried to melt into the table while the Q& A went on and on. Finally the doctor finished and they all left the room to start the radiation.

I heard the door do its Star Trek Enterprise door sealing sound, then I was then alone in the room, pants down, with enough bling taped to my frank and beans to supply a hip hop video. All I was thinking was; *"Fuck you Universe, laugh it up!"*

The treatment over, the lights came back on and everyone returned, eager to collect the crystals. Doctor Spotlight/ Uncle Cozy took his seat and began to slowly remove them.

I had had enough of this shit.

"Unscrew my mold please," I asked the tech.
"Just a second," the Doctor said.
"Unscrew the mold *now*," I said. I was getting really angry. The doctor knew I wasn't fucking around and the techs freed me from the

humiliation chamber. I sat up and began pulling the crystals off of myself and tossing them into the dish. Like the sick bastard that I am, I made sure to throw a bunch of pubes in there too, thinking they could check me for crabs while they were at it.

When I was done, I swung off the table and gathered my shirt and whatever else was on the chair. As the team filed out they all thanked me. I was red with anger and embarrassment and just nodded. It turns out I wasn't sterile but I sure was pissed that I had to find out in that way. In all fairness to the doctors and staff, I was probably told before-hand about the test but forgot, seeing how I was in a bit of a fog most of the time in those days. You see if I wasn't so proud I would have had someone with me and they would have probably remembered that little detail....

Come to think of it, when you start treatment you should probably know your blood type and have someone that you know has clean blood willing to donate some to you in case of emergency. Take no chances my friends. Take no chances.

Last but not least, keep your pubes neatly trimmed during treatment. Not only does it make your penis look bigger, it doesn't allow as much tape to stick to you. As satisfying as it was to give that guy a pube salad, it hurt like a bastard to pull them out. I'm just sayin', you never know when you are going to be the star of the *Holy Shit this is Embarrassing* Show. I hear the girls like it neat too....

So that was another little example of why it is good to just keep breathing, keep writing and keep moving forward. It is also a good exam-ple of why you need a sense of humor.

You can be sure that given all the surgeries you might have to endure, they can never remove that!

Moving through treatment is all about flexibility and patience. Your body is going to react to the treatment. Uncomfortable things will happen to you physically. That is why it is so important to explore and get familiar with the inner landscape. Become an *inner* space astronaut. This is important for life, period. Let's say you strongly identify with how you look. I think most of us humans, guys included, are in that boat. What happens when all your hair falls out? What happens when you lose a shitload of weight? What happens when you stop looking like yourself? I don't say this to scare or shock you; I say this to *prepare* you.

Unfortunately our mainstream western media is constantly bombarding us with airbrushed, digitally altered images of "beautiful" people in magazines, movies and pretty much anywhere they can advertise. We are led to think that youth and beauty are the only aspects of life that matter. For all the guys that are rolling their eyes I say give me a break. I see so many of you young bucks out there working as hard as the ladies to look good. Holy shit, the plucked eyebrows, the pretty hair, the tans, the tight clothes!

Gentlemen, I hope for your sake that you have *some* clue as to who you are when the shit goes down because the last thing you are going to want to do is go to the tanning salon during treatment. I know, I know, you are just trying to look good. I'm just ragging on your pretty asses. I bet there are as many guys or at least a higher number that have body issues. I had them but in a different way.

I should be putting this in the post-treatment section but I will tell a little tale of body image bullshit now while we are in this neck of the woods.

Shortly after treatment I was in bed with my girlfriend at the time; she was rubbing my chest and making advances on me and the more she touched me, the *angrier* I got. I didn't understand what was happening. She was beautiful, I was attracted to her, but for some reason

I really didn't want her touching me in a sensitive, loving way. Now before you start with the dumb-ass jokes, let me tell you that I went to talk to the free therapists down at the local community health center. I talked to this crusty old counselor; he listened to me ramble on for awhile, then told me I had body issues and that I was clearly angry at my body for betraying me. I told him he was fucking nuts and laughed it off. He shrugged, told me he was going out for a smoke and seemed to not care either way.

I got into my old station wagon and drove home, thinking about what he said. The more I thought about it, the more I realized he was right. I think I even said out loud, *"But that is a fucking girl issue!"* After chewing on the idea for a little while longer, I realized I *was* angry with my body *and* my mind. I was angry with a lot of things. I hadn't realized I was feeling this way until I had that episode in bed with my lady. There was a time when I went into a grocery store and saw a bunch of damaged cans of beans for sale at a discount. I remember getting mad because my immediate reaction was that the beans in those damaged cans were as good as any. That just because the can was banged up didn't mean that the insides were any less "good" than undamaged cans.

I really hadn't had the time to work things all the way out yet, so it really came as a shock to me that I might have these feelings toward my body. So of course I wrote about it and started to figure it out. So maybe you think that this body image stuff is bullshit. I think we all fall victim to the advertising messages sometimes, and us guys can sometimes fall victim to unhealthy thinking that leaves us painted into a tight, angry corner. Take the time to monitor how you are feeling. Again, I will beat you over the head with the journal thing, but my god does it help sort things out.

When we are in treatment, we can change a lot on many levels, inside and out. So it is really good to meditate, get inside, recognize your feelings and develop those strong inner bonds and that rich inner life. I believe that internal strength and connection is what allows people to move forward through very difficult situations.

It doesn't hurt to practice letting go of all those emotions too. Spending time practicing *just being*. It depends on where you are at in your own trip I suppose. I spent years trying to hang on and then years trying to let go! I'm still working at it today.

Damnit.

Imagine that you completely based your identity on what you saw when you looked in the mirror. Then one day you are trapped in a fire and you end up nearly burning to death. When you come out of your medically induced coma, you look like something out of a horror movie. You are no longer "you." What happens now?

There is a stranger in the mirror.

All you have left of your former self is whatever you feel inside. Your identity now becomes something intangible to you, other than what you *feel*. But it is also something others can feel. I know I watered down a very complex situation, but the basis of what I am saying is that you are not only your body, and to hang all of your identity on that one thing is dangerous and ultimately disappointing as our bodies are constantly changing and will eventually fail us.

To read an incredible story about identity and body image, check out "The Gift of Fire" by Dan Caro. This dude had his face and his hands burned off in a horrible explosion at the age of two and well, you just gotta read the book.

When you die, people will remember you for different things but hopefully they remember you for how you made them feel. How would you feel to others if you kicked off right now?

This body image stuff applies to both the treatment and post-treatment period. It applies to our whole time here on earth! So as you progress along these paths, spend some time inside and root down into those places that "feel" like you and can't ever be touched, no matter what happens to your body.

If you don't have a clue as to what I am talking about, buy a book on meditation and start spending time inside. Buy "Being With Dying" by Joan Halifax. Thank me later... If you don't read, YouTube that shit. Explore, open your mind to these concepts and ideas and your world, inside and out will expand, so might your heart! Good deal!

Get your inner astronaut suit on and start exploring! I know its trippy stuff but hey, you aren't exactly on familiar ground anyway, so why not check it out?

When I went through the mental illness trip, I constantly felt like I didn't know who I was. I would look in the mirror and "see" my image but could not connect emotionally to who I was. I can't describe it, but let me assure you it was really scary. I couldn't even come up with a *concept* of who I was. The sense of disconnect was huge.

Without any physical disfigurement I still looked like a stranger to myself and had to go inside to start piecing it all together. Like I've said before, I was grateful to get that cancer diagnosis and be thrown into that world, because the shit I was going through was too scary to handle.

Whether it is during the crisis/treatment phase or after it, prepare yourself to become something different. Be open to "becoming," period. Sometimes the stuff we hang onto is holding us down and is not worth the effort, but we don't know until we drop it or feel something different. In life we will lose things and we will gain things. I look at nature and am reminded of that every day. Is a tree still a tree without leaves?

THE BAD TIMES BIBLE

Nothing stays the same in nature. Everything changes, and eventually so will your situation and your attitude towards it.

I always seek to gain wisdom (that's part of my problem...) and try to keep an open mind and an open heart to do so, even in the midst of a shit-storm. These days I try to keep my mouth shut and my eyes and heart open. Besides, if you have your mouth open in a shit-storm, you know what happens. So if the body changes during treatment observe it and let it go. If others tell you with their eyes that you are changing, *let it go.* You will end up alone if you let your pride dictate the action.

I had a friend who passed away years ago from a very aggressive cancer and on his last day here, before he lost consciousness for good, (*or gained absolute consciousness or awareness for good, we don't know!*) he told his dad he didn't want anyone seeing him in the condition he was in. He looked terrible and was the first to admit it. He had lost a leg, a pile of weight and was jaundiced. He knew it was going to get even worse. The trouble was, his friends were showing up to say goodbye.

Lot's of them...

His father managed to convince him to relent and let his friends come in. His father stood in the hallway, completely blown away by the love that he and his son were receiving from those friends. He hugged them and he told me he was honored to be a part of this. My friend lost consciousness quickly, but I believe that he *felt* every person who came into that room. He could have remained fearful and embarrassed by how far his body had degraded. He could have shut the door and left his body with only a couple of family members around him. But he decided to say, "*Fuck it*" and in doing so he gave a gift to his friends, his family and to himself. He was sent off to wherever he went with the love of his friends to carry him. You don't need a body for that.

Be brave, be open, and if you lose your hair, get a crazy-ass wig. Wear clothes you like, be how you like. But remain open to the process and the transformation.

The world's most beautiful swords were all hammered on the anvil after coming out of the forge and then they were submerged in water. They weren't pretty—they were beaten and cooled and beaten and folded and heated, over and over until they became a polished, beautiful thing.

Like a sword, your soul is going to get thrown in the fire, hammered and drowned. Know this. That being said, allow your heart and soul to be a beautiful sword that comes out of the forge sharp and gleaming. A perfect, beautiful instrument of love and compassion, designed to live well, love well and cut through the bullshit and the illusions of this life.

No pressure though, hopefully we are all working on this stuff. I am also learning daily how to let go of all expectations and just *be*. But *that* is next level shit and I'm still a big, dumb animal. Maybe that trip will be in the next book.

Now go look for a funky tracksuit and wig while you digest this madness.

6

How to Be a Kick-Ass Friend

"Friendship is the hardest thing in the world to explain. It's not something you learn in school. But if you haven't learned the meaning of friendship, you really haven't learned anything."
MUHAMMAD ALI

ALCHEMY STILL EXISTS and happens everyday. Right now, flesh is being turned into gold without its owner even knowing it. Through actions of massive kindness and consideration, and simply being there, a person can be turned into a gold-plated, Kick-Ass Friend.

Every person in crisis needs a Kick-Ass Friend. They are also known as the four o'clock friend, the person you can call at four in the morning, no matter what. I was fortunate to have a few of these friends. I tell you man, being able to pick up the phone and talk any kind of crazy shit to someone at any time of day *who was willing to listen* was gold in the vault.

There are things you won't want to tell your family. There are things you don't want to post online. There are fears or concerns you may have that you just don't want to tell anyone save for a couple, or even one close friend. Here are the loose rules of the deal.

Rules for the patient a.k.a. "Sick Bastard"

Be honest with your friend and don't ask for something you know they can't provide.

Remember that this is tough for them to deal with, maybe even more than you realize. Being a caregiver or friend is hard because you can only help so much and have to watch your loved one suffer some aspects "alone".

Don't be an asshole to someone who is trying to help you, even if they are annoying the shit outta you. Just tell them what you need and don't need. Remember to show your gratitude and love for them. It will mean more than you know, especially if you check out.

I think people in crisis are called "patients" because it is so close to the word "patience". If there is one thing you need to develop outside of a bulletproof sense of humor, it is patience. You will be waiting for tests, waiting for treatment, waiting for results, waiting for this to be over and waiting for the dissipation of that feeling of wanting to smash that table of whiners next to you in the restaurant because they won't stop complaining about the most meaningless shit in the world. They should also call patients "waiters", come to think of it.

Go with the flow and remember life is messy and there isn't a perfect way to "do" this. Just show up with a "heart on."

Permission to smack me granted sir. I Loooove you! (Said in an annoying morning voice)

Rules for the friend or caregiver aka "Kick Ass Friend"

There is no right or wrong way to do this. There is only showing up to try to help.

Know that just being there for your friend is more than what most people can do and that makes you awesome. Don't think you need to know all the answers. Just be there to the best of your abilities.

Try to figure out what your friend or loved one needs without asking. They may be too messed up to be able to think straight. Making decisions when you are stressed out and sick is really hard. Keep things simple. If you do ask them what they need, just be aware of what they are not saying as well. Communication is mostly non-verbal anyway so *feel out* the situation. Respect your friend's wishes and don't take shit personally.

Even though these types of situations may bring up a lot of things inside of us, don't make it about you until you are alone with your journal writing about it. There is a time and a place for that. Being of service isn't easy, so also remember to be easy on yourself if lines are crossed or you feel you have offended your friend or messed up somehow. You are just trying to help. It's cool.

Remember that in a crisis situation there are many "players" involved. Medical staff, family, friends, ex partners, you name it. People come out of the woodwork and everyone has an opinion. We all want to be the hero that saves the day but know where you fit into the situation. Where are you most effective and most *comfortable*? Go there and do that, whatever that is.

It's good to push our boundaries in life but know *when* and *where* to do it. We can't be all things to all people. It doesn't work and can get messy. Sometimes "helping" in our minds is actually hurting people in reality. Don't be like Lennie from the fantastic book "Of Mice and Men," we all know what happened to him.

Learn how to listen. We sometimes talk too much, or make it about us, or try to soothe or "make it go away" when we should be listening. We do this when we are nervous or don't know what to say. I have been guilty of this unskillful behavior myself. It's cool, shit happens, and you are probably really freaked out and just trying to help your friend to the best of your abilities. Be an active listener and recognize when silence is better than words. Don't panic, you will get it.

If you are uncomfortable about something, talk about it. This relationship is a two-way street.

Realize you are going to change too, and that this experience can be for your benefit.
Be prepared for the worst. Do this to the best of your abilities and have the courage to be there for your friend/ loved one, even if it means helping them die. I'm not talking about smothering them with a pillow, I mean just going all the way with them. I promise you, as hard as it is to do this, you will *never*, ever regret it and the experience will make you a more enhanced, deepened person. There are books out there to help you learn how to do this. Seek them out.

If your friend has a long illness you may find yourself burning out emotionally and physically. Remember to take care of all *your* needs first. You don't need to have a nervous breakdown. Take the time you need to get the rest you need. If you need help, get help. Ask for it. Don't be proud or feel your needs come second. Martyrs are mostly dead and are super annoying. Just be aware of where you are emotionally and what you need.

There is no right or wrong way to do this. See the first rule.

I can actually laugh thinking about some of the truly awful encounters I had when I was sick or out of my head. Running into people when you are in crisis can sometimes be a really awkward, terrible experience. For both of you!

If you are mobile and able, I always suggest you keep being social, stay around life and involved with life. Yes, there are times to retreat and heal alone and contemplate, but you must also stay in the flow of life in one-way or another.

That being said; prepare yourself for awkward moments of sometimes epic proportions. Sometimes when you are sick you don't look great, you don't feel great and you even smell a bit. I remember going through the radiation treatment and being grossed out by the way I smelled. I thought I smelled like death.

I am serious. It was nasty. I suppose I should have allowed myself to smell that way, given the fact that my body was trying to rid itself of the dead cell material and so on, but I was really self-conscious regarding that smell issue.

My hair was burned off at the back. A friend once told me that it looked like I was wearing a hair helmet and that I had Lego hair. You know, the removable black hairpiece that comes on those little Lego toys? Yeah, funny, but it looked terrible. I would shave my head, but it was still all red and puffy back there. Sometimes you just can't look cool when you are sick I guess.

In fact, one of my best friends thought it was the funniest thing in the world when I asked him how the back of my head looked before going out to play pool one night. He said it looked fine, no worries. Once I was in the pool hall washroom and realized it had a mirror set-up that let you see the back of your head, I found out how it *really* looked.

It looked terrible! He lied to me, and at first I was so pissed off! You know? What an asshole, I thought! When I walked out and he knew by my expression that I had seen my shitty hair. He just burst out laughing and suddenly so did I. It just sucked so bad that it was awesome. Believe it or not, that is a good friend.

Post-treatment, I had another awesome friend named Catherine who was the living embodiment of tough love. I could go to her house any time of the day or night, feeling freaked out, rough or whatever, and she would make me soup or tea, talk to me, listen to me and let me sleep on her couch. She also had a really cool store where I would go to visit her.

However, if I showed up pissed off, she would kick me out and only let me back in if I came back with a coffee for her. It made me mad, but I understood what she was doing. She forced me out of my darkness, or at least made me try to fight my way out of it. Catherine also sent me a care package one day that was just amazing. It was just a random care package that really hit the spot. Catherine continues to do amazing things for so many people to this day. She is a legit; five star general *superstar* human being. I hope you have a friend like that because they make a *massive* difference in your life and in how you adjust to it.

It is a lot less likely during these days of Facebook, but if you are going out in public or to social events while in crisis, you will eventually run into people who don't know you are sick or messed up. I suggest you tell them what's up in a way they will be able to handle. It sucks that you have to do this but sometimes you have to. It is part of it.

I remember running into a girl from college out in a bar and her telling me I looked like shit. She didn't know I was sick. I looked at the buddy I was out with and he smiled and gave me the "Drop the Bomb on her" look.

I told her that it was nice of her to mention how shitty I looked since I was currently in cancer treatment. She fell apart, crying and apologizing. The best part was that she was there with her fiancée, whom I didn't know. As she started crying he offered his hand and was like, "Hi, I'm Dave." Classic! I laughed and made her feel better. This was before everyone was online and everyone had a cell phone. That brings us to Social Networking sites.

The beauty about today's social networking sites is that you can get whatever message you want out there in a hurry.

Simply post what you want on your favorite social networking sites and people will know what you need or don't need. Before I forget, a little word for those reading this who are friends of the P.I.C. (person in crisis).

It is a strange phenomenon that occurs when the news goes out that someone is sick or has died. People love to be the first to spread the word. I have been a victim of this uncouth behavior myself. A strange power seems to come over us as we text, phone, tweet and drunkenly spread the word about so and so who is dying, sick, ill, divorced whatever. People, heed these words: respect, restraint, courtesy, class and couth.

Please take the time to speak to the person or their family before you go spreading the word. I say this because when you are going through the wringer it is sometimes really hard to process what is going on around you and inside you. Life can take on a surreal quality and your worldview and perspectives can change quickly.

So, as exciting as it is to be the person who tells everyone that Terry has a brain tumor and is surely going to die, stop. Take a breath and call Terry. Better yet, drive over there with a bag of candy or something ridiculous, maybe a cupcake with sparkles on it. Ask Terry how he is and if there is anything you can do to help. Terry might be too messed up to even think what you can do to help so just do something. Anything. When I was laid up at home after a large chunk of tree crushed me last year, a buddy would show up unannounced and take out my garbage. It was a small gesture that had a huge impact. Thank you Danny.

I know it is human nature to spread the word about events in our lives as quickly as possible. We have been doing it since we first stood upright and maybe even before. But behind all that information is a human being with very real feelings. They may be going through something that they may want to keep private. So if you hear something, confirm it with the person in question, ask them what they want to do and who they want to inform and be respectful of them and their wishes.

Public posts online without proper information or more importantly, permission, from the sick person, are in my opinion a no-no. It is best to talk about these kinds of situations in person. Show the person in crisis some respect and have some class; they probably have enough to deal with don't cha think?

Side note: it's weird how they call someone's death their "passing." If life is a test and we are here to learn lessons, does that mean when we die we have learned all we need to know? Have we passed the test and graduated to the next level? The same goes with calling someone "late." Late? Dude isn't ever going to show up, he's already gone, baby. More on the leaving behind of the meat suit later.

Perhaps we can't make sense of it and we just keep talking about it as a way of trying to process it. But remember that words have power. There is emotion behind those words and energy is being put out there into the world with them.

This may sound like a far-out concept, but I believe it has merit. If someone tells you they love you, you feel it in your body. There is a chemical reaction and you feel good. If someone comes up to you and tells you they are going to rip your fucking head off, you undergo a completely different chemical reaction. Both these scenarios started with words. The same concept applies when you think thoughts about yourself, too. Good thoughts, good feelings, bad thoughts, bad feelings. Where should we try to put most of our focus?

Words are powerful, and unfortunately when people start talking about other people in crisis it often gets negative or dark. We automatically start thinking the worst and get caught up in the drama of the event, forgetting that this is a person's reality we are talking about.

What if we found out that our words could help or hurt people in a tangible, *physical* way? What if we found out that the energy of our thoughts and words added light—or darkness—to the energy around those people? To keep it simple, what if we knew FOR SURE that good thoughts helped people and bad or worrisome thoughts actually harmed them? What would you do? To take it a step further, what if we found out that whatever you thought for someone else *automatically happened to you*? THAT would seriously change the way we use our thoughts and our energy, wouldn't it?

If a P.I.C. is diagnosed with a serious illness and has a family, the question put forth shouldn't be *"What's going to happen to those poor kids?"* as if the poor bastard has already died, but we should instead ask *"What can I do right now to help that man and his family?"* If he has kids, offer to babysit, clean the house and maybe take him to treatment, anything that you *can* and *are willing* to do.

Do you know how nice it is to receive a meal when you are in the shit? Of course, you have to find out what they can and can't eat. But it is the gesture and the fact that you are there cooking for them that makes the difference.

What happens when we go over and cook? We spend time talking and enjoying ourselves. We connect and we are engaged in life. Beautiful.

Words have energy and power in this world. Use them wisely. Ask simply, what can I do to help? If you arrived at an accident scene that just happened, you don't sit there and think *"Oh, what about his poor family,"* or immediately grab your cell phone and tweet or post on Facebook, *"At an accident RIGHT NOW!! So intense!!!"* No—you would ask *"what can I do to help?"* or, you may drive by and do nothing, like a douche. Yes, I love the word douche.

Be a good friend and do the classy thing. Check that. Do the *right* thing.

Too many times, a P.I.C. ends up alone. Sure, many of them choose to be that way because they don't want to be a burden or they feel really weird and out-of-place in social situations. They also may keep strange hours. They may go to treatment in the morning, sleep all afternoon and be up all night. Figure out when you can go over and spend some time with them. Sometimes you don't even need to talk about anything at all. Just having someone there with you can be comforting. Communicate, talk to your friend. If you really want to help and don't know how, tell them that but again, don't stress them out. It is easier to just say, *"Alright, I'm here to cut your lawn and clean your house and then we are going to watch old movies, cool?"* If they are too burnt out, they will tell you.

When I went out to the bar to play pool and I did meet up with friends, it was sometimes weird and uncomfortable till they got drunk. *Then* their true emotions came out. I got a lot of love from my buddies when they were loaded. Not that kind of love, gutter mind!

They would explain why they didn't call, told me they didn't know what to do and so on. I told them I understood, because I really did. It can be pretty weird and uncomfortable for people to deal with this shit. I also think they were freaked out about me losing my mind too.

My friends weren't sure how I was going to be. The truth is, I couldn't face my friends before the cancer diagnosis. I felt ashamed for losing my mind. I felt like a weak piece of shit and felt like I couldn't look people in the eye.

Like I said before, the cancer diagnosis really was a blessing for me. It gave me back my honor in the sense that if the cancer took me out it was an honorable, acceptable death. If I went and drove my truck into a wall, stepped off a bridge, blew my head off in the woods or killed myself in any way, it would have been dishonorable in *my* mind. This was a messed up view of things but it was quite clear when I met some people when I was just "crazy," that they were *very* uncomfortable with the situation I was in.

When I ran into people as a cancer patient, I was met with concern and support. I even had one friend say, "*Oh THAT'S what was wrong with you!*" As if the mental illness episode was related to the cancer. I have thought the two were related, and I'm pretty sure they were, but that's up for debate at a later time. So the cancer diagnosis allowed me to breathe a *little* easier in public. It allowed me to walk around and not worry so much about running into people I knew.

Cancer is simply more acceptable to people. You can see tumors on an x-ray and blast them with chemotherapy and radiation. You can mark your progress with blood tests and x-rays. It is a more *tangible* experience for people. It is still difficult for people to deal with on a lot of levels, but it is definitely more acceptable than mental illness is in our society.

A lot of people with mental illness suffer in silence. They are often misunderstood and fall through the cracks. I find this unacceptable and tragic. I really hope that we can one day as a society become as accepting and understanding of mental illness and the people who suffer from it, as we are of those afflicted with cancer. More importantly, I hope that one day we learn how to just love each other, strive to be a more tolerant, compassionate species and just roll with it all, regardless of whatever the label or outcome may be. But I guess that's farther down the road.

Being a good friend in ordinary circumstances requires effort and commitment. No relationship grows without nurture and attention. When you get sick, things change. I just hope that you have the kind of friends and family that know how to help you with this experience, and that they have the courage and the love for you to see you through it.

Like I said before, with open minds and hearts we can *all* benefit from crisis, regardless of what the physical outcome is, or what side of the proverbial fence we are on.

Besides, we are all in this world together.

Kick-Ass Friends, I salute you!

—∞—

7

LOVE—THE MOST POWERFUL FORCE IN THE WORLD

"Take away love and our earth is a tomb."
ROBERT BROWNING

ALL RIGHT, BEFORE you judge what this chapter is all about, let me tell you this: I don't care who you are, how tough you think you are, how strong you think you are, whatever your situation is, you absolutely, positively, must have love and compassion to fully experience what it really means to be *alive* in this world. When I say love, I mean self-love, love from others, love in *all* its forms, and lots of it.

If you have no issues regarding emotional communication with yourself and others, then move on, or read this chapter as a refresher. However, if you feel you are *too* soft, feel free to go on and read the chapter in this book entitled "Unleash the Beast." It's your choice friend.

Okay, back to the love business.

I know. I can see you there, rolling your eyes and calling bullshit on me, but let me tell you something. Love is the most powerful force on earth. Love is the world's greatest natural resource that will never run out, and the only one that produces more of itself the more it is used. In this lunatic's opinion, love and compassion are the *only* forms of currency that will *always* hold their value in society as long as we humans are stumbling around on this earth.

Again, you must understand I'm not some patchouli-reeking hippie wandering around with glazed eyes, high as a kite and telling everyone that love is going to make everything okay. Man, I'm hard on the hippie kids eh? God bless em. They have the right intentions. That's not the case. I do know this though; learning to love yourself and others can be hard work. If it were easy there would be a lot less problems in the world and fewer douche-bags out there.

On that note, please don't confuse loving yourself with the superficial bullshit of being in love with your physical body. The truth is, while it's awesome to be a big strong physical specimen, stomping around this earth, the body sometimes fails and *then* you get to meet *who you really are* underneath the meat. So strive to be balanced. Take care of the body that carries your soul, but don't forget the soul in the process. Don't panic, I will talk more on the whole body and soul thing later.

Take care of your health and work on yourself. Women love a well-balanced man. At least the women who aren't out of their minds with daddy issues who seem to want to fight for no reason other than to make up. Save the drama for HBO, 'nuff said on that.

Back to love.

Most guys would rather drive a hot rusty nail through the heads of their dicks than talk about their feelings. Love in particular. Maybe that's why you are holding this book and reading it in private. Don't be scared, homie, what you read is your business. People don't know what this book is about so relax, you sissy. Kidding, but honestly, grow a pair of soul balls and read on.

Love is the one thing that can save this goddamn place. It is seriously powerful shit. Don't believe me? Imagine all the love removed from you and your life. Seriously, take a second and think about what it would feel like to have absolutely no love in your life. I mean, if not even your dog loves you (or your cat, Forrest Griffin). Shotgun sandwich anyone?

Love, or the lack of it, in this man's humble opinion, is the reason people do crazy things to each other. It's why we work hard, go to extreme lengths, persist, strive, create and help each other. Love, I believe is also the reason we steal, kill, suffer, blame, agonize and torture each other. Now, I'm no shrink and I understand many factors determine our behavior, but in my experience, love or lack of it seems to be the prime motivator in a lot of situations.

For instance, it has been scientifically proven that babies who are cuddled and shown verbal and physical affection grow more quickly, are stronger and get out of the hospital faster than babies who don't receive the same treatment.

The same theory applies to plants. Plants that are fawned over and talked to lovingly grow faster and bigger than plants that don't get such attention. You don't believe me? Google it. See for yourself.

Come to think of it, don't tell me that the doctors or researchers who conducted those experiments with the babies weren't loved as babies. I mean, who does that to babies?

Sadly, lots of people I would bet. It makes me scratch my giant head that you need a license to hunt animals, but any two morons can go get drunk and make a child. I'm a big fan of freedom of choice and all that business and I'm not trying to start any big brother type society here, but I'm just thinking that maybe some sort of testing or license should be in order when people get to baby-making. Now that I've opened that can of worms, let's move on.

Crimes of passion wouldn't exist if love weren't as powerful as it is. There are many people in prison who snapped and did very, *very* bad things to people they loved. I am not saying they were totally right in the head to begin with, and crystal meth is a bitch, but in some cases, they were upstanding citizens that made one horrible mistake. You see, love is a force we don't completely understand; yet it is the supreme motivator. If you love somebody, you'd do just about anything for them. I mean, no one ever killed anybody in a bizarre love triangle because somebody asked him or her to, right? That would be *crazy* right? Yeah.

Yes, of course that has happened and will continue to happen because love is powerful—we're still learning how to use it. I'm sure a lot of people got fucked up when they were inventing gunpowder.

It's the same thing with love. BOOM!

Remember your first heartbreak? That sucked pretty badly, didn't it? It's horrible, but we live through it and hopefully learn to love again. If it didn't happen yet—wait for it—you will feel the pain of loss someday. Unless you live in a cave and take no emotional risks whatsoever.

It's kind of insane when you think about it.

If you love anyone or anything you will feel loss and pain when they leave, die; say bad things to you etc. However, if you don't allow yourself to love and be loved, your life will be empty and meaningless. What a world!

It would be nice if suffering or loss didn't happen, but hey, if you ain't hurtin' once in a while, you ain't really playin' the game, son! Come to think of it, if everything was safe and nice we would probably lose our minds from the resulting boredom. Looking back at my life, everything really meaningful that has ever happened to me came from loss or struggle.

The experiences that created me were, for the most part, difficult. I'm not talking about my parents having sex on a high wire; you shouldn't be thinking that either, you sick pig. It's not that you can't learn from positive experiences too. I just think the impact of the lesson is deeper when you suffer a bit. Telling a kid not to touch fire because it burns and is dangerous is good, but that little bastard is *really* going to remember never to do it again when he sticks his finger into those flames.

Regardless of the event, it's the meaning we give to it that determines its worth in our lives. So getting cancer sucks balls for sure, but we can turn it into something we can benefit from. Now back to love.

Loving and developing kindness and compassion towards yourself is a good habit to develop in life, but is crucial to do so when you are in crisis. For some reason, some people think that being mean and vicious to ourselves is a good strategy when we get sick. Yes, you can get frustrated and angry with your body for "failing" you, but being angry with the body isn't going to do a damn thing to help you. We will talk about letting all that sweet, sweet rage go later on, don't worry, it will be fun.

When I say loving, I mean just being kind to yourself and your body. To make it simple, how would you treat your dog if he were really sick? Would you yell "Bad Dog!" and give it shit for being sick? Maybe kick it a bit? I am not trying to compare you to a dog, but if licking your own nuts makes you feel better, by all means go for it brother, and do it for the less flexible guys out there.

What I am saying is, if you don't have your own back, if you aren't comfortable with being kind to yourself, no one in the world is going to be able to help you. It is really tempting to beat yourself up when you are sick. It is really easy to get down on yourself when you are sick. The irony is that you need to love and care for yourself *more than ever* when you are down and out.

At the very least you need to allow those that do love you to help you in the tough times. For too long men have had this mindset that we need to go into a cave when we are feeling sick or emotional. Men are taught to be tough, suck it up and not to show feelings. What a load of horseshit. We love athletes that "play with heart" and "go on emotion" but we can't express those same things in real life unless we are playing sports? Total bullshit. How many men "just had something in their eyes" when they realized Dale Earnhardt hit the wall for the last time?

I'm not saying that we need to sit in a circle crying and holding hands, but we do need to learn how to feel and express ourselves without being completely wasted first.

Nothing is going to rob you of a full life quicker than trying to be some emotionless zombie. Now, I talk about meditating or contemplating and observing the inner world quite a bit in this book. To be clear, there is a difference between being an emotionless zombie and someone who meditates to achieve a state of awareness or emptiness. I have experienced moments of awareness that were the most real, powerful states I have ever felt. Even hardcore meditators can "play" in the emotional realms for fun. The difference is they don't buy into the common idea that your emotions are "you" and aren't enslaved or controlled by them either.

Emotional states are a part of being human and there are those who believe that all emotions *are* suffering. Given that the majority of people are not hardcore meditation experts and you deal with a boatload of emotions during crisis, I want to talk about the more *helpful* emotional states in this chapter. I don't want to go *too* far down the whole "lose yourself" road as this book is for the young dude *just starting* to figure shit out on this level. Baby steps boys, baby steps.

Oh and don't kid yourself, even skilled, experienced meditators can, and will lose their shit at some point during a crisis experience.

Why do you think they became expert meditators in the first place?

So, bearing that in mind, let's look at the fascinating world of emotions!

Cue African Safari jungle music soundtrack.

Getting back to the emotionless zombie thing.

Honestly, when is *not* showing love, or feeling positive emotions in a healthy way *not* a good idea? For arguments sake, let's just say that our emotions are there to guide us. It can also be argued that expressing and being aware of your feelings makes you better at everything you do.

For instance, ask a Navy Seal about using intuition and going on gut feelings. Better yet, buy the book "The Intuitive Warrior" by Michael Jaco. This dude was a U.S. Navy Seal that relied heavily on his intuition and emotional intelligence to keep himself and countless others alive throughout his career as a high level operator. Those things are all in the same spectrum that we are talking about here.

While you are talking to that Navy Seal, ask him about how he feels about his teammates and what he would do for them. Those boys go balls to the wall daily. At the end of the day, they do what they do so effectively not only because they are highly trained, but also *because they care about each other*. Ask a New York City firefighter how they feel about the guys they serve or served with. And has no MMA fighter ever hugged his corner men and or their opponent before or after a fight?

Now don't go making dumb Navy Seal gay sex jokes. That's plain disrespectful and if I catch you doing that shit I will find a gay Navy Seal and let him teach you about respect and love. Then again, just go ahead and live a life being a stone. Enjoy the loneliness, tough guy, cause I know the ladies are lining up to hold a big hard COLD stone. Oooooohhhhh. Oh yeah, have fun dating the ones who think they can "change" you. I won't even get into that sad world.

The point here among many is that the more dialed into yourself you are, the more in tune you are going to be to those subtle feelings and instincts that are designed to serve you. When you get tuned into those feelings, you become a superman.

You get stronger, mentally and spiritually. You could also say you build up your resolve. You really need this strength when your body is sick or messed up. The beautiful thing about building that inner strength is that when you do get better, you are a healthier, stronger person for the experience. Now you have deepened yourself and strengthened yourself. How is that going to hurt you in life?

I only say this because I wasted a lot of time and blew some pretty good opportunities because I didn't want to let the guard down. It could be argued that this behavior is part of being a young male. There are times to shut it down emotionally. Times when the emotion is running so high that you can't process it fast enough or it is overwhelming to the point that you can't function.

So guys have trouble with their feelings sometimes. *Imagine that!* When you get thrown into the cancer experience, it can become a daily battle. All of a sudden you are being shelled with intense feelings, some completely new to you. I remember feeling so overwhelmed at times that I somehow made myself numb.

I turned everything off to be able to maintain my sanity through parts of the cancer treatment process. That was a blessing and a curse. Did it help with treatment? Sure, it allowed me to go through the motions and battle through it, but in the end, feelings want and need to be expressed, especially if we don't yet have the skills to help us deal with the crazy.

The chickens come home to roost and when they do —those bastards come a-cluckin'!

I don't quite understand that last line, but I do know it is essential to get those intense, confusing feelings out. Having that friend or family member that you can talk to is fantastic and crucial. If you are lucky enough to have other patients to talk to that are going through the same situation, take advantage. I stayed in my head way too long, was a little too proud and paid for it by feeling like shit when I didn't have to.

It gets *weird* when you keep everything inside too long. You start worrying about what is going to happen if you let all this emotion out. It's a real head-trip. That is why journaling is so important. Not only is it getting the stuff out of your head, it allows you to do so in private. So if you have trouble talking to people, journal or maybe sit in front of a video camera and spill your guts, whatever it takes, just get it out.

Again, I am adamant about this topic because I really feel I wasted a lot of time and energy on trying to be some kind of tough guy with myself. I see it in the world around me too, young dudes trying to be all hard and tough. Strength can be shown in many ways but I believe that none is more powerful than being compassionate. The idea that men have to be strong and tough has probably *hurt* more people than it has helped.

We have the influence of media in all forms to thank for that, along with the same old stories we tell ourselves about how we are supposed to act/think/feel, picked up from wherever and whomever.

Going through treatment, I felt like I was at war with myself sometimes.

On one hand, you have one eyeball looking inside all the time to see if this cancer thing is going to get you. So you distrust your body and your "self." Somehow, I felt it necessary to kick my own ass on a daily basis. I believed that was going to help me with my problems. Calling myself a stupid fucking useless idiot over and over (*because I felt like I created all of this, still do.*) and sending horrible energy through my body really helped speed me towards healing, recovery and renewal. Not.

That makes about as much sense as when I "rewarded" myself with drugs and alcohol for working hard all day. Okay, so that was fun a lot of the time but in the end it really didn't help me. I know mutants who can pull that off for years but I am a different kind of mutant. The truth is, like many people, I didn't know how to relax or shut my mind off back in those days, and I chose drugs and partying to do so, but hey, I'm still here.

I know you may think at this point that I am crazy and I really hope that this doesn't apply to you in any way, I *really* do. But let me be the first to tell you that if you recognize yourself in any of this, you have to ease up on yourself.

That's right. If you want to get through this experience in a better headspace than when you got into it, you have got to stop with the name-calling, the torture and the punishment. Stop blasting yourself with hateful, terrible venomous feelings. It does not help. No matter what you have done, how big of an asshole you were to someone, how terrible the crime, the only way out is to be honest with yourself, with others, and to love and forgive yourself and others too. Figure out what the motivations were then, or are now, for you to have done what you did, and then correct the behavior.

If you don't have the answers, ask for help. The only thing we do best by ourselves is taking a dump. That will never change. The rest of the time we can probably use a little help. Come to think of it, my father had to wipe my ass once in the hospital when I had a collapsed lung so forget that previous statement. Sometimes you need people to wipe your arse. That is a humbling experience let me tell you. So I will say that rule only changes if you are in a body cast or are incapacitated somehow. Moving on.

Love and forgive yourself. I said it. As much as I don't like using those words for the reaction they often receive from people, in my opinion, it is really the only way "out" or at the very least is a damn good place to start.

I don't care who you are, in order to heal and to feel genuine happiness, you gotta love, forgive and move on. And that love and forgiveness starts with you. You don't have to join a church, be religious, take a course or spend money. You can if you want to, but most importantly, it starts with a simple yet powerful commitment to oneself. It starts with a simple choice to love your own damn self, warts and all and be happy.

How do you do that? Find the words that feel right to you. Say them out loud, a lot. *Feel* them. If you feel like a jackass while doing it, that's okay. It's better to look and feel like a fool trying to learn how to let go and love yourself, than never trying, never finding peace and living a half-assed, pent up life. That seems pretty foolish to me.

Here is an example of something you could say to yourself:

"I _____ do solemnly swear on this day to love myself and forgive myself for all the actions in my life that have come to harm myself and those I care about. I understand that I don't know everything and haven't got all the answers. I promise to have an open mind, an open heart and will do my best to care for myself in these difficult days."

Or, for you tough guys:

"As much as I think this is the stupidest fucking thing I have ever done or said, recommended by a total fucking nut bar who went and wrote a book because he thinks he knows something, fucking jerk off that he is, I _____, will try really hard to

be more open to the fact that maybe I need to love myself and that somehow this will help me live a better life.

I fucking hate what I just said and can literally feel my balls shrinking as I say this, but there is also a part of me, that part deep inside me that cried when my first pet died that I loved so goddamn much, or the part of me that gets all emotional in war movies when the shit has totally hit the fan and the guys are all fucking dying and they love each other but not in a gay way, that knows that this asshole is right. There is a part of me that wants to be a better guy and if it means having to do this dumb shit, well then okay I'll fucking try. But if you fucking laugh at me I'll fucking kill you asshole."

Not as good, but it's a start right?

By the way, for all you homophobes out there, let that shit go. It makes no sense to hate people based on their sexual preference and quite frankly it is none of your goddamn business what people do in that respect anyway. If gay people offend you *that much*, you better look inside because there might be something you aren't seeing or accepting. Live and let live. It's not like there are roving packs of gay dudes trying to convert people in the streets are there? No, they are too busy living their lives I would bet.

Speaking of emotion, hate is one that serves no one, least of all its master. I gotta stand up for my gay brothers and sisters. For the record I think it takes a lot of guts to live that particular reality in a world that has people that will hurt you or *kill* you for doing so. I'm looking at you Russia.

Talk about being tough and having resolve. Think about it for a minute before you give in to the collective asshole pressure to be a homophobe.

Getting off my soapbox now. Once again I welcome your emails and letters. But if you *do* actually email me, to call me a "fag lover" or whatever the cool term amongst idiots is these days, use your real name and address so I can visit you and have a nice healthy discussion about this stuff when I'm out in the world promoting this book. Don't be an Internet coward. It's played out. Stand up for what you believe in, even if it makes you look like an asshole. I will respect you more for it.

Geez, speaking about taking a look at yourself, I got really wound up there didn't I? I better have a peek at myself. That Ryan Reynolds *is* pretty handsome, and funny too!

I'm not gay but if I was I bet it would be awesome. When you fought you could actually *fight* each other, you could meet someone the same size as you but with a way better sense of style and *instantly* double your wardrobe, *and* farting would never be an issue.

I can see all the gay dudes shaking their heads at me thinking,

"Just another hetero trying to figure out our world and getting it all wrong."

You know what I mean boys.

The same goes for racist idiots. Life is too short to truly *hate* people. What a waste of energy. Make all the jokes you want about other cultures and ethnic groups in your own worlds like everyone does, just don't put on an "adult ghost costume" if you know what I mean.

If I have forgotten to upset, challenge or piss off any particular group, just write in and I will include your party in the next book, *"People and Groups that are Destroying Our Humanity and Our World."* I'm kidding... Sort of... Not really.

So, now that I got yet *another* rant out of the way, let's get back to it.

Cutting yourself off from feelings of love and forgiveness will not serve you well, my friends. You will never learn to love another with all your heart and you will never be a fully functioning human being. You simply won't. I am not telling you these things because I am trying to turn you into sappy, crying, baby men, all right?

I am doing this so that you can become highly operational super-dudes. The overemotional baby men are men in progress too, but they aren't finished yet. They just started on the other end of the spectrum. So please, for your own sake, give yourself a chance and try to let some love and forgiveness into your life. You will benefit from it, I promise.

To be effective in life is to be focused, aware and clear. This applies to all situations and to all people. Whether you are a single mom or a drug dealer. In order to get done what needs to get done, you need to be F.A.C. I will end the chapter with exercises on how to start working on this clarity so I don't leave you screaming *"How, you bastard! How?"*

This is hard work when you are in crisis. The irony is, sometimes the lack of these traits are the reason you are in crisis in the first place! If you apply the F.A.C., you will automatically be FACing in the right direction. Slick, eh? I know, I know, *another* acronym. No matter what the problem is, if you are focused, aware and clear, you will be moving towards a solution in no time. It is also a fact that when you are working the F.A.C. you tend to be in the present moment and that leads to more flow experiences, and *those* experiences lead to a more authentic life. Life is authentic when lived in the moment. Its just learning how to be there that takes some work.

So…how do you generate feelings of love and forgiveness for yourself?

Well, the first route I would suggest would be to try and get professional help. If you have access to a mental health professional, take advantage of it. This is especially true when you are dealing with life and death situations or serious illness. It doesn't hurt to talk to a pro before ruling it out. It's not for everyone, but it often does help.

I wouldn't get into a cage to fight or jump out of an airplane without some professional help and guidance. Nor would I try to do my own dental work or perform a vasectomy on someone. Why should taking care of yourself on a personal level be any different? Even the crazy bastards that do train themselves (Evan Tanner, R.I.P., buddy) eventually get help from professionals if they truly want to be the best in their sport/ profession. Your inner life is no different. When we can apply the same principles of martial arts or sports training to our personal lives, we will truly be champions of the spirit and better people for it.

Write music or poetry. If you have a creative talent, use it. Maybe this is the time to discover a talent or pursue something artistic that you were previously afraid of pursuing. I was a drummer before cancer and depression. When I got sick and beat up from the treatment, I felt too burnt out to play drums so I grabbed the old acoustic guitar in the closet and started to plunk away on that. Sometimes I would just sing stupid little songs to myself. I remember sitting in the living room on the couch one-day singing, *"I am alone, this fucking sucks, I am alone, and this fucking sucks!"* I did this over and over until it became ridiculous. I ended up trying to make an opera type song about it and ended up laughing at how badly it sucked. I enjoyed doing it and singing like an idiot took me out of myself for a short while. Anything that does that and doesn't hurt you is always a good thing.

I ended up liking the guitar and singing thing so much that I wrote a bunch of songs and started a band a few years later (loudlove.com). I got a few songs on local radio and then across the country and ended up playing many, many gigs. Did I become a rock star? Nope, well not yet anyway, but I was able to turn a coping skill into a really fun thing to do which I still enjoy. I always tell people who can't afford shrinks--write rock songs.

So even if you can't sing, try and express yourself through song. The English, Irish, Welsh, Scottish and all the other "ishes" have got it right when it comes to using music in life. I get goose bumps when I watch

Football (soccer for the North Americans) and see those crowds singing the team or town songs. It is a powerful experience. Come to think of it, most countries that love that sport use a lot of music too. After the game, people are in pubs drinking and you guessed it, singing!

You can generate lots of good feelings when singing. For the non-singers that love hip-hop, write a rap tune. Any genre works. Singing or being creative lets things out, good, bad or ugly. The end result is you feel better, and you've made some art.

Laugh your ass off too if you can, that is a sure fire way to feel better.

So we got off the topic, but in closing I hope you have the courage to open up your heart and allow some light and love in. Take off whatever emotional armor you have created for yourself and just feel the lightness of not carrying it. Imagine all those shitty feelings, stubbornness and macho bullshit as very heavy armor. Take it off one piece at a time and imagine yourself without it. Imagine not needing it. Standing there full of confidence and love and power. Standing in your *true* power bare-assed naked like a Berserker ready to be unleashed upon the world. Yes you will feel vulnerable, but beyond that is a beautiful sense of *being* that is truly powerful.

Imagine how effective the Spartans would have been if they hadn't loved each other or their king. Not very I would imagine. Those guys were feared because of their ferocity, courage and skill. You don't get that good without a good reason. Figure out what it was.

Bottom line, if you love yourself and those around you, you become more powerful than a gun or a fist. If your only agenda is to love and be compassionate towards yourself and others, you become a grounded, happy, calm person who is *unflappable*. We all know how scary those guys are! You know your own heart and that allows you access to more of the world than you would ever dream of. Does it mean you are "less" of a man if you do this?

Hell no, it makes you more *human*.

So explore love and compassion, let it in and let it out. Allow it, create it, give it and receive it. I promise you the world will reward your courage.

Or don't, and see how that works out.

—⊷⊶—

8

BECOMING THE NEUROLOGICAL NINJA

*"The significant problems we face in life can not be solved at the
same level of thinking we were at when we created them"*
ALBERT EINSTEIN

IN THE GRAND scheme of things, the simple fact of the matter is we are
all going to die. Yes, that rock-hard body you have been working on so
much all these years will be dust one day. The human suit will give up
the ghost.

Harsh words? Maybe, but here is the kicker: it's all up to you. Well you,
the environment, maybe your genetics and many other factors, but let's
focus on you and what you do on a daily basis for now. We have a lot of
control over how and when we get released from these bodies of ours.

Like I mentioned before, every thought that goes through your head
is your responsibility. Even if it is a thought that someone else put there,
it is still your responsibility to believe it, or not. Every word that comes

out of your mouth is yours to be responsible for and has consequences. Every move you do or don't make will steer the ship of your life into the harbor or onto the reef. This is never clearer than when you are in crisis. Now before you freak out, thinking I'm putting even *more* pressure on your stressed-out ass, just remember that this also means you have *huge* power. The greater the responsibility, the greater the power. Yeah, yeah and vice versa, I know.

There are many people who take their lives for granted. Oftentimes there is a sense of entitlement that goes along with that attitude. I have been there myself at times in my life but was fortunate enough to have had lady life kick my ass back into line.

When crisis hits you may suddenly feel the *weight* of your life, or perhaps an overwhelming sense of responsibility *for* your life for the very first time. What was once taken for granted is now a precious, guarded thing you may be in danger of losing.

Having a body can suddenly feel like a huge responsibility. For the most part, it is. Having a body is also a gift of the highest order. Sure, it's a gift you have to give back at the end of it all, but it is still an awesome gift to enjoy while you are here.

Knowing that fact and more importantly *accepting* that fact can be a constant source of inspiration throughout your life, or a source of fear. But I don't remember the last time the doorbell rang and it was fear and worry holding a huge bag of money saying;

"Thanks for thinking of us Pete! Here is a little something for your efforts…"

The frailty of life and the sense of impermanence that go along with being alive is what makes it so damn precious.

That would be great save for the fact that so many young people act like they are going to live forever and are immune to these concepts *until* life kicks you, or someone you love squarely in the nut sack. Even then you may still think you are ten feet tall and bulletproof.

The wise man realizes he is but a grain of sand on a beach or a drop of water in the ocean. By himself he is *insignificant*, but as part of the collective he is *immense*.

But that is part of being young and dumb I guess and ignorance can be bliss.

I'll put the bong down and we will continue.

Like I mentioned in the first chapter, it is my belief that we are *spiritual beings* having a *human* experience in the body on earth. I really feel that is true. So in order to experience the trip to its fullest potential, you could argue that we need to take care of the body we ride around in.

They are like pets, these meat suits of ours. We need to feed them and take care of them. If you neglect and abuse a dog, that motherfucker will light you up someday and I don't mean with the radiance of its love for you. Our bodies are the same. If we abuse the body too much, it will bite back with poor health. The mind is no different.

Nothing would make me angrier than those patients at the cancer clinic who were smoking outside with that "why me?" look. Not to rag on smokers or anything, but do you really think that sending death messages to your body in the form of cigarettes is going to inspire the body to rally and fight? Give your head a shake and get off the butts.

Or, if you really don't care and want to die, stop the treatment and give your spot to someone who really wants it. I know smoking is a difficult addiction, but you are in treatment for cancer. FOR CANCER!!!! FOR CANCER!!!!!! Holy shit! What other incentive do you need for quitting? I may sound harsh, and I know I just kicked a hornet's nest, but I think it is ridiculous and insulting. I welcome your e-mails.

What's worse is seeing staff smoke. Yeah that's what I want, a technician or nurse with smoke breath hooking up my chemo. Beautiful. Would you see staff or patients smoking a joint or drinking a beer outside of a drug treatment clinic? Of course not... So let's keep it simple, no fucking smoking near the cancer clinic. Period.

To all you bastards and fat cats in the tobacco industry that make it possible for cigarettes to exist, wait for it...

FUCK YOU! A *curse* on you. You disgust me. You took something sacred and turned it into an instrument of death. I can't believe you go home at night and kiss your children and think you are good people. You are greedy, heartless leeches. A curse on you. You prey on the weak and line your pockets. Can you *please* stop with the cigarettes and do something positive? The only thing more ridiculous than someone defending the tobacco industry is hearing a smoker defend his or her right to smoke. I love you bastards but seriously, get off that shit.

Yeah, yeah, email me about it you beautiful blockheads. Now that we got that out of the way, let's move on.

So I hated seeing people in front of the clinic smoking, and the fact that the parking got more and more expensive the closer you got to the front doors of the place. Hey, maybe the tobacco companies can subsidize the parking lots of hospitals since they are so good for business. Just a thought.

We are all dying, and to quote from Braveheart:

"Everybody dies, not everyone truly lives." Or something like that. The point is, *that* fact becomes crystal clear when the shit hits the fan. We are all dying, but some of us are getting there a little quicker by our own hands and heads. Yes, the thoughts you think have weight and consequences. Yes, your attitude matters, and it matters most when you are in deep shit.

When your back is up against the wall, it becomes clear that you have nowhere to run. You may feel stuck in this body and in this situation. The truth is there are ways to "transcend your reality" so to speak. Getting smashed on booze, high on drugs, gambling and using porn all take you out of yourself for a little while, but they are not the greatest forms of release from your stressful situation. It's like rubbing food on your stomach when you are hungry instead of eating it. Does that make sense?

Of course, the point is to live. I know that, and say that with the greatest respect for anyone sick and struggling. I know how terrifying it is to be in that shitty, leaky, busted- ass boat.

The thing I am talking about is taking the time to find that inner space, that part of your "self" or "soul" that is pure and untouchable and to go there. If the whole "self" or "soul" thing freaks you out, just go *inside*. If we focus too much on NOT dying, we lose the living time we have left.

The crazy thing is, the more you focus on relaxing your mind and body and *not* focusing on the terrible things that are happening, the more you actually are able to heal.

If you are relaxed and present, you are giving yourself a gift. Get it? Being "present" is a "gift." Let me beat you over the head with that. You are going to be more relaxed and more focused. This is going to make you a better person to be around and put your body in a better position to start to heal itself. If you are dying, your friends will talk about how great you were before you ejected from the flaming wreck of your body. I'm just sayin'. No pressure, do what you gotta do.

There were many times in cancer treatment and during the crazy depression days where I felt like my soul was trying to leave my body. I remember feeling sick or anxious and wanting to get the hell out of my body. I had the feeling my soul was a WW2 pilot and my body was a shot up spitfire in flames streaking towards earth. My soul kept yanking at the canopy to open it and bail out, but it couldn't open the canopy. It was a strange and oftentimes disturbing feeling, but most definitely a really powerful one.

I remember that sense of separation between my body and my soul, or whatever you want to call it. It became apparent to me during the tests the doctors were doing that my soul or consciousness would go somewhere else while they did things to my body. It scared me at first but then I started thinking—what if this body isn't "me"? What if my body is like an avatar that "I" or the energy that represents me is riding around in? What if it is simply what a spacesuit is to an astronaut? That sounds like things you may think about while you are *really* high, and they are, but they really started to make sense to me in the context of illness.

Thinking about these possibilities started to make me feel a little better about things. I started to feel like I was more than this body, that I was bigger than I could imagine. I felt that my body was where my energy congregated and focused so I could participate on this earth mission. I started to think that not unlike astronauts, when my mission was over, I would no longer need my suit and crying over my useless suit was as silly to me as the image of astronauts doing the same.

So back to my point: be concerned about the body. Take care of the body, love it, nourish it and do all you can to make it better, but know in your soul and in your guts that the body you spend your time on earth in is not "you." If you can do this, you will take pressure off of yourself, and if you *reduce* the pressure and stress that you generate and *increase* the compassion and care, you will see a result in your health and well-being.

Speaking of caring for yourself, to all my brothers who work outside for a living, two words: face cream. Do yourself a favor and get an unscented moisturizing cream. You will thank me when you are 40 and don't have a face like a catcher's mitt from the 1920's.

Ask a girl to help you pick one out. It's a great way to meet women in pharmacies. Another tangent I know, but trust me, it's good advice! While you are at the pharmacy, buy sunscreen and use it. Melanoma is no joke and it can kill you. I too struggle with this but have had a small hamburger patty cut out of my arm because of melanoma. Sunscreen, bitches!!!

Its tough, friends. It's not like you want to stop caring so much about losing your body to sickness, but it does help to adopt that mind-set a bit. It is total mental ninja stuff here. I know you are reading this thinking;

"I am in the fight of my life and you want me to forget about it, or stop worrying about my body?"

I know, I know, all the love yourself, mind/body crap used to make me furious too, but here's the thing, in *my* experience, it is one of the few ways out of the misery that seems to have the most powerful, lasting effect. It is the only light in the dark that lasts. You have to go "in" to get "out." There is a reason why we say "in love" I suppose.

Even now, when I am mindful of how I treat myself and make sure that I take care of myself, I get great results. When I get lazy, distracted or tired and I don't, my life seems to go to shit.

There is also great power in dropping all expectations period. I started to learn this later on in life. I used to catch myself in moments where I wasn't obsessing about my situation and I only caught myself because I noticed I wasn't freaking out. These moments were few and far between and were like little zen breaks that happened without planning. It was like not existing for a few seconds and it was a relief when those moments happened.

Can you train yourself to do this? Of course you can!

Dropping all expectations and having the resolve to stay that course takes skill and dedication. No expectations, no pressure. Next level shit for sure, but something to think about.

Like I said before, in our western culture we are youth-obsessed and have ridiculous body image ideals and expectations. We are bombarded with images of perfection by the media and hold youth up on this pedestal like it is the greatest thing in life. People spend thousands of dollars chasing a dream and standing on a dock waiting for a ship that has steamed long ago. First of all, being young and beautiful is great, but it doesn't last. The body fails, we get old and we must surrender this body at some point. Can we eat well and exercise and feel fantastic? Hell, yes! Do we have to look 20 forever? Fuck no! What lasts? Character, having passion, being compassionate, loving and having a radiance pour out of your old wrinkled face and a twinkle in your eyes. THAT lasts forever. Or at least the memories and the impact you made on people do.

I don't ever remember being at a funeral of an elderly person who lived a good long life where the topic around the casket was how sexy the deceased looked and what great tits she had when she was 20. Now don't get me wrong, I'm positive that conversation has happened. But I doubt it happens often. In fact, even when people die young the topic is always, "*So young, so young, they never had a chance to live.*" No one stands up there and says, "*Ladies and gentlemen, let's bow our heads for a moment and give thanks to the fact that Sarah died so young and so good looking.*" Enough of that bullshit. Strive to live well, age as best as you can and leave the earth one day, worn out and happy.

Being able to see your body as a vessel for your soul can ease the pressure. Have some fun with the idea of this. Try this exercise. Once again, find a comfortable place where you won't be disturbed, get as relaxed as possible, start your deep breathing and then begin. If you feel anxiety or fear when doing this meditation, let those feelings leave you every time you exhale. All right, here we go.

Picture your body in front of you. See it as a container. Look at your own eyes and see them as glassy or mannequin-like. It is a very freaky exercise, I know, but try it anyway. Now, for fun, see a huge ball of energy and light, filled with colors and sound and vibration pulsing above the body. Slowly turn that ball of energy into a tornado-like form that swirls around the top of your body's head. When you are ready, slowly drop that energy into your body starting from the top of your head, see the color come into your skin, see how your body goes kind of transparent and glows with a powerful radiance as each cell of your meat suit is filled with your energy and comes "to life."

When every cell in your body is filled with light and energy, see the light of life return to the eyes. Stand before your body. See it fully charged and fully healthy, pulsing with incredible energy, ready for life. Disease and fear melt away from this body. The high frequency energy, which is vibrating through this body, literally shakes the disease off of it. Disease and low frequency, heavy energy type dark thoughts disintegrate instantly. They can't take the pure light energy and the high vibration that now encompasses every single cell of your body. It's glowing brightly and it feels incredible just to see it. Now, just as you are almost rendered unconscious with awe, realize that you can step into this body any time you wish. When you realize that this is your body, you are filled with an excitement that you have never felt before.

Step into this incredible being of light and energy and claim it as your earth vessel. Feel the INCREDIBLE surge of energy as you become one with this body. You are healthy, powerful and filled with an energy that you have never experienced before. You raise your arms, throw your head back and the sound of 10 million lions roaring fills the world. It is earth shaking and powerful.

You are alive.

Stay with the breathing till you feel ready to open your eyes and then "come back."

Yes, it's true I have a tendency to go a little overboard with my freaky ideas, but try nonetheless to have some fun with this type of visualization. If you are on medication and feel like you can't visualize, simply close your eyes and try to see every cell in your body filling with a bright pure light. Or just breathe. That works too!

To add power to this exercise, when you breathe in, breathe in light. When you breathe out, breathe out a dark red or black mist. Fill your body with light this way and see if it helps. Again, the main purpose of these exercises is to get control of the body through breathing and through the focusing of the mind, we learn to relax it. The more you gain control, the more you can let go. Mental Ninjutsu! You could also say that ninja's were assassins and that through mental ninjutsu we are assassinating our bad habits and negative tendencies.

Now, for those of you with body image or body attachment issues, you can try the opposite exercise. You can close your eyes and fill the body with light, really get the energy going, and then visualize the body melting away from the light, so all that is left is this pure light pulsating and vibrating. All that is left is the essence. See if you can feel a difference between having a body and not having a body. I know that this shit is weird but it can really help with anxiety and stress if you let it. It can also get you out of "yourself" for a while, too.

Another simple way to "see" the difference between body and soul or your essence, whatever the hell you want to call it, is to picture a glass with water in it. Now, picture fingerprints on the glass. Do the fingerprints affect the water? No, they don't. Think of the glass as your body and the water as your soul or essence. The fingerprints could also represent the cancer, or whatever else may be messing you up.

The glass and water are two different things but are still "one". To go even farther with that analogy, you could say when we die our glass of water gets poured back into the ocean. I like the way that looks in my mind's eye. Regardless, life gets messy and even more confusing when we think the two are the same. In my experience, they aren't and it works for me. Maybe this makes sense to you or maybe it doesn't. But hey, you got this far so keep going!

I know that those of you who are suffering from anxiety or panic disorder may feel very uncomfortable with this concept, but let me explain how this will help you. When we are anxious or stressed, we sometimes feel trapped by our bodies. We wake up and wonder if the anxiety is going to be there. We feel like slaves in our own bodies and farther removed from the world because of it. Our bodies become prisons which we look *out* from, instead of being the awesome, feeling, tasting, earth experiencing machines that they are designed to be.

So play with these visualizations, *push* the boundaries of your comfort zone and expand what you *think* are your limits. Don't accept your current reality as concrete because it isn't. Have some fun, use your imagination and play around with the idea of what you are and see if it helps. It's cheaper than drugs and better for you! *I say this knowing full well how terrifying it is to be in that state of anxiety or panic having lived that experience myself.* But please, give it a try. It helped me tremendously. I hope it helps you too.

When performing these kinds of exercises, you may feel a lot of emotion well up. Sometimes you feel anger, frustration and fear. Anger is a great fuel and it can serve you. But anger and fear left unchecked turn into depression and will eventually bring you down. So what's left? Love, compassion for yourself and others aaaand...

This is making you mad, isn't it?

I know—it is so hard to muster up those feelings in the midst of the fury. It's like trying to keep a white tuxedo clean in the middle of a shit-storm. It is next to impossible. God help me I love a good shit-storm analogy.

The tough part is that during the cancer experience a lot of the anxiety you feel is coming from the fact that your body is sick. One more time: your *body* is sick. Not to mention that if you take some of the modern medical treatment options, you will get even sicker. So sometimes during all this, your *soul* is freaking out. The "you" inside is freaking out and wants to get out like you were in a car on fire.

It seems near impossible in times of crisis to get calm and to try to generate feelings of love and compassion for yourself. Yes, treatment can render you exhausted and beaten, but you know what I mean. This is why it is important to release those feelings with journaling, breathing exercises, meditation, physical activity and sometimes blowing shit up. Sometimes you have to shoot up an old car with a shotgun and scream. Sometimes you gotta visualize some crazy shit to release the pressure. Sometimes you gotta drop it all and do nothing. Do what works for you. We touched on a couple of those exercises here, but there are so many more you can do to help you release the pressure.

As children, we needed permission to do everything. We were told when to sit, when to eat, when to sleep, when to get in line and when to go to bed. We even needed permission to go use the bathroom. Then we grow up and all that conditioning is still there, deep within us. So when the shit hits the fan, we look to the authority figure to save us and to lead the way. *"Tell me what to do!"*

Well, here is the thing—you are in control. You need to take the reigns and get a hold of that wild horse you call your life, your mind and your body and take charge. The first step towards getting control is simple and free and more powerful than pretty much everything else in this book.

You must learn to breathe.

I remember having to remind myself to breathe so many times during treatment. It seemed like I was holding my breath all the time.

We forget to breathe. We make ourselves very still. We get small inside. It's that old caveman instinct that tells us that when a rival tribe member or some big animal is near. We need to get very still and very quiet. So what happens? Our breathing almost stops. We're on red alert--tense and ready for the inevitable attack.

If you would have tapped me on the shoulder during certain moments in my treatment I probably would have jumped out of my skin or hit you. I used to feel like a hand grenade with the pin half out putting on a happy face. We are creatures with old instincts to get low, hide, be quiet and be very still. We also have instincts deep inside us to be prepared to kill and fight for our lives at any moment. Our bodies have chemicals that prepare us for all of those scenarios and pump them through us, sometimes all at the same time, it seems!

So as these reactions gear up inside us, we are also waiting for the outside world to give us cues. We are waiting to be told what to do. Doctors will tell you and your family to go home and make yourself comfortable. That is good, by all means, relax and be comfortable. The reality is you need to learn discipline and focus as well. The absolute start of it all is learning to breathe. Learning how to simply sit and breathe and get settled inside of yourself tells your body that you are in control, there is no danger and all is well. So learn to breathe.

Here's a little exercise for you: find somewhere comfortable; preferably somewhere you won't be disturbed. This works anywhere, from sitting in a waiting room to waiting at the lights in your car. Take a big breath and scream your head off. If you can, hit something as hard as you can. Okay, don't do this part in public unless you are cool with the consequences. I loved hitting a heavy bag (punching bag) with a baseball bat. I loved just beating the shit out of it. Focus all your rage and frustration, all your fear and anxiety on that bag and just beat it like it called your momma something nasty. When you are completely exhausted, carry on with this exercise.

With your feet firmly planted on the floor, your hands in your lap and your eyes closed begin by grounding yourself by seeing roots come out of your feet that go deep into the earth. When you feel rooted down, start with a long, slow, controlled, steady inhalation through your nose. Count to 8 in your mind as you do this.

At the "top" of the breath, begin a long, slow, controlled exhalation out of your mouth for an 8 count as well. Focus your awareness on the space between your nose and your upper lip. This will help you maintain focus.

Try to do this exercise for five minutes when beginning. If five minutes is too long, try for a minute and build your times up from there. Try to keep your mind free of any thoughts. If you have a thought or hear mental chatter, just return your focus back to your breathing. Let the thoughts and chatter dissolve.

Always bring your focus back to that spot under your nose. Focus on your breath. Sit and breathe. Do this as much as you can. Breathing helps with anxiety, pain, and general feelings of helplessness. When you take charge of your breathing you are taking charge of your body and your life. The body follows the breath. The mind follows the breath. That is a powerful first step.

When you do these exercises keep your journal handy. Take a minute to write after doing your breathing exercises. You may be surprised at the insights that pop up during these sessions. For the tough guys who are shaking their heads, calling bullshit on this powerful exercise, *do yourselves a favor and try it before you write it off as bullshit.*

Here are some examples of activities, jobs and situations where breathing exercises are crucial to prove my point:

- Being a sniper or competition shooter
- Being a deep sea diver (old school, no equipment)
- Being a fighter (what does the coach say between rounds? Breathe, control your breath)
- Being a martial artist
- Being any kind of athlete
- Being a race car driver
- Having a baby or watching your partner have a baby
- Being in line at the check out when it is long as hell and the cashier is an idiot or there is a professional coupon-er ahead of you.
- Robbing a bank

- Waiting for test results (medical and scholastic)
- Lifting weights / power lifting
- Doing Archery
- Asking a girl out
- Asking a boy out (especially if you happen to be gay but trying to hide it and are pretending to be some super macho dude in a very small town)
- Having sex (when you don't want to "finish" too quickly)
- Waiting for a pregnancy test to come back.
- Standing up for yourself
- Doing stand up comedy
- Coming up to a Ride Program when you've had a couple after work (don't drink and drive you fucking dumb-asses)
- Awaiting the jury decision for anything, especially the one that involves the hit and run you did because you were drunk... just sayin'
- Doing prison time (you try clenching your ass that hard that long and see how easy it is... pretty little fish)
- Waiting for lift-off in the space shuttle.
- Waiting for lift-off in the space shuttle after "repairs"
- Basically anything involving being alive.

So you see how important breathing is, right? I could go on all day with the list but here is the other list just to be sure.

This is the list of activities and situations where deep breathing and learning how to stay calm won't help you:

- Being dead.

Am I clear? Thank you. So go become the neurological ninja, take control of your meat machine and learn to breathe. It takes a bit of work but it works as well as the work you put into it. You dig?

9

THE SELF-ENTITLEMENT TRAP

"Life is a compromise of what your ego wants to do, what experience tells you to do, and what your nerves let you do."
BRUCE CRAMPTON

THERE MAY COME a time when you start feeling like you deserve certain things. Or perhaps because of the raw deal you feel you've been given, you may feel you are *owed* certain things.

You may then start behaving differently, acting as if you are special or above some of life's rules. This dangerous attitude is the S.E.T. or the Self-Entitlement Trap. We can SET ourselves up for major disaster if we set and then fall victim to it. I know, another stupid acronym. I can't help myself.

Sickness sometimes turns people into monsters.

People sometimes act differently, say different things and become different people when they become ill or experience crisis. I will use the example of my own life because to talk about someone else at this point wouldn't be nice now would it?

When I got cancer I felt like I was special. Then again, I always felt special, but that was because my upbringing allowed me to develop confidence in myself, and in my abilities to successfully navigate life's torrential waters. Look how well that has gone. Sigh.

Now some would argue that this same confidence allowed me to delve deeper into destructive behaviors because I "knew what I was doing" and could "stop at any time." The truth is, my self-confidence has been my greatest asset and my biggest detriment. That confidence in my behavior is what has sometimes sent my life into the deep dark shit tank. Well, that and a raging ego, but hey, lets start somewhere.

For example, as a teen and a young man, I always justified drug use and other potentially self-destructive habits as a reward for good behavior and a release from hard work. I worked hard, so I would play hard, even if it hurt me. This could be seen as a relatively harmless attitude to have when you are talking about occasional minor drug and alcohol use, but without the *discipline* and *responsibility* required to keep your life together when making those kinds of choices you now have a belief system that is setting you up for disaster. Yes, I believe it takes discipline to be a hard living mutant. It seems counter intuitive but there are many people who pull it off. They amaze me. I know plenty of people who can live that lifestyle but sadly I am not one of them. I learned that the hard way. A simpler way to live is the tried and true *"is this going to help me or hurt me?"* question. I always found a way around that one, too.

This sense of entitlement I speak of can lead you down some pretty dark roads.

We've all met the raging, banner-waving survivors who have become angry fanatical champions of (insert cause here). They sometimes make us uncomfortable and are constantly annoying us with their ribbons, wristbands, car magnets and inability to listen to anyone else. They've become a monster with good intentions.

No one wakes up and decides they are going to be this creature. This state is achieved through great stress and tough conditions. Getting sick doesn't make you special; it makes you a person who is going through an experience—with the right to choose your own interpretation of that experience. You can and will do whatever you want.

I do believe that the banner waver people have the right intentions. The lives they lead and the people they become are the result of how they decided to interpret and give meaning to their experience. Simply put, their attitudes and actions are the direct result of how they processed their experience. I guess I just said the same thing twice but you get it.

We are *all* the end result of the decisions we have made to interpret the experiences we've had in life *up to this point*. But life changes on a daily basis. Your life can change in a *second*.

Let's say you are a cancer patient who feels that because they got sick, life *owes* them something. This attitude manifests in your life in the form of you being a bit of an asshole to people. You go to the bar to have a drink even though you aren't supposed to, and you get a bit mouthy and somebody punches your lights out. You wake up shocked and confused. *"This can't happen to me! I am this special being! Don't they know what I am going through?*

I DON'T DESERVE THIS!!!!!!"

Well, sometimes you do.

The underlying truth to me seems to be that some of us are scared, hurt, broken little people running around and bumping into ourselves. We do and say things to get us into more and more trouble. I got into massive debt trouble because of this entitlement bullshit. Well, that and the fact that back then I really didn't think I'd be around long and I made some dumb ass choices. It was a feeling I didn't share with many, if any at all. I didn't realize how much my mentality had changed throughout this whole process and I stayed in survival mode a little too long. I didn't think about tomorrow and even though that can be a great mind-set to possess, it can also cause you to make some *terrible* decisions.

I lost some pretty good opportunities because of my attitude. I felt totally justified in my actions at the time, but the reality was, I was still scared, still hurt and puffing up to make myself seem bigger and tougher like a cornered cat, or a puffer fish going into defensive mode around a scuba diver. BTW, I just love the word scuba. I like the way it sounds and I like saying it. *Scuba*. Moving on...!

What was the result of thinking I deserved to somehow be above common sense? Financial ruin and *more* desperate feelings that I had been fighting for *years* to get away from. I was back at square one, just older and finally a *bit* wiser.

When looking at the data from my life, I see patterns. Stress and bad decision-making, reinforced by a sense of entitlement plus a stubborn refusal to ask for help equals terrible results. Good results have always come when I deal with the stress in a positive way--slow down, take stock of the situation and ask for help when feeling overwhelmed.

If I was an army general and had led military campaigns the way I have led my life at times, everybody would die every time.

Rushing in without proper information, or the time to digest the info you do have, causes problems. I always thought that things would just work out because in my mind, I was a good guy who got fucked over in life. But all that mindset did was set me up for more reaming's.

You really are what you think you are.

I became the good guy who gets fucked over. I *believed* the story my ego was telling me. Finally, I decided that I wanted to be the guy who had lived a pretty interesting and challenging life and then went on to use those experiences to help millions of people and make millions of dollars to be used to help *even more* people. You feel me? *This* is the kind of cycle I want to get "stuck" in.

So what is the lesson here?

Don't set those traps. The world doesn't owe you shit. You owe the world your best effort possible. The irony is that the world seems to reward you more when you give of yourself without expectation. The more you give to the world, the more you get back. The trap is in *expecting* to get something back.

Pure hearted intentions have power boy, don't kid yourself, but the minute you do something, *anything* with selfish expectations, you lose. On some level, you lose. A piece of your humanity, a piece of your soul, a piece of your good heart is gone.

So take that sense of entitlement and send it packing. You are entitled to what you feel you are entitled to—*if* you are *willing* and *able* to do the work to make those results happen. That's it. Anything based in anger without the will or the plan to feel that anger, use it as fuel and move forward, brings pain and suffering and certainly won't bring peace. They can't be in the same room together.

I stole many years from myself because I was pissed off, frustrated and felt entitled. I robbed myself of basic happiness, enduring stress equal to or worse than the stress of illness. My logic was that I got a raw deal and deserved the best in life. Well, after reviewing the tapes, I realize that I put myself in those positions and screwed up all on my own. Now over to Jim with the weather....

Here is the truth. We all deserve happiness! Who deserves pain? Really? That is one sick person who says that someone else deserves pain. Okay, maybe you could argue those who *cause* pain deserve pain, but it doesn't stop the cycle, does it? What you focus on, you receive. I know this to be true!

Being angry, acting from that place of anger and making angry demands of yourself and from others doesn't bring the results we truly want *unless what you really want is to be angry.* But that doesn't make any damn sense now does it? Who truly wants to be cynical, bitter and angry? Does that sound like a good time? Really? I have lived that existence and it *sucked.*

I have encountered people who defend their shitty, negative attitudes like they are precious jewels. God bless em, these energy vampires refuse to see things any other way but negatively. If that is what makes you feel secure (because you sure as shit aren't feeling happy) or vindicated, well have at it. Like I said, I have been there and that attitude leads you nowhere good. I personally want to feel at peace and motivated to keep evolving as a human. It gives you something positive to do and is a goal that is always out of reach. This is a damn good thing in my opinion.

If I could go back in a time machine and had to give myself advice back in those days, I would tell myself to forget about chasing happiness and seek to be more loving and compassionate, first towards *myself* and then outwards into the world. That takes work and is the kind of work worth doing. The best part is that in the end it helps others. When we do that we *all* win. But then again, I'm grateful to have eaten the amount of shit that I have up to this point because even though I am still striving and struggling with *many* aspects in my life, my experiences have given me a perspective in life that is for the most part positive and hopeful. To me that's a win.

The challenge in any crisis is in understanding and managing all that nasty, challenging stuff you feel inside on a day-to-day basis. It's dealing with the hurt, fear, pain and the frustration. It's hard work sometimes. It's embarrassing and it leads to uncomfortable places, but just like you gotta wipe your arse after you poop, you gotta pick up the pieces and clean up the mess of your life. Because if you don't, you'll walk around with a dirty arse, smelling like shit and no one will want to play with you.

Now at this point, if you were like me years ago, you are feeling ready to drive, fly, take sled dogs or roller-skate to my retreat center in the country (on a private lake, no less) storm up my long driveway that winds through a beautiful enchanted forest and run screaming into my personal dojo, with the intentions of kicking my ass for being so full of shit that I deserve a beating or at the very least a serious talking to.

It is here that I greet you with a hip throw to side control, where you soon realize that all your anger has gotten you pinned to the floor by someone who is lovingly smiling at you and waiting for you to stop screaming, raging and crying so we can talk.

My chain-smoking monkey butler arrives with a tray carrying two tall, frosty glasses of iced tea. He then monkey slaps you in the face to get you to calm down, and you lie there, stunned by what has become of you, pinned to the ground and being slapped by a monkey with a smoke in his mouth who only wanted to bring you a cool refreshing glass of iced tea.

Don't go and call PETA, the smoke isn't lit. He's trying to quit and I wouldn't let him smoke in the dojo anyway. He also knows how I feel about cigarettes.

At that point you realize the ridiculousness of the situation and start laughing. You laugh hysterically at which point I help you up, Clive the monkey butler takes your hand and walks with you to the water's edge of the private lake beside my house while I change out of my Gi. I come to join you in that perfect place by the lake where the view is *spectacular* and we sit and have a great talk about your life and what brought you here.

You soon realize like the rest of us, that you are just angry, frustrated, hurt and scared and don't know what to do. You realize that *that* is a great place to start. The iced tea tastes perfect and you are glad to have come.

We take stones and put all our anger and fear and disappointments into them and hurl them far into the lake, smiling as we think of those problems sinking towards the muddy lake bottom. We move on to the firing range and I laugh as you blast away at targets with all your fears and disappointments written on them. Even when you miss, the release still feels good.

Soon, we head over to the Calming Field where an old bulldozer with "Captain Calm" spray painted on it is waiting for you. After a quick driving instruction and the choice between an old army helmet and mirrored shades or a Viking helmet and goggles, you begin to push a very large boulder across the field from one big red circle to another. The grinding sound the rock makes on the blade as the powerful old machine pushes it along pleases you, and you realize that resistance is futile. You scream to me over the noise that the bulldozer should be called "My Intention" and I agree after you explain that with clear, focused, powerful intention and skill, you can move mountains one rock at a time. I tell you that you are starting to get it and you laugh like a maniac.

When the rock push is over, you drive the bulldozer over a car after you once again spray-paint words that represent the things that frustrate you on it. You are not able to stop screaming and laughing this whole time. You feel lighter and more powerful than you *ever* have before. As we dismount Captain Calm, I tell you to remember how it felt to move that boulder and crush that car. I tell you that Captain Calm has become a part of you forever and you will have access to his power whenever you want it, to move any obstacles in your life. I tell you I am going to steal the intention analogy you came up with and claim it as my own. You don't seem to care. We then move on to the wood chipper.

At the wood chipper I ask you to choose a cedar log from a pile. When you make your choice, I give you a de-barking tool and you begin to strip the bark from the log. Amazingly, at the precise moment that you begin to get really thirsty, Clive shows up with another *perfect* glass of lemonade. You ask if you can pet him and I ask if I can pet you, and Clive makes a funny monkey face and we all bust up laughing. You receive no monkey slap this time.

I ask you to do this de-barking work in silence, telling you to think about the people you feel have wronged you in your life. When there has been enough bark stripped from the log, I ask you to take a marker and write down names of people and situations that have brought you pain on the bare log. You smile as you realize the first name you write is your own. Then I fire up the wood-chipper. I show you how it works and then smile as you feed the cedar log through it, watching the past be chewed up and spit out, becoming the chips for a beautiful footpath for others to walk on. You figure that one out by yourself pretty quickly, enjoying the image in your mind's eye of people walking along a path comprised of your released frustrations and disappointments.

After an incredible dinner, I show you to a room where there are body paints and all kinds of cool shit to transform you into a warrior. I leave you there, telling you that the next version of yourself I meet will be your warrior-self that has always been there to protect you and others. Reluctantly—feeling more than a bit foolish—you paint yourself and feel something standing up inside you. With a primal excitement and your new self-revealed, you follow the sounds of drumming and chanting down to a fire pit where others are gathered around a huge fire. When you meet me down by the fire pit I ask you to simply take in the moment.

You see others like you. Bodies of all ages, shapes and sizes. There are some with physical scars and others with eyes that reveal a ferocity and life force that you recognize coursing through your veins. When all have arrived we celebrate our rawness and our warrior spirits. We give thanks for our courage and our newfound strength. We are reminded that it is okay to feel powerful and raw, and that there is a strength in each of us that is old and wise.

Circling the fire, each person gets a chance to take a chunk of wood, stand up and deliver whatever message moves him or her. Some say that the chunk of wood represents all the fear and hate in their lives and after giving thanks, they throw the log onto the fire and watch it burn. Others stand by and simply scream in triumph and throw their logs into the fire.

Every tossed log is greeted by three loud and fierce "ah ooo" screams from all around the fire, borrowed from the Spartan tradition. The smoke rises up and away, carrying our hopes and dreams, our fears and our pasts with it. As we each stand and deliver our message, you realize that *you are not alone.* You feel the connection between all of us. You realize and feel deeply, what great strength is contained within us all and in the human spirit. You realize you will never be the same and that *this is such a good thing.*

Afterwards we dance around the fire, chanting and singing and allowing ourselves to let go, to move and to be free. Knowing that we can't shake ourselves free of these bodies that hold our spirits, we try our best to shake the fears and things that trouble our spirits *from* these bodies. We celebrate and we give thanks. When the celebration of life is over, Clive is waiting to take you back to your room. As you are led there, you realize that the monkey is off your back and is now leading you away to rest. The irony makes you smile.

You sleep like you have never slept before.

In the morning you leave with a new perspective, a wallet-sized picture of you in full warrior gear, an autographed picture of Clive and a newfound sense of peace. I tell you my door is always open for you to return for a chat at anytime. I remind you to call first though, as I am always off doing awesome things around the world. You leave, feeling fantastic and better for having had the experience, promising to show others the way.

Your life becomes one of compassion, trust and complete *awesomeness*.

You die many years later with a huge smile on your face, worn out and happy. The last image in your mind is of you dancing around that fire so many years ago with Clive looking on and clapping, monkey slapping *the shit* outta people.

Wouldn't that be nice?

I truly wish that this had happened to me. I wish I would have run screaming into a dojo and had my ass kicked and then led to a beautiful place where wisdom was imparted upon me. The classic Karate Kid Fantasy... except for the washing and waxing cars part.

Hell, I would have even loved the whole monkey butler, iced tea, bulldozer, and warrior, fire pit thing. But that didn't happen. Not yet anyway, but the proceeds of this book are going to make that happen when I open *The Hillbilly Healing Center*. Mark my words!

IT WILL HAPPEN!

Even though I had started to learn and implement a lot of the stuff in this book, it still took a while to "feel normal."

No, I didn't have the magical, awesome experience I just described. What happened instead were 15 years of soul searching, anger, frustration and an attitude of "*I can do this myself because no one understands me.*" At times I had a big shovel nicknamed resentment and there were days I *loved* to dig.

I would dig at the past, chastising and tormenting myself for the decisions I had made. This would bring up more feelings of resentment, frustration and anger and that would make me dig even more. I would find myself in a huge hole surrounded by negative energy until I was trapped by it. Oh yeah, as I dug, I also had the energy of self-entitlement to fuel me.

Eventually, I did find a dojo where I found Brazilian Jiu-Jitsu, a martial art that allowed me to find real peace within myself through hard work and long hours of training. I found that I had created most of my problems because of my beliefs and my inability to slow down and release the anger and frustration that drove me unmercifully. I realized one day, after years of trying to figure it out, that my life was not working. I had hit that classic point where so many have gone before me. I truly felt like a walking cliché.

I was tired, broke and alone. I laughed as I realized that I had completed the trifecta of being spiritually, physically, and financially bankrupt. I felt that I had huge potential but just couldn't get it together. I realized that I hadn't yet reached the bottom when I went nuts and then got cancer all those years ago. Those experiences had created a fucked-up monster that then led me to the *real* bottom.

The hardest part was keeping up the front that all was well. The good news is that I eventually found ways to build myself back up. I found a way to rise above the shit.

I married a really rich woman whose father owns a brewery.

Kick me. I deserve it for that one.

That's not true but if you can make that happen, well... to each his own, I suppose. Yes Dad, I know that is your joke by the way. Now everyone knows. You probably stole it from someone else.

Realize that beating yourself up is useless. It's an easy fight to win with no satisfaction. I mean it's like beating up a child or a handicapped person. Who does that? Right? A fucking jerk does, so don't be that guy. Take the past and figure out the reasons things went the way they did. Write it down and read it. Let it sit.

Realize you aren't perfect--you are a soul driving a meat suit around and you are going to get in fender benders, and sometimes the driver is going to get hurt too. It depends on what you hit and how hard you hit it. *Where* you end up in life also depends on where you focus your attention.

So remember, the world doesn't owe you *shit.*

But I believe *you* owe your best effort to the world and to yourself every damn day.

Why?

That's up to you to figure out my friend.

—⊗⊗⊗—

10

PERSPECTIVE

A PUNCH TO THE face is a very different thing to experience depending on which side of the fist you are on.

This crisis you are in is just an experience. You can even choose to look at it as *not* being a crisis. Hell, you don't even need to define what it is that you are experiencing. It is what you are going to make it. The energy you put into this current experience is going to feed it and nurture it. What are you going to pay attention to? What are you going to feed on and what are you going to let go of? If fear was a fish that could be caught, what kind of fish do you have on the line? What kind of body of water are you on? Are you on a raft or on a crab boat? Are you reeling in a shark or a sunfish? Is this shark dragging the boat backwards like in the movie JAWS? Crisis can feel like that sometimes. Fear can feel like that sometimes. Like you are being dragged down into the deep waters.

I was at my grandmother's funeral and had a fantastic talk with my cousin Ron. He is one of the heaviest thinkers I have ever met, and is, in my humble opinion, brilliant. We were talking about life and heavy shit as we usually do when we see each other and he told me something really cool.

He told me that people forget that we all float. Yes science guy, some people don't float as well as others, or float at different levels but for the sake of writing something poetic and beautiful lets just agree that in theory, we all float. Sheesh!

I'm paraphrasing here because I could never be as eloquent or as deep as Ron, but the gist of it was that if we all stopped thrashing around in the water, wide-eyed and terrified of drowning, we would realize that we float.

We could take the time we need to regain our senses, our energies and our focus and find our way back to the proverbial shore in a number of ways. He planted such a simple, powerful image in my mind; *that we all have what we need to feel good about ourselves and life in general somewhere inside us already.*

I like to think that we are born with it and that spark lies deep within us waiting to be fanned into the flames of awesomeness - that there is nothing to do but remember that fact and be quiet and still enough to let it manifest again as a healthy life full of joy.

I believe this to be true but I also know how hard it is to remember that when you are up against it and the mind is running wild. So don't panic, just keep reading my friend.

We all float. Just think about it for a bit. What does the water represent? Crisis? Suffering? Doubt? Life itself? At first, the water is a dangerous thing that is threatening to take us under. But switch perspectives and suddenly the water, that same thing that was once threatening to drown us, is now something completely different. It holds us up, carrying us gently along until we find our way back to shore. If it was a body of fresh water, you could even drink it! You could fish in it! You could live off of it!

What allowed us to switch perspectives was that we calmed down enough to realize that we could float. We realized that we could make it to shore. I find it interesting that the difference between the words *scared* and *sacred* is one letter position. One small shift in the order of the letters and the word becomes something completely different. Some could argue it becomes the polar opposite of its original meaning. Sometimes a small shift in perspective is all it takes to see things differently.

Life can be seen as something threatening or as something that will support us, depending on our choices and our perspectives. My cousin Ron is a heavy, brilliant dude and I hope I didn't totally mess that up or embarrass him by including him in this mess of a book.

It is also really helpful to remind yourself that nothing in life is permanent. Nothing stays the same forever. Not love, financial markets or our bodies. Every moment, things are changing and we can *influence* them.

It is super fucking annoying when you are down and out and some well-meaning jackass is trying to make you feel better by comparing your situation to someone else's.

"It can always be worse" they say, or *"look at the positive side of things."*

Although both of those statements are absolutely true, pick your shots, people. I understand you are trying to help, but review "How to be a Kick Ass Friend." People know it can be worse. It can *always* be worse. I have been guilty of this behavior myself.

Side note: I hate seeing people in pain and sometimes want to push them through it. You can't hurry people through pain, grief, or any emotional experience. It's gonna take as long as it's gonna take. Even though you want to hurry them through it for the right reasons, you can't, so don't. We tend to make things about ourselves when we should just shut up and listen.

When trying to help someone who is messed up and in a bad place, remember that *it's not about you*. Yes, there is common emotional ground and that's what we look for when trying to bond with the person, *but the most powerful thing you can do is listen with all your heart.*

Now if someone is being a victim, lovingly kick him or her in the ass, call them on it and then crush them with love. You are doing them a favor.

A real friend is someone who knows who you are when *you* have forgotten and won't hesitate to kick you in the ass to wake you up.

Now back to our scheduled programming.

What is 'better" anyway?

Is being happy and mentally healthy but confined to a wheelchair "better" than being able-bodied and schizophrenic? Is it "better" to survive a horrific car crash unscathed, only to find out that your best friend, your child, or another loved one was killed in that same crash?

What about being in financial ruin, and you beg and plead the universe to save you and deliver you lots of money—then suddenly someone you love with all your heart dies, leaving you a lot of cash. Is that "better"? What's "better" to you? The examples can go on and on.

Comparing yourself and your situation to others is a really bad thing to do. Ask the guy who had to take a piss in a urinal next to John Holmes back in the 1970's.

I remember sitting in the waiting room at the cancer center and feeling sorry for myself. I raised my heavy, thought-filled head just as a nurse wheeled this old guy in who had had half of his jaw removed. BOOM! I'm feeling better.

As terrible as that is, it is true. I wasn't thinking; "*better him than me*," I was just brought back into perspective by the sight of him. Yes it sucks to have cancer, BUT I can still make out, smile, literally, chew my food and grow a beard. *I have a complete jaw!*

Well the beard came a few months after treatment but you follow me. My armpit and parts of my chest hair still haven't really come back and yes I look like I'm wearing a hair-kini but who gives a shit about that? Oh, and I can go out in public without being stared at. Does that mean I am "better?" It means whatever I decide it means.

Here is another situation I got into that made me think a bit:

I was in a diner having a cup of coffee during my treatment days. In the booth next to me were college students, about my age. I was alone and I was listening to their conversation about how "depressed" they were about this situation, and how "sick" one of them was last week and their nose was totally running and how it was so HORRIBLE. I sat there trying not to turn around and just tear them to shreds. It was at that moment that I realized two things: the first was how unlucky I was that I wasn't a fucking sheltered, mindless twit like the kids next to me, enjoying my youth and clueless to the kind suffering I was experiencing. The second was I wouldn't trade anything for my experience because of everything I had gained from it.

I felt I was learning more than any degree could give me—and that was in the midst of it! The truth was, I wanted the best of both worlds. I wanted to be young and stupid and clueless and free in a good way, but I also wanted depth and understanding. I was frustrated because I felt alone and not at all like most people my age felt. At 21, I felt like my youth was over and that I was an old man. I felt *zero* connection to my peers and that sucked. The good news was that I felt more connected to the things in life that mattered to me, but at what cost? Which is better? It is up to you to decide.

Going back to the man with half his jaw removed—I felt better about my situation after seeing him because I saw someone who seemed to have it rougher than me. Again, I didn't know his particulars, but I knew I didn't want to have half my jaw removed. I was grateful for my situation; I don't think there is anything wrong with that. For all I know, that dude found bliss. I used to feel that I wasn't a "real" cancer patient since I didn't have the *worst* cancer you can have. I felt like a lightweight compared to some of the cases I saw, although I am quite sure no one would have wanted to trade mental health situations with me at that time. But like I said before, comparing yourself is such a bad idea.

I will tell you this, I sure feel like a "real" cancer patient when I am going back to the cancer clinic for x-rays and blood work during my annual checkup. Sitting there, shitting my pants as I await results and hoping I will be fine gets harder every year. I know I am lucky to be alive and I am grateful to be here, but I still feel freaked out. This is coming from someone who has been working on his mind for a loooonnng time. But hey, I'm a slow learner.

Speaking of feelings, think about the feelings you have after a funeral. The sight of that casket going into the ground and the sense of permanence that death brings is sobering.

You may look around and think, *"Shit, I'm glad to be alive."* We actually don't know that it's "better" to be alive than dead, because we have nothing to compare with besides other people's opinions. I'll tell you this though, I'm pretty sure I saw the afterlife coming out of surgery not long ago and it was *awesome*. I didn't want to come back "here." Maybe I'll tell that story later.

Regarding death, what we *do* know, is we *don't* know, so let's go live our lives like the precious gifts that they are for whatever time we have left!!

I remember watching my uncle die and being completely overwhelmed with child-like awe in his last few moments. I remember how all the little muscle contractions beneath his skin reminded me of a shimmery, glittering lake—how the light dances across the water in the early morning.

My relatives were weeping all around me as he left, and all I could think about was, *how fucking awesome life is*. I was completely in the moment, my hands on him, as I watched his soul bail out of his busted-ass body.

When it was over, I went outside; it was a beautiful morning. I left the hospital in a state of total gratitude. I was glad my uncle was out of that body and that his brothers could grieve and move on. Watching him die was extremely painful for them as he was the youngest brother. It crushed them.

As I walked to my truck my Zen-like trance was quickly shattered by the blast of a car horn. I looked over at the intersection and the next thought I had was how fucking stupid people were, rushing here and rushing there and blowing horns at each other. I stopped and looked at the beautiful sun and felt the cold air fill my lungs. I was so overwhelmingly grateful to be alive, I wept. I cried tears of joy and I gave thanks to life. Was I sad my uncle was gone? Yes, but it didn't *outweigh the joy I felt for being alive*. As I drove home I marveled at life and felt once again awed and humbled by its power.

Now you may be thinking I am full of shit. That's fine. I would have felt the same way reading this in the midst of my crisis. Remember, I am many years down the road here folks. I have taken some time to observe my life, myself and to *really* digest my experiences before going and writing a book on something as intimate, sensitive and as delicate as cancer, mental illness and life in general! I am also sure that when I read this at 70, if I make it that far, I will have a completely different perspective once again, too!

Taking the time for reflection, digestion and introspection of my life's experiences had led me *to be able* to have that moment where I was *able* to feel gratitude, joy and awe as my uncle was dying. All that time put into myself allowed me to have that powerful experience.

I didn't tell you that it felt like my heart was going to tear itself in half when my father showed up right after my uncle died, and saw his youngest brother's lifeless body. My uncle bailed out while my dad was on his way to the hospital. The sight of my father mourning his little brother just *crushed* me.

I have always said it is harder to be the caregiver than it is to be the patient and seeing my dad softly crying over his brother's body brought that home once more. I felt helpless knowing that he was hurting. I rubbed his back just for a second to let him know I was with him and then left him to let it out. I know how my dad mourns; I knew to just let him be. I also felt grateful to come from such a fierce and loving family.

As I write these words, I am struck once again by how hard it must have been for my father, mother, sister and those close to me to see me go through the things that I did. I can only imagine and would spend little time doing so, what it must have been like. It is too much. I am once again reminded of the power of love and its importance in my life.

So many perspectives from a single event. So profound and personal, but so universal.

What a heavy, beautiful, intense trip this life is. I am endlessly grateful to still be a part of it.

It is very easy to get caught up in the moment when you are sick; it's easy to be caught in the drama of the moment in life *period*. Perspective is everything in life, or at least a very powerful part of it. Perspective is the ability to think outside of yourself—this can be a relief when you are anxious and scared and also quite handy when you are dealing with nasty situations or people.

Putting yourself in someone else's shoes or at least *trying* to see things from someone else's view can help you understand their anger. It might also diffuse the anger in you, allowing you to think clearly and deal with the problem with a clear, calm mind. It can also activate the compassion inside you. So that's good right?

There are many ways to change your perspective. A very simple exercise, which I'm sure most people have experienced involuntarily, is simply called "*Racehorse.*"

Racehorse is basically getting stuck in traffic with a twist. I know you are scratching your head, but be patient, you bastards! Now I'm not talking about just being stuck in traffic although that can be a real test of patience in itself. Nope, I'm talking about waiting till about a half an hour before traffic really gets bad and drinking as much water as you can in one sitting. Let's say two or three liters. Chug the water back and then get in your car and look for any sort of containers, and get rid of them. Now the rest is easy, sort of.

Get in the car and drive onto the highway or wherever the traffic is going to be the worst. Make sure you get right into the thick of it as your bladder starts to talk to you. The idea is to be stuck in traffic having to piss like a racehorse. We have all done the squeeze and squirm (squeeze the steering wheel and squirm in your seat). This is such a powerful exercise, *and* you can do for free. Let's see what it can teach us....

Patience: Well, you are stuck in traffic and are going to piss yourself. It is pretty obvious that you are going to need some patience.

Will: Lets see how much willpower you have. Are you going to hang in there or piss yourself?

Resourcefulness: Is there anything in this car I can piss in while stuck in traffic? One of my best friends can drive and piss in coffee cups at the same time like he was born to do it. It is quite a feat! Too bad I got you to empty the car of containers first... hee hee.

The Power of Prayer: I'm not religious but I have prayed to NOT vomit, get speeding tickets, be a father, piss myself and crap my pants. Sometimes all at once!

Perspective and Focus: Nothing puts things into perspective like being trapped in a car in traffic while having to piss like a racehorse. You focus very hard on one thing, and that is not pissing yourself. Very simple and very powerful!

Gratitude and being thankful for the simple things: When you finally take that leak you will COMPLETELY understand what I'm talking about. Taking a leak has sometimes felt better than having sex and winning the lottery at the same time.

Humility: If you can't hold back and you do piss yourself, you may experience this powerful emotion.

Relief. Take a piss...'nuff said.

With this one simple exercise, you can learn so many valuable things. You don't always need the big, mean, horrible experiences in life to learn powerful lessons. You don't need to buy anything or take a seminar. You don't even need to do this in a car. This simple exercise can really open your eyes to concepts that are very important. Whether you are dealing with cancer or you are trying not to piss yourself in traffic, the concepts, reactions and thought processes are very similar.

Sure, pissing yourself in traffic is not going to kill you unless something goes horribly wrong. But it is a good example of how we can deal with crisis in a very small way. If you want to up the ante, add laxatives and prunes and a big meal beforehand. Shitting yourself in traffic is no joke. I don't want to even get into that one. It's hard to cross your legs and hold back a deuce while driving standard, *especially* on a hill. (Don't use the handbrake.) In fact, you can learn about persistence by thinking like your body does when it's trying to make you go for a poop. Talk about drive, will and persistence!!! ANYWAY!

I really don't think any of you will do this exercise but I hope I made my point. If you do, *please* film it and send it to www.thebadtimesbible.com!

Sometimes when we are in crisis, we need to dial it back to something we can handle and understand. It is really easy to get caught in philosophical, existential and mind-melting mental traps. It is good to explore those aspects, and very much part of the experience, but only to a point. Then we need to dial it down, scale it back, and regain control. We can also breathe, meditate and drop it all. Do whatever works for where you are at in your life at the time. You understand.

Simply holding back or interfering with a simple, primal, vital and ancient ritual like voiding our bowels and bladders can really bring a ton of perspective to the table. Well, you could just hold your breath but that wouldn't be as much fun, would it?

So take a second to gain some perspective. Hell, take a minute. Be creative. You can literally change the course of your life by simply changing your perspective. A piece of paper can be 10,000 or more things depending on how you fold it.

So go ahead and ask yourself questions like *"What am I not seeing, Universe?"* or *"How can I see this situation in a different, more positive way?"* How many ways can you fold that piece of paper? Keep asking questions and keep adjusting your perspective; it can make a huge difference. Remember to take the time to give yourself and your mind a break everyday too. You aren't going to crack *that* nut in a day.

Remember, a punch to the face is *very* different thing to experience depending on which side of the fist you are on....

———— ∞ ————

11

Stop Kicking Your Own Ass and Get Into the Time Machine

"The man who has no imagination has no wings."
Muhammad Ali

In order to dig yourself, sometimes you gotta dig into yourself. Ya dig?

This chapter involves the concept of inner-child work. As much as that term made me want to vomit the first time I heard it, I realized that if I modified the inner-child exercise in order for it to have more meaning to me, it might be of value.

I can handle this concept when I think of it as visualizing the most sensitive part of your being as a small, child-like version of yourself. I just really don't like the term "inner child." There is something about it that irks me. Moving on.

The point is to access the sensitive, innocent parts of us and get re-acquainted with what they *feel* like. We want to break through the layers of fear and armor that keep us away from our genuine selves. So give it a chance, you might be surprised at what you find out and feel.

As I mentioned before, one of the hardest things to do in a state of crisis is to stop playing the blame game. It's so easy to kick yourself while you are down. Why do we do that? Why do we beat ourselves up when we need to do the complete opposite?

We do it because it's easy and we need to blame somebody, right? The question is; what does it accomplish? Do we feel better? Does it make the problems go away? No! So why do we do it?

If you had a child you truly loved and they did something wrong, would you scream and berate them? Would you whisper horrible things in their ears as they slept?

If you saw someone else doing that, you would probably beat the living piss out of them to stop them from doing it! So why are we so fucking mean to ourselves?

Because maybe sometimes we feel we deserve it. And that is just a goddamn shame. So little time on earth to spend and we spend so much of it hurting and punishing others and ourselves. Man, I'm really hung up on that one, eh?

It's time to try something new here.

Remember, I am not asking you to film this next exercise and put it on the Internet. I am not asking you to do this stuff in front of your friends and family.

I am asking you to open your mind and heart and try something different. There are now theories that suggest that the past, present and future are all happening *at the same time*. These theories suggest that time is not linear. Google that shit. It is really cool and mind bending stuff to think about. With that interesting and awesome theory in mind, we are going to try something.

We are going to use the Time Machine embedded in your head.

I want to take you on a little trip. I want you to turn off the logical part of your brain for a moment. I want to tell you that you have an incredible ability inside you. You all have the power to travel through time. Yes folks, if you close your eyes, you can take yourself anywhere you want to go at anytime in the past present or future. Believe this with all your heart. Try hard. Well, just close your eyes and get out of your own way.

This time machine can take you to the places where you got hurt, hurt someone else, or screwed up somehow. This time machine will allow you to go back and protect that small innocent child you were (even if you were a little bastard) when you most needed it. It can take you anywhere you want to go, to any place in your life, or into a future that does not yet exist. Unless of course the theory that suggests that all time is happening at once is real, in which case that future and possibly many more exist and are playing out as you read this. You get it.

I don't know how this works, or the science behind it—but when you really try to do these exercises, sometimes something really cool happens inside.

When you go back and spend time with those versions of yourself, and talk and listen to them, a healing or at the very least a *shift* occurs. Seeing your child-like self cracks you open to an innocent place and makes you want to protect that child. It is really weird, but it works. Something happens, energy shifts; you *feel* things. It is quite remarkable. Give it a shot and a chance. At the very least you might release some emotion or remember that you care about yourself, and those are two good things!

The beauty of this exercise is that you can visit anyone. Imagine for a minute if you could go back and talk to your parents when they were children. Imagine talking to *their* parents as children! Go as far back as you want, tell them what they are about to become and what they are going to do and how it is going to make people feel.

Talk to them before they become the people that they were when they hurt you. Do the same for yourself. Do you think when you were a kid you thought to yourself: *"When I grow up I'm gonna be so mean to myself! I'm gonna say terrible things to myself and I'm gonna take drugs and beat myself up and hurt myself and other people too!"*

No! Of course not.

And if that child saw how you were treating yourself now, would they encourage that? See, the freaky part of this exercise is what comes out of the people's mouths that you talk to. If you can focus and commit to the exercise fully, some really freaky shit starts happening.

They start talking back! They start giving you information. The really weird thing is you FEEL it. If you are having an emotional response to this exercise, you are having a real experience. Believe me; you will have a real experience. And these experiences can change you.

I have reduced myself to tears with this exercise. The child in me has *berated* me. I did this exercise once and the teenage version of me totally ripped me a new asshole. I have had some intense discussions with parts of myself to say the least. No, I wasn't high when I did it, either.

Sometimes when I am stuck, I close my eyes and get in that time machine and I go see the Pete *of the future* and I say *"Hey man! I'm fucked up! I'm stuck! I am alone here dude! Help Me!!! How do we get outta this one?"*

Then the older wiser Pete with the epic white beard smiles, puts his arms around me and gives me a big back-cracking hug. I feel safe and relaxed there. I listen to what he has to say. I thank him and I leave. The other thing about going back is that you can go back and just love yourself. Instead of just going back to console, to warn or to question, *just go hang out*. Spend time with versions of yourself. Go visit yourself on your deathbed. Ask some questions. Sit by your pregnant mother's side and talk to her about the upcoming birth of yourself! Freaky, eh? But do it! You will have some fascinating experiences, I promise you.

This exercise allows you to go anywhere at anytime to do, say, or experience anything you want. Generating positive feelings through these exercises only makes you more relaxed and more receptive to healing. Releasing negative feelings that may be trapped in you through creative visualization exercises is a safe activity you can do anywhere you can close your eyes and be quiet.

It is mental work once again, but any time spent controlling your own thoughts and creating images in your head that generate positive feelings is less time spent reeling in that bastard fish called fear. There is no end to these types of exercises. I have included more here to get you started but feel free to make some up on your own. Be creative and try to have some fun. See what moves you. And now, Let's Get Visual!

Visualization Exercises for ANYTHING!

All right, I know there are some people out there reading this that believes visualization is stupid new-age bullshit. I know that some of the people that present this type of material come off as really, *really* flaky sometimes, and that can be a turn-off. I get it. I am also here to tell you to give your head a shake hard enough to open up your mind a bit. The mind-body connection is something that has been explored, with interesting, *encouraging* results, for a long time.

There is a reason it gets so much attention and that reason is that it is a powerful tool to possess—and you can use it as often as you can for whatever you want. Pro athletes use it, corporate kings use it, and we all use it to a certain degree without even knowing it. Like whenever you imagine banging some girl you will NEVER get a chance at. I kid, I kid. It really is a most important tool to be included in your arsenal, my pea-headed friend.

I know you are sitting there on the couch, hung over with an orange penis (because you got drunk, ate Cheezies and watched porn last night), saying, *"But what exactly is this visualization that you speak of?"*

Well, first of all I can't take you seriously with an orange penis, so go clean that up first, or at the very least put on some pants and we'll get started.

That is a great joke that I didn't write, by the way, so if you wrote it, thank you—and don't sue me either, because this is a book to help people, you greedy bastard. Now, I know you may be thinking I was going for a cheap laugh there with the whole orange penis thing, and if you knew me personally you would be correct in thinking so. I was also using it to illustrate a point. When you read that orange penis bit, if you made some kind of mental picture in your head of that hung-over dude sitting on the couch with an orange penis, put your hand up. A lot of you did right? We do it all the time. Visualization is simply making pictures in your imagination. The real power to this exercise is in linking powerful emotions *to* those pictures. If the pictures are the cart, the emotions are the horses that pull it.

So why is this such a powerful tool, you ask?

Well, for one, if you are spending time making pictures in your head and evoking emotion with them, you are focusing your awareness rather than letting your imagination mess with you. This is always a good thing, right?

The second reason that this is a powerful activity is that it is the kind of exercise that really lets you gauge what matters to you. When you are visualizing, you can tell what is really close to your heart. What are the situations or visualizations that cause the biggest, most powerful emotional responses inside of you? Is employing this technique just you simply *tricking* yourself? Well, sort of, but only as a means to an important and real goal—to gain insight.

The argument against manifestation and visualization has always been that you can't simply manifest *anything*. Well, I believe that if whatever you are trying to manifest or visualize resonates within you as a possible, attainable reality and feels *authentic* to you, let er rip!

These types of exercises help us sort things out and figure out where we want to go. What I mean is, you may try to visualize something and not have an emotional response to it. In my experience, that is always a sign that I am barking up the wrong tree. If you are sick, you may visualize yourself healthy and stronger than you have ever been. You may see the affected areas of your body in perfect health. The possibilities are only as limited as your imagination.

Try it right now. If you are someone who is experiencing some cellular misbehavior right now, try some of these out.

For Stress

The Shop Vac: *In this one, we imagine a set-up where we have a shop vac (vacuum cleaner), rigged so the suction nozzle is attached to a hockey helmet, which we then wear. When we turn it on, imagine all the stress getting sucked out of your head and into the shop vac.*

The Ghostbuster: *In this one, we see all our stress leave our bodies and manifest into a giant cloud of angry shit floating above us. Throw out your ghostbuster trap and capture that shit! Go to Youtube and look up the Ghostbusters movie to see what I'm talking about.*

The Boiler room: *In this one we see a wall of huge valve wheels and levers and stuff. Label the valves and levers with whatever titles you want, stress, anger etc and turn the dials to wherever you want them to be.*

The Tsunami: *See your problems as a small village by the sea. This village is filled with all your angry thoughts and all your pain in the form of loud obnoxious villagers. See a huge wave come from the ocean and smash that village, pulling it out to sea. Drown those fuckers. Not P.C., but very effective.*

The Crash Test Dummy: *Load your problems into a car and smash it into a wall. (Again, see your problems as the dummies themselves.)*

The Ground and Pound: *See your stress manifested into a MMA fighter and see that fighter getting smashed to unconsciousness.*

The Boiling Pot of Heart Water: *See your heart as a container of boiling angry emotion. When it hits a boil, pour it out.*

Firing Your Cancer: *Seeing it as an employee and making it clean out its desk and send it away. You are the boss—fire its ass!*

The Poor Man's Treasure Hunt or Scoop the Shit Outta the Cat Box:
This one is really simple—just see all the problems in your life as the shit and piss clumps in the cat box and scoop them out! It's even better if you have the flushable litter and you load up the toilet bowl and then flush it down.

The Ultimate Supreme God of Love: *See yourself as an all-powerful deity that can create anything, including perfect health for yourself. See a movie in your minds eye of you healing yourself and others by blasting them with powerful loving vibes. Conversely, you can imagine a deity pulling all the sickness out of you and radiating pure awesomeness.*

The power of the mind is limitless. You have nothing to lose but time trying these exercises. We all know you are going to end up with that orange dick at some point anyway, you filthy little monkey, so why not do this first?

Then again, this may still be horseshit to you. Have some imagination and go for it. Who knows? It may just work.

———

12

THE MEMORY TRAP

"I don't want to repeat my innocence. I want the pleasure of losing it again."
F. SCOTT FITZGERALD, *THIS SIDE OF PARADISE*

WHEN STUCK IN a mental rut or when struggling with stressful situations, we may be seduced by the powerful and intoxicating Lady Memory. Like that exotic dancer that made you believe you actually had a shot at sleeping with her then "took" all your money; Lady Memory can sometimes seem to be a heartless wench.

The thing about memories is that we tend to sugar-coat them; we romanticize them and make "those days" seem so much better than what we are experiencing now. Sometimes those memories really are great and the times we are thinking about really were innocent and fantastic compared to the tough times we may be currently experiencing. That being said, I refuse to believe that the best times are behind me. I refuse to give in to the powerful pull of the past. Sure it is nice to escape into the past and think about the days when you felt free and untainted. Yes, *untainted.* Put your hand up if the cancer or depression experience has left you feeling dirty or unclean. Remember the body image stuff? Now remember the glass with the water in it.

Sometimes those mini-escapes are great for releasing yourself from the pressures you are feeling today, but we all know that until someone invents a REAL time machine, you can never go back. That house is burned and that ship has sailed.

Have you ever taken a trip somewhere hoping to recapture a certain feeling or memory? Have you ever carved your name on a tree? Why do we do that? I used to find myself visiting places from my past when I was sick or down and out.

At first there is that nostalgic feeling of remembering days gone by, and *then* I would realize that here I was, sitting in my car outside my old elementary school in the rain like a scene from a shitty movie, while people I went to school with were more than likely living their asses off.

I left feeling worse and ripped off, and that is never helpful.

So why did I go to those places? What was I actually in search of? Well, I was looking for glimpses of myself. My *old* self.

I was looking for traces of the past that would somehow help me make sense of my present. I was looking to escape to a time where I felt life was good, if only through a memory. The funny thing is, now I can look back at my treatment days and feel the same way. However those days were far from rosy when I originally lived them. They were terrifying and painful. This kind of thinking is what leads us to sometimes sleep with our ex-girlfriends, too. Well, that and being drunk and alone late at night. It's all good until you get the "poison" out and your head clears and you realize all the reasons things didn't work out between you. Yeah, fun times that always end in tears!

The thing about being in crisis is that you may sometimes find it hard to be with people who don't understand what you are experiencing. It can be *really* uncomfortable to be the sick person in the room. In my experience, I found it much easier to be alone. I didn't want to be the topic of conversation. It is weird because some people really *do* want to know what's going on and some just want to ask you how you are out of politeness.

If you aren't comfortable being around people, don't torture yourself. Do try to engage in life though. If you can, go out into the world and talk to people. I don't mean online either. Go and talk to real people. Get into conversations with strangers. I would sometimes talk to strangers and not tell them what I was going through just to *pretend* everything was normal. Take it a step further and lie about who you are and what is going on in your life. Introduce yourself to someone using a *ridiculously* fake name, like Lawrence Orenthal Von Elatious the *third*. Step outside yourself and see if you can pull it off. Have fun with it!

Quiet time is nice and all, and meditation and reflection are important, but getting out into the world is crucial to maintain that connection to something *outside* of you too. Completely cutting ourselves off from people isn't a great strategy. We can get caught up in our heads and that can *really* suck.

We look to our pasts for guidance and escape but we can look to the future for that as well. There is a difference between using visualization as a tool to investigate different aspects of your life and *living* in the past. Remember, if you spend your life looking backwards you end up bumping into a lot of things. Just a thought and all the more reason to be in the here and now taking it all in and letting it all go.

Oh, and the whole stripper thing? Well, you are gonna have to figure that one out on your own.

13

UNLEASH THE BEAST— RELEASING OUR ANGER

*"Angry people want you to see how powerful they are... loving
people want you to see how powerful YOU are."*
CHIEF RED EAGLE

"Your Anger is a Gift"
ZACH DE LA ROCHA- FRONT MAN FOR RAGE AGAINST THE MACHINE

BELIEVE IT OR not, I really don't think "the war on cancer" is a good term
to use when we are talking about the cancer experience. We make cancer
out to be something alien, something that invades us from an external
source or place and tries to kill us. *We* - are the cancer, our *cells* are the
cancer. If you search, "What is Cancer?" on the web this may come up:

*"Cancer is any malignant growth or tumor caused by abnormal and uncontrolled
cell division; it may spread to other parts of the body through the lymphatic system or
the blood stream."*

Although it does *feel* like you have been hijacked and your life threatened, you need to remember one thing: cancer isn't the Taliban sneaking into the villages that are our bodies at night to take us over.

Cancer is not a physical "thing" that *enters* your body. It does not hide in the dark, plotting to kill you, waiting for its chance to strike. If a village existed somewhere where cancer somehow took a physical form and lived and trained to kill us all-myself and *millions* of others would have found it and burned it to the ground. I would have killed cancer with my bare hands for what "it" has done to myself and my loved ones, my friends and their loved ones. But there isn't. Our bodies are the battlefields and it could be argued that our minds are the training grounds for everything that happens *in* our bodies.

There is advertising that depicts people getting ready to fight cancer. I understand the emotional motives behind this type of ad, but I find that when it comes to the actual healing of the body, it is much more effective to declare love on our-selves and our bodies, than to declare war on them.

That's correct my friends. I said declare *love*. Release the rage and fear and declare love.

Before you smash my head in with an axe handle, hear me out.

Even if cancer is doing crazy shit to us, it is still *our* cellular material at work here. It is still part of *our* bodies. Declaring war on our own bodies makes no sense and is counter-productive. Our bodies are housing the cancer experience and declaring war on ourselves is not going to work.

I know it feels better to point the finger, raging and screaming at *something*. It may help to make the cancer a foreign enemy, something outside of our-selves, but it simply isn't. Cancer is a complex disease that we are only just starting to learn about. I know first-hand the anger and frustration the cancer experience generates, but I never benefited from just being pissed off without directing that anger somewhere outside of myself.

Speaking of pointing the finger, please remember that awesome Native American saying that when you point a finger at someone or something, three point back at you. I really like that one. I think of it all the time. I am not saying blame yourself for your problems—there is a big difference between *blaming* yourself and *taking responsibility* for your actions and thoughts—but it really doesn't hurt to take a look at our inner and outer actions and ourselves when the shit hits the fan. Okay so maybe it does "hurt" a little bit but hey, you gotta start somewhere.

We do need to focus and direct our energy but it has to be a loving, positive energy and not one of anger or violence. THAT energy needs to be released FROM the body in order to prepare the body for maximum healing. That is what this chapter is about.

Sometimes when we were kids, and even as adults we are told to "be nice" and to "behave." We are sometimes forced to keep our true feelings inside. If we don't have the skills to cope with these feelings, we may end up bottling these powerful emotions up. When things go sideways in our lives we can be left boiling and fuming with no way to let these powerful feelings go. Sometimes the feelings are so strong they border on being primal. They can be a lot to deal with.

Whether you are the patient or the caregiver/friend, the cancer experience can leave you feeling intense anger, frustration and helplessness. There may be times when you may feel that your anger is going to overcome you. These feelings left unchecked are not conducive to healing and they must be released. An angry body is a tense body and a tense body is one that will resist the good vibes that will make us feel better and allow the body to properly heal itself. An overheated engine doesn't run as well as one that has a proper cooling system. You feel me?

The levels of anger and frustration I experienced while going through my cancer experience were very intense. For some men, feeling anger is the *natural* response when feeling threatened or vulnerable. Men want to *physically* control situations that are threatening them. It is easy to punch someone's lights out that is threatening you. Problem dealt with right? Now if the "threat" is an *emotional* one, such as feeling terrified by a disease like cancer *and* you don't have the skills to deal with those feelings, well you now have *two* problems.

In my case, feeling angry felt better than feeling afraid and it did give me *a sense of control*. The thing about anger is that while it is a fuel and a motivator, left unaddressed, it can quickly turn on you and burn you down. Anger can also get you into some trouble, as we all know. The following story is an example of a form of release that is ancient and global. It is an ancient ritual known as bar fighting. I don't recommend it as therapy necessarily, but it makes for a good story. I also don't tell this story to stroke my ego as it contains within it some really powerful insights. So knowing it is not just another bar fight story, please grab your popcorn and read on.

I kept strange hours during treatment. There were times when I would be up all night. Feeling cagey and unable to sleep one of these nights early in my treatment, I decided to take a friend up on an offer to go out and play pool.

The night started off really well. A bunch of my friends were at the bar and we were all having fun, shooting the shit and playing pool. I was playing at a table with some girls we had just met and I was having a pretty good time. I remember looking around and smiling at the people around me, innocently having fun. I remember thinking that *this* is what life is *supposed* to be like.

I wasn't allowing myself to get caught up in the sadness and frustration that had become my constant companion for the past while. It was nice to forget for a few seconds at a time at least that I had cancer, and was struggling with my mental health. It was great to be amongst people having fun and not sitting in a tension filled waiting room. It was nice to *be* someone having fun, if even for a few moments at a time.

In those precious moments when I was laughing at a friends joke, or flirting with the girls, I felt free from the heaviness and craziness that had become the default emotional setting of my current life. There were times back then when situations like this would leave me feeling resentful and jealous of these seemingly happy, stress free people. Not tonight. Tonight I was just a guy with his friends playing pool with a bunch of girls. It felt good.

Damn, what a treat it was to feel this way.

The trouble started when the boyfriend of one of the girls I was hanging out with came into the bar a couple hours after I had already been there playing pool with his lady and her friends.

The girl in question was *very* flirtatious and had never mentioned to me that she had a boyfriend. To be honest, I didn't really give a shit either way. I wasn't there to pick up a girl, I was just happy to be out playing pool with the boys having a nice "normal" night. So there I was, head down, lining up a shot when this asshole came up to the table with a pool cue, raising it like he's going to smash me in the head sucker-punch style.

Dickhead didn't realize that the guys at the next table were my friends and as he started his wind- up, one of my buddies noticed, turned, and just smashed him in the head with his own pool cue.

As the guy was howling and grabbing his head, one of the doorman who was good friends with one of the guys I was with, came over and asked me if I wanted the dude thrown out. The bouncer told me that if the sucker punch king goes, my buddy who nailed him goes too. I said

I didn't give a shit if he stayed, that *he* was the one bleeding while I was laughing.

The guy was screaming at me, telling me he was going to *teach me a lesson* as the doorman took him to the other side of the bar, away from us. His girlfriend went with him. Pity.

Here is a word to the wise.

Never tell a cancer patient at *any* time, or at *any* age that they are going to be taught a lesson. It's just a bad idea. The irony here is that the day before I had spoken with a shrink at the cancer clinic and she had asked me how I was feeling. I told her that I was angry and she wanted to know *how* angry I was. I told her that I wanted to throw her, her desk and everything in the office out the window. I wanted to burn the world. She didn't like that. I stopped seeing her. I was begging the universe for release from my anger and the universe had seemingly answered my prayer with this idiot.

So this asshole is telling me that he's going to kill me and all this shit and I just told him that we'd do it when the bar closes. Then something inside me started to *burn*.

This guy had no idea of the state of crazy I was in. I watched the clock for the next two hours, just smiling, thinking about how good it was going to feel to unload on this guy. I stayed stone cold sober and he was getting more and more drunk.

He was a hockey player at the bar with guys from his team. My buddies were all telling me how they weren't going to let me fight. It was actually really nice to see my friends all-clamoring to destroy this guy. It was twisted and wrong, but felt oh… so, so right. That's how some dudes show their love. I told them I was good to go but if it went to the ground and I was getting pounded out, to pull him off and beat his ass.

I know that wasn't fair but this was a street fight and I was feeling less than awesome at the time. I also didn't know Brazilian Jiu-Jitsu at the time so there was that too.

I was sick and my body had recent holes in it from surgery and a re-inflated lung from a biopsy needle that missed the mark and collapsed it. I wasn't exactly in the best shape of my life. I was, however, a little out of my mind and looking to release my rage on this poor bastard.

So closing time came and we went outside as Douchey MacDouchbag and Co. were bravely slamming their last shots of rye into their block-heads. I took off my coat and my buddies were still pleading to let them fight him and I told them again what I needed them to do.

So the door opened and it was like a terrible 80's action movie. The idiot screamed and came down the stairs at me full-bore. Like Steven Segal, but less fat and with a shaved head, I stepped aside at the last second, grabbed his arm and the back of his head and introduced him to the side of a Honda Civic. I switched grips and hammered him twice behind his right ear. Douche bag dropped onto his hands and knees, turned back to face me, screamed and leaped at me again.

I did the exact same thing, swung him into the car again and nailed him with three good shots. However, something different happened this time. I felt a blow to the back of *my* head and turned to see his girlfriend screaming at me. I laughed as she was dragged away and turned back to the guy, who was on his hands and knees again. The best part happened next. One of my friends was kneeling down and screaming at the guy: *"My friend here is sick with cancer and he is KICKING YOUR FUCKING ASS!!!"* he then screamed at the guy to get after me, and then he yelled at me to keep kicking his ass.

I will never forget the look on that guy's face when the situation registered. I say that because it was at that moment that the pin fell out of the grenade. I pointed to him and told him to get up (totally like a bad action movie). He just looked at me and I yelled at him to *get the fuck up*. I was burning in a white-hot righteous rage and felt like a killing machine sent by a vengeful god to rid the world of assholes like this.

I felt like I was going to kill him, and it felt *fantastic*—*I* was in control, he was not and *I* was dictating my life at that moment. *Not* cancer tumors or mental illness or doctors. *I* was in control and I wanted to really hurt this guy. I wanted to make *him* pay.

So he stood up and started toward me, confused and really freaked out—that was when I unloaded the one and only sidekick I have ever used in my life on a human being in anger. I even did the side step over move before I unleashed it for extra power. I felt like Bruce *Fucking* Lee as I blasted this dude in the chest with a perfect 80's ninja movie sidekick that drove him into a telephone pole and unconsciousness.

I swear to whatever god you believe in or don't—the crowd roared and I was in heaven. My friends swarmed me and it was *mayhem*. I never fought for a title, but I imagine that is what it feels like to win one. Just like in the movies, sirens pierced the cheers and we all made the mad scramble to not get arrested.

As we reached the cars, I realized that I'd left my jacket behind, with all my I.D. and my house keys in its pockets. The cops were already in front of the bar and I had no choice but to try and sneak back and get my jacket. I grabbed a friend's jacket and baseball cap and headed around the other side of the bar. As I got closer, I saw my coat between two cars where we were standing before the fight.

I convinced myself that I was invisible and casually strolled over to my coat and picked it up. Luckily, no one noticed me. As I left, I glanced at the guy. All the anger was suddenly gone from my body and at this point I was worried about getting caught and charged if I'd hurt him. I walked back around the corner and got into the car and left.

The interesting thing about that situation was that I had asked the universe for some release from the anger and I was rewarded with a random douche bag to beat on. That fight could have gone differently and I could have added more injuries to my current situation. That would have sucked. I could have also been charged or hurt him badly and that wouldn't have helped my situation at all. The *best* part of that story was how all my buddies were looking to help me, and were worried that I might get hurt. It was nice to feel protected and to know that I wasn't alone in *this* particular fight.

I won't lie, it felt good to scrap that guy, but street fights are dangerous and unpredictable. Especially when you are sick. Everyone that knows me personally knows I am not a fighter; I fought when I had to, but never enjoyed it. It's just not for me. I don't like hurting people in any way. I'm a big strong guy and if I punch you in the face it's going to hurt *a lot*. I know this and don't feel the need to prove it.

I like the challenge of diffusing human time bombs BEFORE they go off. I would rather a guy buy me a beer for talking to him and not beating the piss out of him, like I did so many times as a doorman, than have him waiting for me out in the parking lot at the end of the night with ten of his closest friends ready to kick my ass. Besides, I always found talking to women and wrestling with them in the sack a *much* better pastime.

Releasing your rage in a safe environment is a very healthy thing to do. Anger builds up inside you and makes relaxing very tough. When you are stressed, the body doesn't work right—we need to get rid of the anger.

Here are some great (and safer!) ways to get rid of anger.

The simplest form of releasing anger is to recognize it as an energy that needs to be expressed and dealt with. See it for what it is. It is fear and frustration and disappointment and there are reasons for all of those things. We are never angry for no reason at all. Simply feeling vulnerable can cause angry or resentful feelings.

So before you can write about it in your journal it really helps to physically release the energy of anger from your body. If you have access to a punching bag and a baseball bat, go ahead and beat that punching bag until you literally can't lift your arms anymore. Chances are after you release the anger and rage you will get down to the tender emotions and may cry for a bit.

Now all you tough guys are rolling your eyes again, but let's think about every championship that was ever won in any sport for a second, shall we?

So there is adversity, a challenge and common goal--both physical and mental, perhaps even spiritual. (They *never* pray before football games right?) There is a goal, which to accomplish requires both a singular and a team effort. After a struggle of sometimes-epic proportions, there is a result of either "victory" or "loss" for the competitors involved. Those results are met with emotional responses of elation, anger--a whole host of feelings, some of which are new to the participants and can't even be described.

There are always tears on both sides from the players and the fans alike. *Tears* people.

TEARS!

We have the ability to cry for a reason. Get over the whole "real men don't cry" thing. It is such a waste of time to try and be some emotion-less tough guy that I don't even want to talk about it anymore.

But I will.

Personally, I like to be alone when I feel the need to shed tears, because it is a personal thing for me. Some people like crying in front of others, do what you gotta do, but release that emotion. Whether you are playing for the super bowl or trying to rid your body of a disease, you'll have emotions to contend with. Emotions are there to enhance our life experiences here on earth, so use them. It is the new millennium for CRYING out loud, we don't need to be such fucking cavemen anymore. If men were taught that emotions were in us to be experienced and used, the world would be a better place. Period.

Speaking of being a caveman, destroying anything is a great way to get rid of anger.

If you have access to heavy equipment, old cars, shotguns, find fun ways to release your anger. I shit you not; I want to eventually have an old farm that I will name *The Hillbilly Healing Center* or something to that effect, where this type of release work can be done. Driving bulldozers over cars and pushing giant rocks around can be very therapeutic. I once dated a girl whose dad bought an old bulldozer and had a giant pile of sand delivered to their property. She told me he would go out and push the pile of sand from one spot to another. It was therapeutic for him. I thought it was awesome.

If you have access to a quiet place where you can shoot up an old car, I wholeheartedly suggest it. Old houses are great to shoot up as well. Add dummies or mannequins to the mix and you have the beginnings of a great day of release. You take the dummies and put them in the car. You take a piece of paper and write down what it is that you want to release and why.

Then you tape those papers to each dummy and start talking to them. You can have a lot of fun if you have an imagination. How you blast those dummies is up to you. I suggest screaming like a lunatic as you blast away, because that feels good too. Dummies can be made with old overalls and old clothing. Be as realistic as you like. Beat them, burn them and run them over. Build your own grappling dummy and beat the crap out of it. Choke it and submit it. All you are doing is making a mental experience physical. You are putting the anger in a different place, and *that* place is out of your body.

If you don't have access to this kind of firepower or you are too tired and beat up to do it, you can still get it out in other ways like playing video games with your buddies. Play first-person shooter games, alone or with a friend. Pretend that whatever town or environment you are in (in the game) is your body. Then pretend the bad guys, zombies, whatever, are the cancer cells. Hunt them down and destroy them. You can have a lot of fun "cleaning house" like this.

Driving down the highway screaming your head off while cranking Slayer or any heavy music feels great. Throwing a bowling ball through a wall or a window feels great. Filling a pillowcase with newborn kittens and smashing them into a telephone pole feels great. Kidding!

Shame on the part of you that liked that idea.

Speaking of pets, animals are *fantastic* creatures that are designed to help us release stress and reduce blood pressure. Spend time with animals. Go for walks with your dog. Pet your cat. Those furry little buggers will love you even if you are sicker than sick, smell like shit and are the most miserable bastard in the world. God bless them all.

Animals are truly amazing at sensing your sadness or pain. They will come up to you and rub up against you when you are upset. Oblige them with some affection. If you can't show your feelings to a human yet, show them to an animal. They will never judge you or laugh at you or do anything but sit there and love you. However, if you are the type of person who likes to hurt animals, please come see me and I will end your sickness by drowning you in a children's pool. There will be love in my eyes and heart when I do it.

Fish are relaxing to watch. There was a fish tank in the waiting room at the cancer clinic that I used to watch and it would put me to sleep. Well, that and the drugs.

The point is to release that anger. The more you can move your body the better. If you are still able to exercise, get as much as you can. Like I said before, if I didn't have the release of grappling, I would climb the walls everyday. If you are well enough, try a martial art. Brazilian Jiu-Jitsu is the best therapy in the world in my humble opinion. It is better to be healthy and strong to train at this sport, but I am sure the right dojo would accommodate a person in crisis or someone who is physically challenged. BJJ shows you who you are, and who you are most definitely not. It also seems to attract amazing people.

As soon as you are healthy enough to try this humbling, powerful sport, try it.

There is something so therapeutic about grappling: the way it elicits the focus you need, forces your mind to let go, be in the moment and *act*. I love the combination of the primitive, animalistic nature of the physical part of the sport combined with the mental strategy required. It is a satisfying sport to say the least.

Grappling, for me, is an *external* manifestation of our *internal* struggles. The body loves it and you have to be creative, too. It welds the mental, physical and the spiritual together. I really encourage people to try a grappling sport because of the many benefits they offer. I have never left the dojo feeling worse than when I went in, even if I get hurt.

After the physical release is taken care of, write.

The combination of the physical and the mental release is powerful. Write down any thoughts or revelations that may have happened while doing the release work. If you are not able to do any of the above exercises, I suggest writing in your journal about the anger you are feeling. Get to the bottom of it.

At the end of the outpouring of anger, read it out loud and find somewhere safe to burn it and as you do so, say aloud, *"This anger does not serve me anymore, and I release it right now,"* or something to that effect. Find and use the words that work for you. If you have access to a fireplace or a bonfire, burning something that represents your anger is a great way to relax and release it. Writing by a fire, reading what you wrote aloud, then tossing it in and watching it burn is fantastic. Every piece of wood you put in the fire can represent something that is troubling you. As you watch them burn, feel the anger or troubles dissolve energetically in you.

Make love to someone by the fire, too. That is always fun and relaxing. Please don't masturbate alone by the fire though, it's just wrong. It ruins the whole fireplace thing for me. Ah hell, if it's gonna make you feel better, go for it. Just don't stain the rug.

Talking about how you are feeling with someone *who knows how to listen* is also good. I find if you can get out into nature and do this kind of release work it seems to work better. Stop thinking about masturbating in the woods! When you do, squirrels laugh at you and make jokes about your nuts. I will always remind you to try to speak with a professional or find a support group. Blowing shit up is fun and does help, but it doesn't hurt to try to have a pro take a crack at you as well.

Remember to be safe when doing any kind of release work. Blowing yourself up is kind of pointless, so be careful when you get into doing the crazy stuff. Have someone there to help you or to make sure you aren't going to hurt yourself, or someone else, or get arrested! If you do hurt yourself, don't blame me dumbass!

Regardless of the method or the methods you choose, find a way to get that anger out. It is always good to find some peace through release.

And speaking of release....

14

SEX AND THE CANCER PATIENT

"Sex is kicking death in the ass while singing."
CHARLES BUKOWSKI

THIS IS A short but sweet chapter, not unlike a lot of your sexual experiences. Low blow when you are already feeling down, I know.

All right—this is a fun topic to talk about, my friends. Sex can be an awkward, uncomfortable experience in the best of situations. Throw cancer into it and we now have a really interesting dynamic.

When I was in cancer treatment I would run into girls I knew (and some I didn't know), tell them what was going on and knew I could probably work the situation to get some fantastic sympathy sex. The problem was I felt like shit, looked like shit and didn't want to run the risk of not being able to "rise" to the occasion.

What's worse than having cancer? Having cancer and trying to have sex with someone and you can't get it up. Pity is never good in any situation. Empathy is much better. However, if a beautiful woman wants to take pity on you and make you feel good in the sack, then by all means, accept this wonderful gift.

Let's say you are in a relationship when you are diagnosed. Hopefully you are going to be talking to your partner and not shutting them out. Whatever the situation is between you two, use this time to make your relationship better.

If you have intimacy issues, use this time to learn how to just be together in the sack and develop some tenderness. Believe me, when you are really feeling like shit, its nice to have someone just rub your back or even hold your hand. Watch the episode of "Deadliest Catch" when Capt. Phil is dying. This dude was a hardcore Bering Sea crab fisherman. In the end, he just wants his hand held by his son. It's touching to watch, and it is a real good example of the grace and simplicity that sometimes comes over us as we get ready to leave our bodies.

Besides, ask a very pregnant woman if she wants sex or a foot rub. I'm betting you'll be rubbing hoofs and not knocking boots. If you have a partner when you are sick, tell them what you need. If you aren't feeling it, don't do it. If you are going to be a dirty bastard and keep asking for "your last blow job," be prepared for some trouble. But hey, if it gets a laugh and the odd sexual favor, go for it. There is a real opportunity for closeness here. We have talked a lot about developing an inner relationship with ourselves in this book, but crisis brings just as many opportunities to develop our relationships with others as well.

To the partners of the patients:

As much as it may be increasingly difficult to maintain a sexual relationship with your ailing lover, it is essential that you try to do so. Sex is a fantastic release for everyone. Yes ladies, I can see your eyebrows going up and you crossing your arms but bear with me for a second!

At a certain point, your partner may not be able to have full-on "traditional" sex with you, but there are alternatives. We mentioned the blowjob. I'm just putting it out there for the sake of my wounded brothers, but in all seriousness, it is important to maintain a physical connection of some sort, even if it is just holding hands.

Be open; ask what your partner needs, tell him you are here to help. At the very least, make physical contact and try to make him feel wanted. I know you are thinking *"He doesn't do that for me!"* Ladies, please lead the way—hopefully your man will follow. I guarantee it will be appreciated. Remember that the things you do in these tough times will *never* be forgotten, good or bad! Always look for an opportunity to deepen your relationship. If you are trying to be close but your partner needs space, respect that. Lots of crazy shit goes on in the mind of a cancer patient and sometimes they need room.

For instance, if I may bring up the body image thing again.... Without even knowing it, patients sometimes feel angry towards themselves and their bodies. They may feel "dirty" or broken or unworthy of affection because of the disease or the way treatment is making them feel. So they may get angry and push you away in bed, or push you away in general. They might not even know *why* they are doing that and may feel even worse afterward. Believe it or not, like I said before, guys can have body image problems too.

If your lover is struggling with these issues, the symptoms will likely manifest themselves in angry or reclusive behavior, be aware. Ask if they want to talk and tell them that you are here to listen and that you aren't trying to *fix* anything. Then, do as they wish.

In a perfect world, you get sick or a loved one gets sick and the experience opens your eyes to what really matters in life. You get closer to each other and within your own selves. The experience concludes one way or another and everyone is left better for it, deepened and more in tune with themselves and those around them. Strive for that.

So work it out, talk, laugh and try to maintain that physical relationship with your partner in any way you both feel comfortable. Having someone willing to be with you is a gift at *anytime* in life. Having someone willing to hold your sick ass when you are down and out is a real nice situation to be in, even if it's a horrible situation overall.

If you are alone when this is happening, I hope that you have friends or family that you can be with. If you feel ballsy, go out and find a girl you like and tell her you aren't sure you are going to make it and cannot die without making love to her. You may have the greatest sex of your life. Be careful though, Karma's a bitch sometimes, and if she has a boyfriend he may help speed you to your death.

Compassion, intimacy, and simply being there for someone you love are essential components to a happy life, more so when you are sick. So don't be afraid, ask for what you need and have some fun. What do you have to lose? Well, your life, yes, but at least you may go out with some tenderness…

15

WICKED WISDOM

"Whosoever is delighted in solitude is either a wild beast or a god."
ARISTOTLE

WHEN I WAS a kid I used to watch my parents and their friends party their asses off down in our basement. The music was cranked and the drinks would flow. My family wasn't afraid to dance and have a good time and the parties my parents had were legendary. I used to sneak to the top of the basement stairs and watch this madness through a three-foot-thick cloud of cigarette smoke, and I loved every second of it.

One night, my dad saw me at the top of the stairs and came up to get my ass back into bed. I settled into my bed and my father began to lay some of the *heaviest* shit I had ever heard in my young life on me.

I respect my father a lot. He left home to join the Air Force when he was 18 years old and lost *his* father the next year while he was away doing his service. Dad traveled the world and lived life to the fullest, working hard and enjoying all that life had to offer. When he talked to me I listened.

My dad pointed at the world map I had on the wall and told me that I could do anything I wanted and go anywhere I wanted if I put my mind to it. There were no limits. Then he told me something, which struck a chord deep inside me that has helped me more than probably anything else anyone, has ever said to me. He looked at me and said,

"Son, you can't get 'em pregnant if it's just spit..."

Kidding, that gem came later on in my life and I took it to heart as well.

What my father did say was that as a young man, while waiting at JFK airport, he suddenly realized that he was completely alone in this world. Not that he *felt* lonesome or didn't have friends or family, but alone in the sense that at the end of the day, when the shit hits the fan and things are falling apart, you really only have yourself to rely on. You only have yourself to keep you company when life is kicking your ass all over the street.

My father told me to get right with myself and figure out who I was, to really understand and be cool with who I was because in the end, you are all you have.

I guess how you process and integrate those kinds of ideas into your psyche will affect your views on the difference between loneliness and solitude. Even at that young age, I figured I'd better put some thought into this stuff if dad thought it was important.

Now this may sound like a heavy thing to tell a kid, but it really ended up helping me later on in my life. Dad was feeling no pain from the Lambs Navy rum no doubt, and maybe he wanted to plant that idea in me at a young age to let it grow. Regardless, it was good, honest wisdom from a man who had made it work for him. I put it in the vault, and went to sleep to the throbbing bass lines of ABBA.

I didn't think about it again till 13 years later, when I found myself freaking out in a hospital bed as I awaited biopsy surgery of the tumor in my chest.

My family had left for the night and I was alone for the first time since the initial diagnosis. I was alone, away from home and in the hospital. I remember the anxiety creeping up on me as I lay in that bed, my mind racing. Then those words my dad spoke all those years ago popped into my head. I imagine the thought must have hit me as hard as it had my father back in the day. I was in a hospital with a few thousand people, but I was truly alone. I wanted to run, but I couldn't outrun my thoughts. I wanted to scream, but I couldn't open my mouth. Cold fear welled up inside me. I started to sweat. I suddenly really understood what my dad had warned me about 13 years ago. This was what he meant.

I was alone.

Don't take this the wrong way or freak out but you are alone *inside* with your sickness, your crisis, and your pain. Unfortunately there are thousands of people who are rowing the same shitty boat you may currently be in, but take heart in the fact there are also millions who have also rowed that same boat who are screaming at you from the shore telling you to *keep rowing*. When it comes down to it, you are alone in those dark trenches of your life. The perfect friend, lover, or partner of any kind can't save you from that truth. They can't crawl inside you and do the emotional work. They can't protect you from whatever is haunting, hurting and causing you stress and pain. They can rub your back, hold your hand, say nice things and listen to you, but at the end of the day it is you and your guts and your heart and soul that have to walk the hard road and do the heavy lifting.

This can be a totally unhinging revelation to experience for the first time and it can shake you down to your core. The only saving grace is that it is also an opportunity to figure out just who you are. If you "get it" it means you get right with yourself and figure out that even if you don't have all the answers, and *no one* does, you are going to show up for yourself. You are going to be there for *yourself*.

When it's three o'clock in the morning and you can't sleep, when you're terrified and reeling in chaos, *that's* when it really hits you.

You are alone.

It is just you. You and this experience.

If you are a young adult when you go through this experience you may have a moment when you realize your youth has just ended. It's hard to go back to the carefree, uber-naive youth you used to be after a cancer diagnosis. There is no more map. There are no more signposts. There is seemingly nothing but uncertainty. This sounds terrible I know, but before you go and jump off a bridge, remember, where there is uncertainty there is also opportunity. They walk hand in hand like lovers, those two bastards. However, when the realization that you are alone first hits, it hits hard and nasty and it feels like you are in a horrible place, naked and alone. This is often the point where the terror starts. However, it can also be the time when you figure out what courage is for the first time.

Courage to me is still moving forward when things get tough. Courage to me is being scared shitless and saying; "*Fuck it* ", taking a deep breath and getting up to face whatever the day brings. This isn't false bravado to hide the fact that you are terrified and unprepared. This is simply saying;

"Well I am terrified, alone and unprepared but I say; Fuck this! In the spirit of self-love, and preservation, I choose to move forward and not crumble. And if I do crumble, I choose to rebuild myself the best way I know how and that's that."

Also;

"I give myself permission to fall apart and put myself back together again."

Words to that effect. "*Fuck It*" is also the name of a *fantastic* book by my mentor and friend John C. Parkin. Please check out this beautiful lunatic's body of work. He is a gem.

This terrifying point in the crisis experience is a crucial one. I wish I would have had someone walk into my room at the exact moment the wheels were coming off my wagon, sit down and tell me what an *incredible* opportunity lay in front of me. They could have told me to change perspective, to pull the camera back and to see this whole thing *differently*.

They could have told me that I had been here before, the day I was born. Squeezed, pushed and pulled out of the cozy womb of my mother into a loud, bright, alien land and smacked on the ass to boot. It's not like you are in the womb with your brochure and suitcase waiting to be delivered. Just like babies aren't taken from wombs and expected to know how to handle their newfound environment, you shouldn't be expected to either. This is a new land for you and you need time to figure out the territory. Figure out the lay of the internal and external landscape as it were.

So let me be the guy to come into your room and tell you that the reason everything feels so insane is because everything *is* insane. It's not normal to be sitting or lying in a bed waiting to get tests to see where tumors are in your body. It is scary as hell. So yes, you *may* feel a wee bit terrified. That's okay!

What isn't okay because it doesn't help but sometimes feels unavoidable, is feeding into that fear. Fearful feelings exist for a reason, but in this scenario they need to be brought under control. Do what you want, but let me tell you that feeding that fear doesn't make it go away. Fear is like a playground bully; don't let it push you around. Recognize it for what it is and remove its power. Don't *feed* into it, *go* into it, examine it and *breathe* into it.

It is just chemicals rushing through your body after all. Those chemicals in this situation are probably caused by the fact that your mind is running wild. You are afraid and getting ready for an attack from an enemy that you can't see. Your body might be warning you, like the big dumb animal it can be sometimes, that there is something wrong. Put your hands on your belly; give your body a pat and say,

"Thanks for the warning buddy, I got this. Let's work together and take care of this situation shall we?"

You know what I mean, something to that effect.

Lying in that bed, I imagined the feelings I was having were similar to what a point man must have felt while smashing blindly through the jungles of Vietnam during that terrible conflict. Like that guy at the head of the patrol, knowing the enemy was out there, maybe two feet away, but all he could do was just stumble forward, swinging his machete through the thick jungle, hoping he wouldn't get shot. Hopefully you have a team behind you like a point man does to support you when the shit hits the fan, too.

Speaking of the shit hitting the fan—who came up with that one? Who was the first person to throw shit at a fan? If they didn't throw the shit at the fan, what was the situation that resulted in the shit actually hitting the fan? I would like to know. Sigh. Moving on....

There is a big difference between feeding fear and acknowledging fear. Bust out the journal and start writing. Write down what you are feeling. Be honest. Put all that fear into the pages. Another powerful, crippling feeling you may experience is *vulnerability.*

Shit, I KNOW you are going to feel it because that is the birthplace of most of these other feelings. Vulnerability is one of the hardest feelings to deal with for a human being. It is that feeling of being exposed, being open, powerless even, that makes people cringe and put up the walls.

Especially dudes.

Guys *hate* feeling powerless.

The cancer and mental illness experience can make us feel vulnerable and that feeling may spawn many others like fear, anger and a sense of weakness. It is a bastard of a situation to be in, especially alone in a hospital room at night, but you *can* deal with it and overcome it. You may not *completely* lose those dreadful feelings, but with training, you *can* put that dog on a leash and make it walk beside you.

To work on these feelings of vulnerability, go to a public washroom, one of those big stalls where you can't reach the lock from the toilet and go for a poop. Sounds easy right? Not for some people, I know.

Here is the catch: don't lock the door.

Scary right? How does that make you feel? Vulnerable, I would bet. In all seriousness, if you can, go for a walk, talk to people—engage in life. A quiet hospital room can drive you right off the deep end, so engage in life when you can. If you can go outside, go outside and breathe deeply. Find somewhere to sit and watch people. That is always fun. I used to sing just to keep my mind active and focused and to get me breathing deeply.
Sometimes I would just yell and scream in my car.

Whatever works whenever you need to work it right?

There is a saying; if you have time, meditate for 20 minutes a day, if you are too busy; meditate for an hour. Although it may be difficult to meditate in these times, it is well worth the effort to start to get a handle on your breathing and to calm your mind down. There are many great books and videos on meditating, please explore this powerful tool!

Yes I'm gonna beat you over the head with meditation and deep breathing...

Fear can be a real bitch to deal with, but it needs to be handled, in whatever way works for you.

I remember the first time I felt real fear. I was about nine years old, I think. I was on a dirt bike with a cousin and he took me way out into the woods on old trails and logging roads. He stopped and told me to get off, that he had to check something on the bike. I got off and he sped away, laughing his ass off. I just kind of stood there watching him drive away. I realized when I couldn't hear the bike anymore that he wasn't coming back for a while.

I looked around, realized I had no idea where I was and I got very scared. I was alone in those woods with no clue where to go. I didn't know anything about the woods or how to navigate them properly. I had no tools or compass. I didn't know how to read the landscape or the sky. I also had a huge imagination, which immediately started cooking up worse case scenarios.

Right away my mind took off, not unlike my idiot cousin, and I couldn't stop it. There were bears and killers and killer bears behind every tree. Every sound was *something* coming to get me. I started walking back toward what I thought was the right direction until I heard the motorbike coming back and walked towards it. I was really upset. I didn't understand why he would do that to me.

I didn't get that it was a prank; I thought I must have done something wrong. Guilty conscience I guess and I'm not even Roman Catholic! So half an hour later, he picks me up and makes fun of me because my eyes were red from crying. I told him that I had fallen and hurt my knee. I was ashamed and felt stupid, vulnerable and weak. I was humiliated. In reality, my cousin was being a fucking idiot. I felt stupid and ashamed for having a completely normal reaction to being left in the woods alone. I *was* a pretty sensitive kid though.

That cousin represents life. You think you are best buddies and life is taking you somewhere awesome, on a grand adventure and the next thing you know, life is dropping you off in the woods by yourself, unprepared and terrified, wondering what the fuck you did to deserve this treatment.

You may feel like I did as a kid, vulnerable, alone, unprepared and terrified. The difference is now is that you have tools. You can find your way "home" or build a *brand new* "place to live." Shit, you may decide home is where your heart sits beating if you are a natural born mystic!

I say this because "home" keeps changing on you. Home feels different. Normal is just a word in the dictionary now, and a word neighbors always use to describe the "quiet young man" that has lived next to them for years that has just been caught with body parts in their freezer. "Normal" has nothing to do with what you are feeling and experiencing. To hammer the point home even more—freaking out, losing your mind and being terrified is a pretty "normal" reaction to have, given the circumstances. Feelings on a good day are hard to define and talk about. When things go ape shit, it becomes much more...well... interesting.

I hope you aren't hit by the fear train too hard or too many times in your crisis experience, but if you are, remember the following points;

The feelings of fear you are experiencing are there because you are feeling threatened, vulnerable, unprepared and wanting to know information about an outcome that feels like it is at least for the time being, out of your control.

Remember your body talks to you feelings.

Your mind will fuck with you.

Fear may be your body's way of trying to tell you that something is wrong, over and over again by sending waves of anxiety. Pretend your body is a big dumb animal that "you" ride *inside* of. *Soothe* that beast. Calm it down. Let it know you are aware of the problem and calm it down through deep breathing, meditation or screaming your fucking head off. It sounds freaky, but try it. Scream first, and then do the relaxation stuff for maximum effect.

Face the fear. Go *into* the fear. *French kiss the fear.* Ask the fear what it *is* and what it *wants.* Slow dance with that shit and talk to it. Like dealing with an asshole heckler at a comedy show, put the fear in the spotlight. Tell it that it has the floor and the microphone. Ask it; *"What do you need so desperately to tell me?"*

Like a heckler that is put on the spot, when fully addressed and listened too, your fear will usually just sit down and shut up. Maybe it will leave saying:

"Um, it's cool, its nothing really, I'll come back later."

If not, kick it out. Show it the door through your minds eye. This is *your* show.

Dissolve the fear or let it flow through you. Do whatever gets the best results. Tense your muscles and then let them relax to remember and feel the difference between those two states. Empty your mind and move your body, put clothespins on your nipples, get silly. Whatever works! Sometimes just sitting there and doing nothing works too.

Do whatever it takes to kick fear's ass out the door.

Remember, never once *anywhere* in the world did the doorbell ring and there was fear and worry with big bags of money in their hands to give to someone as a reward for thinking about them and giving them a place to live. It's never gonna happen. Ever.

They don't pay rent so its bye, bye to these unwanted guests. Right?

Being alone in crisis can be terrifying, so give yourself a break. Giving yourself shit or feeling bad for feeling scared is counterproductive. Try and develop a sense of gentleness towards yourself. I know this may be hard for you tough guys, but try it. No one has to know that you are being kind to yourself. Don't worry, I won't tell!

I believe that when you get sick your body, life and whatever gods you may or may not believe in are not trying to punish you. To my religious brothers, I believe religious leaders say that shit to put, and keep, asses in the seats. Get that crap out of your head and put the energy of your thoughts into calming yourself down and releasing the stress and anxiety.

If you begin to cycle through huge existential questions, bring your train of thought back to the present moment by writing in your journal and breathing deeply. Or slap yourself in the face as hard as you can. I'm kidding. Sort of. *Okay, I've done that.*

If you want to focus on one thing, focus on the fact that *all we have is this moment.* This isn't some new age bullshit speak. This very moment is all you have. Even if it sucks, it is all we have, so work *with* it, not *against* it. Breathe into it and calm yourself. Pick your battles and focus as much as you can on being in the moment and getting grounded and calm.

Speaking of New Age bullshit, for all you eye rollers, a fantastic grounding exercise that works well is to see roots growing from your feet going deep into the center of the earth. I have used this one a lot to help ground and center myself. By the way, isn't it interesting that a lot of new age concepts and principles are actually ancient wisdom? Explore these types of exercises—the mind is powerful. Again, if you can, go for walks, talk to people and engage in life.

As scary as it is to go through the "Holy shit I am ALONE" trip, it is a gateway and a rite of passage in your life. This may be the first time you have gotten rocked by anything in life. Take your time and breathe through every moment. You don't have to figure it all out. I believe we will *never* figure it *all* out anyway. Life isn't set up for that it seems.

Now that I have you freaking out thinking you are alone forever I *will* give you a little help in the form of a concept to chew on and digest that *may* help you but may also take some time to sink in. It came to me much farther down the road but it helped *immensely* when I wrapped my heart around its truth. Ready?

Realizing that many people feel exactly like you are feeling in those moments of terror is actually an invisible bridge that can connect you, through the recognition of your mutual suffering, to another human being.

Don't get sad or more distressed thinking that someone else is feeling what you are feeling, recognize and more importantly *use* that suffering as a bridge to connect *with* them, with their humanity. I know, I know. That might be a little much right now, or maybe I just brought you back to shore. The realization that we all feel pain and can *connect* through that pain is a great opportunity to develop compassion for each other. These feelings of compassion then leap out of your chest into someone else's heart allowing you two to meet in that beautiful place called *understanding*.

It's a beautiful place to meet someone, *especially* if that person is your own damn self!

Like I said, in the heat or cold sweat of the moment you *probably* won't realize this truth. You most likely will be too freaked out to even try to make sense of this concept let alone implement it. I thought I would throw that in the mix to give you something else to think about cause I'm such a nice fella!

So focus on breathing deep my friend, that's what matters anyway. Do me a favor and think about that whole bridge thing for a bit though will ya? It's a big one and a *great* concept to chew on. In my opinion there are few "truths" out there that hold any water, but *that* one strikes me as the real deal and still gives me great comfort to this day. It is what allows me to share that sacred space with someone in crisis. Yes, I said sacred. You will know it when you feel what I'm talking about. I hope that happens soon too.

It took me a while to figure out that suffering is mental or emotional, and pain is physical.

What I mean is you can be physically in pain and not be affected mentally, and you can be without physical injury and be suffering greatly emotionally.

As an example, last year I got smashed by a large tree limb resulting in multiple physical injuries while working on a tree removal. I received three facial fractures, a subdural hematoma, a shattered clavicle, four broken ribs and my C7 (vertebrae) and my T 2, 3, 4, 5, 6 (vertebrae) all got fractured.

I was in a lot of *physical* pain. But since my body has been beat up quite a bit in my working life and I have eaten many cosmic shit sandwiches, (which of course ended up being *just* what I needed to eat at the time) and am *well* versed and practiced in the art of personal crisis management, I was able to process the situation pretty quickly.

Basically, I woke up in the ambulance, wiggled my fingers and toes and was instantly grateful to be alive and not paralyzed. Once I found out the rest of the crew were unharmed and everyone was safe and sound, I *relaxed*. With a quick mental scan of my body I knew I was injured pretty badly, but I also trusted that everything was going to be fine. If I didn't have that trust, I would have *also* suffered mentally.

That experience was also made *extremely* easy for me because my friends, family and community stepped up and came to my rescue. My

lady worked her ass off to take care of my needs, our home, and our animals. We live on a hobby farm. Our hobby is shoveling shit apparently.
Her mom helped a lot around our place too. My friends and family were
also there for me whenever I needed help of any sort.

My sister and her husband organized a fundraiser where bands
donated their time and talent in an incredible evening raising an embar-
rassingly large pile of money to help me pay bills and get my life back on
track. Part of that money also helped fund this book project, so those
amazing, generous people that donated to my sorry ass have unwittingly
helped whomever this book is going to help. That is pretty damn cool
in my opinion.

When receiving *that* level of love and support, physical pain and discomfort are easily transcended. The tears I shed were tears of gratitude
and I was in a state of awe many times when thinking about my life
and the people in it. It was another powerful, humbling experience that
proved to me *once again* that even when my *physical* vessel is damaged, my
spirit could soar. No matter how hard I get "hit" these days, I can't be
touched.

The monetary gift was mind blowing, humbling and truthfully a little
embarrassing and difficult to accept. But it paled in comparison to the
love I received from the people in my life. To me, love and compassion
are, and will always be, the best medicine ever. I try to remember daily
that we *all* have those gifts in us to give away for free.

So although I may have freaked you out earlier about being alone,
and on a certain level and in certain *moments* we all are, remember that the
love and compassion that we share with the people in our lives is what
connects us, and can at the very least help shoulder the burdens of life
we all feel at times.

To those who may read this and feel a resentment or jealousy towards
me because I am such a loved son of a bitch let me remind you that I *only*

received what I have been putting out for years. I love and feel compassion towards people and they love me back. Simple.

On that note, if you need love, come see me and I'll hook you up.

On another note, can you come help me muck stalls and clean the barn?

Thought I would throw that in there in case you weren't clear on that whole pain and suffering stuff. I also wanted it known in black and white and for all of time that I am grateful for what was done for me. You people are awesome and I love you.

So yeah, after all that "being alone" stuff I just pounded into your head the *ultimate truth* is that all this crazy, scary shit you are going through is actually a bridge to connect you with everyone in the world. Why everyone in the world?

Because we all hurt sometimes.

No one is immune to suffering, loss or pain. It is part of being human and part of the deal when you sign up to wear a skin suit here on earth.

If you take anything away from this chapter o' madness, just know that should you choose to make this crisis experience a positive, different or less terrifying one by making it about *learning how to live* as opposed to *being afraid to die*, you automatically shift the energy in a more positive, less stressful, direction. Dare I say you might even become *curious* as to where adopting that attitude may take you...

Again, thinking, *"Holy shit I'm scared, what the fuck is happening to me?"* is about as normal a reaction to crisis a person can have. So be easy on yourself! Just give this some thought. Also, watch baby goat videos on YouTube. They help too. Cute little bastards...

So, to really beat you over the head with this concept, in *my* experience, changing our perspective and thinking, "Okay, how can I make this a positive, or *different* experience for myself?" *shifts* the energy. You are giving yourself options to "feel" or experience this crisis differently. It's like sitting in your car waiting to go into a funeral thinking,

"I've got two choices here. I can go in there and see how sad people are that Billy Bob is dead and really feed off of that sadness and let it weigh my heart down, or I can go in there and see their tears and grief as a testament to how much people cared for him and marvel at the power of love."

Same situation, Billy Bob is dead and is not coming back to his body. Yet there are two different choices as far as perspective is concerned.

I guess I should have put this stuff into the love and perspective chapters but this whole book is a goddamn mess anyway. Screw it, my book, my mess.

So remember, if the moment comes that you realize you are alone, feel it, chew on it, write about it and let it pass. Realize it is not a bad thing. This is a moment that will only happen once. Like losing your virginity. *That* might have been a less than awesome moment too.

Speaking of moments, remember that *even when we are alone,* the quality of our lives in general, and the moment we are in *this very second* depend on the company we keep and the attitude we possess. So be nice to your damn self! It will make the difference between a shitty lonely life or, if you *choose* to be alone, a life of blissful solitude.

Know that all this overwhelming emotional energy can be focused energetically to create that *mighty bridge called compassion* that reaches out to your brothers and sisters in this world. To be a total cheese ball, tear down the bricks of fear and isolation around your heart and build a bridge of compassion with them okay? It might not happen today, but keep at it, one brick at a time. How do you eat an elephant? One bite at a time.

But please don't eat elephants, they are truly amazing creatures.

If a knucklehead like me can do this stuff, so can you. I'll be right there with you doing the work.

It might be tough to wrap your head around all of this at first, but you will get the hang of it. That applies to sex and satisfying a woman properly as well, fellas.

But THAT too is another book or DVD, maybe both!

Written by someone else of course.

Besides, you aren't *really* alone.
YOU GOT ME!!!

———

16

DEFENDING THE CASTLE AND FINDING HOME—THE MIND/ BODY BLITZKRIEG

"The significant problems we face in life can not be solved at the same level of thinking we were at when we created them."
ALBERT EINSTEIN

OUR HOMES ON this earth are our bodies. We identify with them so much—lets face it, we can't go anywhere without them and we tend to spend a whole lot of time in them.

If you've ever taken a powerful hallucinogenic, you may have had an experience which some experts might call "out of body." Using drugs when I was a crazy teenager introduced me to the idea that we are more than these bodies of ours and also made me look at the world differently, inside and outside of myself.

Using drugs, I travelled the cosmos and mined the depths of my soul. Well, I went as deep as I could go at the time, anyway. The fact that mission control was my living room and my recliner was my launch pad is irrelevant. I was an astronaut in inner space, a voyager to the outer realms of my consciousness. I experienced separation from my body in a *pleasurable* way. My consciousness went somewhere else. I felt like I went places far outside of myself and at the same time deeper into myself. Elvis had left the building.

It's been said that teenagers take drugs because they are *seeking* something and adults take drugs to escape things. I think it's a little column A and a little column B for a lot of people regardless of what stage of life they are in. In many cultures, vision quests aided by hallucinogenic drugs are part of very important and powerful rites of passage for young men. I know that I used drugs for similar reasons, searching for answers for questions I had that I couldn't even put into words. I just didn't have a shaman to guide me. Well that and the fact that I was in my basement listening to Hendrix but *whatever*.

As an artistic soul, I loved the enhanced creativity that certain drugs allowed. As a philosopher I loved the complex thinking and insights that were made available to me while under the influence. These were sacred events to me.

Not unlike meditation, using drugs had allowed me to "get out of myself." At times it felt like my soul had left my body and went to other places. I'm *obviously* not a doctor or a scientist. I would be driving a much better car if I was, but I do know that there are different levels of consciousness and I'm pretty sure there are other dimensions in this giant hologram we are a part of. When I got high, it was pleasurable to escape out of my body and into those other places. It didn't bother me that I was out of my body. I always came "back."

At the time those experiences made me feel secure because I could feel the difference between being "in" my body and "out" of my body. The drugs were the catalyst for those feelings.

When I experienced anxiety for the first time when I wasn't high, I thought I was losing my mind. I didn't realize that generalized anxiety was something that could occur without drugs.

Your imagination is an incredible thing. I believe it's what sets us apart from the animals. Well, that and the fact that animals don't form boy bands, among other things, but I digress yet again. The point is, the imagination can really help us—but if left unchecked and allowed to run amok, it can also really hurt us.

There have been many books written about the power of our intentions and the law of attraction and that sort of thing. I believe that there is a lot of validity to these concepts if you are going to experiment with them-which we do anyway without realizing it. I know that fear and worry only add *more* stress to our already hard-working immune systems. Definitely not a good idea when we are sick. We need to use our minds to help the body heal and repair itself, not gum up the works!

We all know how tough it is to break old, unhealthy thought patterns. If we aren't able to drop the negative mental activity through meditation or some other means, then we need to *harness* this great power and make it work for us instead of against us. How do we do this? First of all, let's see where you're at in life.

If you've ever experienced generalized anxiety, you know that it makes concentrating *really* difficult. Constant anxiety wears you down after a while. We know it adds stress to your entire body and makes your immune system less efficient. Being anxious interferes with your sleep and fogs the brain or makes it work too fast. Sometimes anxiety, when fed with our fears and worries, turns into a full-blown panic attack. If you have never experienced a panic attack, consider yourself fortunate.

To those of you who just cringed, I sincerely feel for you. A panic attack as defined by the Mayo Clinic is:

"A sudden episode of intense fear that develops for no reason and that triggers severe physical reactions."

Yeah. That's putting it mildly.

A panic attack is an absolutely terrifying ordeal to experience. You really feel like something horrific is going to happen, that you are going to die or that you are losing your mind. The fear and vulnerability you feel while experiencing a panic attack is off the charts. To be clear, they suck really badly. It takes a lot of effort and work to gain your *own* trust back after experiencing one of these bastards. You tend to live in fear of "it" coming back and it can really shut down your life. You feel like a shell of your former self and that you can be emotionally assassinated by anyone at any time.

Anxiety and panic disorders are cripplers. If you do experience a panic attack, know that you aren't losing your mind, that you aren't going crazy, and that you are going to be fine once it is over. Don't let anyone tell you that you are insane or that you are going insane. Just know you are experiencing a panic attack and that it will pass. I have had panic attacks while under the influence of drugs. At the time I thought I was just too high. No big deal, ride it out until the drugs wear off. Yet when panic attacks started happening while I was sober, I thought I had broken something in my head and had lost my mind. Once that train of thought fueled by the emotions of fear gets rolling, it becomes *very* hard to stop. Your life at that point can then deteriorate quite quickly without proper intervention or action being taken.

Remember my wild run through the warehouse that ended up in the boardroom?

The point is, anxiety and panic rob you of being in the moment and having a place to go to in your mind. When you are anxious, you feel like you are running away from yourself all the time. You are like a small furry animal trapped in a burning shed. You are stuck in there, having trouble breathing and running like a bastard, banging off the walls in a panic to escape the flames.

You don't have the option of your imagination anymore. Your reality is reduced to a primal, terrifying existence where you try to hide from this horrible feeling; you are looking both inward and outward at the same time.

If you are in a situation where you are dealing with mental illness and cancer at the same time like I was, it becomes very stressful. So if you can and believe me, I *know* how ridiculous this sounds, TRY to keep some distance between your nervous breakdown and your cancer experience. Don't try to get it all "out of the way" at once. It is a lot to handle. Life can be challenging and stressful "in normal times" so breathe deep and keep reading.

I do bring this up though because the cancer experience can bring up a lot of fear and anxiety for obvious reasons. Staying calm makes everything better and mastering the art of calm is really hard work but absolutely do-able. I think of the English during the second world-war making tea while the Germans bombed the shit out of them. There were posters that read "Keep Calm and Carry On." These posters have recently re-surfaced. I suppose we need to remember the lesson. I love this simple directive. I also know what a challenge it is to accomplish.

I feel it is essential to counter the stress with activities that are familiar and comforting. I will bring up the breathing exercises *again*. They are SUPER important when dealing with panic attacks and stress, overall. When the anxiety hits, sit, get grounded and do the deep breathing. Plant your energetic roots deep down into the earth and let the energy of the anxiety pass through you. As hard as it is to do, don't fight it, don't resist. Empty your mind, meaning release all thoughts that pop up or are screaming through your head. I know it is hard, but give it a shot. If the feelings of anxiety were eggs, picture your mind as a Teflon frying pan coated with coconut butter.

Nothing sticks baby.

Breathe.

Not everyone can walk into a gym right off the street and bench-press 500 pounds, so realize this type of training is no different. Time and practice will show results. Let the anxiety pass through you. Focus on your breath. Breathe in and out, nice and steady. I promise you that the more you do this exercise, the less intense the panic attacks will be and you will experience more confidence and a greater sense of control. I got myself off of medication by learning how to breathe.

Now, don't just jump off meds and start practicing deep breathing techniques, be smart and consult with your doctor or health professional before you do anything like that. In my case, I got so pissed off and frustrated that I just forced myself to learn a different way. My 21 year-old ego wouldn't accept the whole medication thing as a permanent solution so I found another way that worked *for me*. Just be careful is all I ask. Breathing exercises pretty much saved me and gave me a lifelong, life *enhancing* skill. Pretty good advice I think considering this is coming from someone who couldn't leave the house for a while there. It's also free!

Before I move on from the subject of medication, please don't think you are weak or broken should you need medication to function. I struggled with the stigma of medication when I took it and I believe that hurt me more than it helped me. If you need it, even just for a little while, do your research, ask your health care provider a lot of questions and realize you are a partner in your own recovery. Take an active role in your recovery. You aren't a lab rat or a robot. Don't just take whatever is given to you blindly. Be informed about what you are taking. When I lost it at work I eventually saw a psychiatrist and when I asked him what anti depressants did he told me:

"They change the way you think."

That's it, no further explanation.

That was the worst thing he could have told me as I obsessed about what *that* meant. That one answer caused me *more* anxiety about what was happening to my brain. Thinking about it really freaked me out because I didn't take the time to truly press him about what I was taking. Needless to say, the results were not great.

So, once you get a handle on the old bean, you can hopefully use it to help you visualize. When visualizing, you can constantly be generating images in your mind that hopefully cause good feelings in your heart. That is key to this technique. *Create images in your head that cause a positive emotional response in your heart.* Visualization is the atheist's prayer. I know, I know, here come *more* emails.

I was at a workshop lately, and the *very* wise and incredible man who was presenting said that the emotion *is* the prayer. I love this. That simple statement sums it up nicely. For instance, if you are visualizing a result or situation in your head and regardless of what the image is, if the accompanying feelings are of a desperate, pleading and overall anxious nature, think what will come to you. More of the same I would bet. That has been my experience anyway. What we put out *energetically*, we receive. If you are in the waiting room or the treatment room or wherever, create images in your minds eye that make you *feel* good.

You can sit there and think about your funeral (which isn't bad luck, negative or morose, it can really put you in the moment, but we will talk more about the fear of death later), or you can think about yourself as an old person surrounded by great -grandchildren.

Create whatever images you need in your mind to release those positive feelings.

I ran into trouble when I froze or shut down my feelings. I found that at a certain point, the emotion and the fear got so high that I suddenly found myself *emotionless*. I was just a solid block of ice. Numb. That state has also also been called dissociation.

Everywhere I went, I ran into friends and family that were concerned for me in a way that I *perceived* as being fearful *for* me. I felt their fear and I didn't like it. I'm not knocking them; I'm just saying what I felt. Like a clogged toilet at a truck stop, I felt useless and disgusting.

So I think the combination of what I was experiencing and what I was feeling, made me just shut down inside in order to get through the whole affair. The shame, guilt and fear generated by the mental illness was very much alive in me, and that had a lot to do with me just freezing out the world. It's a bit of a paradox—on one hand it is good to not feel too much in stressful times so you can do what needs to be done, like a meat robot. On the other hand, this reaction leads to a very isolating, lonesome, alien feeling—you become just dead inside, a barely functioning husk of a human being.

Not being able to connect emotionally because of this sense of isolation is awful. What follows are some of the ways I found that helped me deal with this particular problem.

When in public, I "faked" it. I would put on my happy face and try to make others feel good or comfortable to avoid the negative, draining energy that I would otherwise feel if they felt bad or afraid for me. (Or afraid OF me as was the case when I had lost my mind.) I believe we can hurt or upset others with "bad vibes," or the energy coming off of fear or pity. If people saw me as the same old Pete, it was easier for both of us to deal with the situation. I also read somewhere that many rock stars like Kiss and Aerosmith pretended they were rich and famous rock stars long before they were actually famous.

Fake it till you make it!

Recognize what is happening inside you. If you feel frozen, go into it. Sit there and focus on that feeling or lack there of. If you pay enough attention to it, it will shift. It always does. It might shift into something shitty or scary, but that's okay too. At the onset of your crisis experience, *especially* if this is the first time you are truly being rocked by something, I do believe you need to regain, attain and maintain some amount of control to be able to *start* moving through the experience.

As you spend more time in those intense emotional realms you may find the benefit of letting go of that control. For example, I got so tired of fighting *against* the feelings of panic and anxiety that I just let it pass through me one day. I said *"Fuck it, come get me."* Well, when I did that, lo and behold the attacks got less intense *almost immediately* and started to happen a lot less.

When I dropped the resistance, stopped fighting the fear and anxiety and gave in to it, I was suddenly freed from the power of it. Again, that is next level shit but give it some thought.

Some men in western culture are taught to fight, defend and win at any cost. These instincts run very deep in some of us, I get it. But surrender in *this* context is actually a huge victory and is a *very* powerful act. Surrendering can lead to freedom and freedom is getting off of that rollercoaster called emotion.

This might not be instinctual behavior at first and may feel counter intuitive for sure, but it is a concept worth thinking about. Remember I'm *way* down the road here and I just wanted you to think about that concept for a second.

We aren't taught *emotional* skills in school and that is society's loss. Can you imagine the society we would have if we were? In school at all levels we are praised for our academic and athletic abilities and are taught how to improve both of those, but when it comes to matters of the heart, or simply how to navigate and develop *skill* in the realm of emotions, we are left on our own. Big mistake founding fathers, *big* mistake there.

This probably happened because the founding *mothers* were left out of those decisions.

Like cement, our emotions can harden quickly to protect us in stressful situations, so be aware of what's happening and keep an eye on it. If high stress situations start to make you feel like a zombie, pay attention to that feeling of frigidity and see what it *really* is.

Write, breathe, and drop the resistance. You won't die from trying.

Conversely, immersing yourself too much in certain feelings, e.g. hysteria and panic will wear you out quickly and diminish your immune system's ability to deal with your illness. Strive to find that perfect balance between awareness and being too "shut off." Those feelings you are swallowing and freezing will find a way to get your attention, so be aware that they are there somewhere. They will put their shoulder to the door and start ramming—so keep writing and stay on top of what you are and are *not* feeling.

Find a place to let it out. Like I've said before, hit a heavy bag with a baseball bat. Scream and break shit. If I was feeling nothing or emotionally frozen for too long, I would try to read a story or watch a movie that would get a rise out of me or un-block those emotions that were frozen. Sometimes I'd punch myself in the nuts. I'm kidding.

Releasing emotion in a controlled way helps relieve the pressure. Movies are awesome. Watch a movie that will make you cry your ass off—just let it go. Let the emotion out and don't be ashamed. Guys have such a big issue with this and I find it really sad. Do this alone to avoid any embarrassing moments. Or, if you want your girlfriend to see how sensitive you are, do it in front of her then have great sex. Life is beautiful.

Being a tough guy has its place. Although that is actually a really stupid thing to say when I think about it. The bullshit Hollywood stereotypes of what men are supposed to be have caused more problems than they have solved. This is real life, and in real life feelings can help you navigate the world.

The "strong" silent type may look good up on the big screen but in reality it makes for a pretty uninteresting existence. There are times to keep your shit together and times to let it all hang out. Decide when those times are for you. I truly believe that a well-balanced human being is what we should all strive to become, male or female. We should strive to be human beings that are in control of ourselves but still capable of becoming filled with awe or allowing ourselves to grieve or release fear and sadness through crying or talking about it, without the fear of ridicule. I guess that is what being balanced is.

I know why Buddhists strive to be free of the ego, or at least learn to *not* be controlled by, or identify with, emotional states. I see the value in those principals and practice a lot of those same techniques. It makes a lot of sense to do so. I also think emotions are like flavors in the ice cream shop of life. You can't expect to be born into an ice cream shop and not taste all the flavors right? Just don't go overboard and make yourself sick. Or sicker! It just helps to be able to pull back and not get caught up in it all. Even with ice cream we can end up with a sick stomach and sticky fingers!

For you younger dudes, or maybe even for some of you older ones too, If someone makes fun of you for crying, showing emotion or being upset, grab them by the throat and throw them to the ground. Handcuff them and throw them into a car and drive them to treatment and let them see what its like. I doubt this will happen but seriously, if someone makes fun of you at all because you show emotion when in crisis or otherwise, smile at them, wish them a nice life and cut them loose from your life. Be done with them and tell them that.

There is no reason to have people like that in your life, none. If people aren't treating you how you want to be treated it might be because you haven't shown them or told them *how you want to be treated*. If you don't do this, people will treat you *the way they want to*, and that might suck. I would rather be alone or spend time with musical instruments, books and animals than be with people who were insensitive and plain old fucking ignorant. You don't need them. THEY are the cancer in your life so cut them out like you would a tumor. Or, ask them what's troubling them. Whatever mood you are in.

The mind is a funny thing sometimes.

By funny, I mean funny in kind of an asshole way because when it is allowed to run wild in stressful situations it can do some *horrible* shit to you.

With it's ability to imagine scenarios and visualize anything, the mind truly incredible. It is such a powerful tool and it really blows my, well... mind.

When we are fearful, we lose the ability to imagine things clearly. We lose the ability to direct our imaginations to help us. Remember this, fear isn't real. Fear is a choice.

In one of Will Smith's less successful movies; *After Earth*, Will Smith's character, Cypher Raige, tells his son, Kitai:

"Fear is not real. It is a product of thoughts you create. Now do not misunderstand me: Danger is very real. But fear is a choice."

I have to say I agree with this. In life there are dangerous, *potentially* life threatening situations, but knee jerk reactions and conditioning aside, given a fresh slate or perspective, *we absolutely have the choice to decide how we want to react to everything and anything life throws at us*. If this crisis you are in is a new situation that calls for new ways of dealing with life, *especially* if our old ways aren't working, try it out!

Instead of being fearful, or reacting with fear or worse, *living* in fear, don't. Just say no to being fearful. No thank you. Then take a big breath and smile.

"But this might kill me!!"

Yes, that is a possibility, but there are many possibilities out there. Which one *feels* the best or most natural to you? You have a choice. You always have a choice.

Exercise that incredible right daily.

Part of healing and dealing with stress is being able to see pictures in our mind's eye and feel the positive emotion they create in us. However, being scared shitless just squashes the natural ability we have to imagine and visualize; we soon revert back to caveman behavior. Like anything else, there are many books and videos on this subject matter and I encourage you to explore them.

I used to say that when Wayne Dyer, a powerful writer, motivator and speaker, could manifest a full head of hair I'd buy into what he was saying, but that was when I was an angry, ignorant young man. Check out his books, they cover a lot of this stuff. Wayne is a force of good on this earth and I hope to give him a crushing bear hug someday.

The mind is the biggest ally we have in crisis. It is also our biggest enemy. They say the mind is the biggest sex organ we have. Judging by the size of my head, I must be quite well hung. But seriously folks, I believe the reason they say that the mind is the biggest sex organ is because *your mind is always fucking with you.* So make friends with your mind. Let the thoughts come and let the thoughts go. *Change* your mind by changing your relationship with it. This next line is important so read it out loud a couple times.

Our thoughts are only as powerful or meaningful as we decide to make them.

Right?

I wish I was a smarter, more eloquent man, or that I could explain this better, but when you no longer buy what the mind or what those thoughts are trying to sell you, the level of stress in the moment drops.

I would say own the thoughts but that's like trying to own your breath. You can only breathe in and out and *feel* the benefits of that function, so I guess it is safe to say you can either *think* and give those thoughts weight and power or *observe* those same thoughts and watch them dissolve, focusing on creating positive feelings instead.

In other words, you can check into your head and enter a wild world of conflicting thoughts that create conflicting feelings or you can breathe deeply and get into your beautiful heart for the real news report. I hope that makes sense. I'm not high, I swear.

Don't let your wild *mind* push you around is what I'm saying.

Create good thoughts then stop thinking *entirely* and start putting out good *feelings*. Is this hard to do? It can be, but it is good training young Jedi.

Here are a few more mental exercises that I found helpful. Feel free to use them and create your own.

1. Invite your monsters to dinner.

This one is classic. You see yourself sitting at a dinner table and there is only one other chair in front of you. A door opens and it is the most terrifying version of yourself you can imagine. I always saw a zombie-like version of myself with yellow eyes and bared teeth. The first few times I did this exercise I opened my eyes as soon as this version of myself showed up—he was pretty terrifying. But when I realized that I could control this vision, I settled down and dictated how things went.

Take control. When the monster shows up, ask it to sit down. Ask it questions. Ask it why it is here in your life. You may be surprised by the answers you get. I found while doing this exercise that once I got past the fear, I received good information from my "monsters." The best part is, it seems the scarier the monster is, the more powerful the gift you receive. Think on that for a bit.

I know it seems like an odd thing to do but it really does work and it stretches out your mind. Also, when you are guiding your imagination, you are in control of that part of your mind, so it can't be running you into the ground with terrible thoughts that cause terrible feelings.

2. Best Possible Outcome Exercise.

In this simple exercise, you simply imagine the life you want to be living. See your life unfolding the way you want it to. Pay attention to the emotional responses you have.

What are you imagining that causes the greatest emotional response inside of you? For instance, if you are experiencing cancer – think of being really healthy and vibrant hanging out with the people you love. See in great detail the setting that you are in. See yourself around a table, laughing and talking about the days when you were sick; use whatever image you feel best defines what being healthy is to you.

Don't panic if you can't "feel" what it is to be healthy. Often when we are sick or medicated for a long period of time, we forget what "normal" feels like. If you only make pictures in your mind's eye of what healthy and happy looks like to you, so be it. Fake it till you make it, or feel it right? The most important thing is that it eventually generates an emotional response. See—and more importantly—feel how good it is to be in that place. Keep trying—it really is important to have an emotional response to these scenarios. That is where the truth, and healing, lies.

3. The Rotting Corpse Exercise

Here is a fun one kids! In this powerful exercise we learn to drop all expectations of any kind of result at all. We offer no resistance to our situation and embrace the fact that we will die someday and be reduced to.. well.. you get it. Now, before you freak out, just remember, the point of this is to drop all resistance. To just see your body lying in the grass somewhere. Just see it dissolving away to a skeleton at first and then see the skeleton turn to dust. Then see flowers growing in the place of where your body was laying. This exercise is hard to do. No one ever wants to think about death let alone when you may be dancing with it. However, doing this exercise for me has always made me feel free. Free of my body, my worries and all the bullshit and insanity that go along with being a human. It's twisted but it is a mini vacation for me. When I do this one I also always feel re-energized and focused on living fully. I find myself feeling grateful for my life regardless of what is happening. Try it and see where it takes you!

4. The Lottery Win.

I like to do this one all the time, shit, who doesn't? It's a pretty easy one. The trick is to think of things you would do for others. It takes the focus off of you and your situation, and can make you feel empowered. When I think about being wealthy, I don't think about having lots of money or nice cars and shit like that. I think about doing the things that money and wealth and good health will allow me to do. Like being able to pay off my friends and families mortgages and take care of the people in my life. This one is just fun in my opinion. In all seriousness though, that is what gives me an emotional response, thinking about what I could do for others. I say strive for that feeling. When you make an emotion, in my opinion, you've made a real connection. Something happens! Okay, fantasize about the big house and the nice car too… Then give them away!

So have fun with this stuff and don't listen to the part of your brain or your head that says, "It's not real, this is stupid! You are sick and you are gonna die!" or any of that bullshit that other parts of your head will throw at you for that matter. Calmly tell your brain in the best "talking to a baby voice" that you have, to be a good brain and do what you ask. Don't get upset by the counter-productive thoughts, just let them pass by and keep re-directing your focus on the positive feelings you want. Run those feelings through you and clear out the sludge inside. Get things moving!

Being skillful with how you use your mind and imagination puts you in the driver's seat right from the beginning of this experience. That is why I like writing so much because when the anxiety is so high that I feel like I can't use my imagination, I can still express myself through words. I can still get the hopes and fears down on paper. To lose the ability to use my own imagination takes away a powerful tool. This is something I use on a daily basis, not just when in a crisis.

The imagination is a very powerful place, and to simply imagine and focus on scenarios and results that will bring us relief and pleasure is an incredible ability. The best part of it is that *it is absolutely free.*

So have fun with these exercises. Let your mind run wild in a *good* way. Talk to the monsters that live inside you. See yourself living the life you want to live, in the body you want to live it in, with the people you want around you. Generate those good feelings inside to the best of your abilities and get your body buzzing with a positive energy. We are all just cells vibrating at different speeds, so why not add to the vibration with some positive energy and move our asses down the line in style?

17

TO BE IS TO BE OF SERVICE

"The best way to find yourself is to lose yourself in the service of others."
MAHATMA GANDHI

I BELIEVE THAT IN life the greatest thing we can do is to be of service. Whether that means scooping a helpless bumblebee out of a swimming pool or bearing witness to someone on his or her deathbed, to be of service is of the highest order. It makes sense to me to help out when you can. If you can help out, you should. In life, the little things make the biggest difference. A smile and a kind word to someone who looks like their world is falling apart can go further than you would imagine. Holding a door open for someone, or showing basic human kindness can change someone's day. The whole "pay it forward" shit is a worthwhile and powerful choice to make, and action to take in life.

Being sick and feeling nuts introduced me to emotional landscapes that were beyond easy description. The beautiful thing about spending time in vulnerable places is that you eventually realize that they are the best parts of us. Now I gotta mess with your head a bit.

In the years since I went nuts and had cancer, I have spent countless hours writing, reading, thinking, meditating and ruminating upon the ways of the world, the human condition and life in general. The following insights are the results of that inner work. For the young person who is in the shit right now, don't let this freak you out. Just read it and see if anything resonates with you. All right? Let's dig in.

Those painful, scary grounds inside us that may seem like your own personal hell at this moment are very powerful places. When we learn to surrender and just experience and observe the feelings that are torturing us, without reacting to them or buying into them as our ultimate concrete reality, they will often fall away. Now, this can take a lifetime to achieve and I have had enough small victories to keep *trying* to do this. But sometimes it happens that it just happens! One minute I am completely engaged with my rage and ego and then all of a sudden I catch myself and boom, it drops.

Do I still lose it sometimes? You bet your ass I do. This takes discipline and like many of us, I can be lazy. It's *easy* to freak out and be an ego driven asshole. Take a quick look around you; the world is full of them.

Look in the mirror first though eh? I kid, sort of...

It takes *skill* and *practice* however, to be able to detach, pull back and drop the hot ego potato. So, that being said, let's go a bit farther down this path shall we? Oh yeah, prepare yourself for some *mindfuckery* too by the way.

Sitting in our own piles of misery is where we can realize that our experiences and feelings can be observed, pondered, felt, and *let go* of.

"Because they weren't real to begin with"- said the old wrinkly zen master inside you, hitting you with a bamboo sword.

It is precisely those places and the time spent in them, that gives people the appearance of being "strong" or of having the "internal fortitude" to help others in crisis.

I would bet that many people who appear strong are 9 times out of 10 just *able* to be present. Those people are *comfortable* just being present, which is a gift you give to yourself as well as the person you are with. I'm gonna punch myself if I use the word present again. Since in theory, my self doesn't exist, *as I am trying to murder that son of a bitch everyday...* I'm going to use that word again anyway. I'm sorry to play with your head like that. I do mean well!

The truth is in my opinion, when being of service or being with someone in crisis, hopefully we learn how to just be there for that person. We give our full attention without expectations, without opinion, or without trying to "fix" them. We are just fully present (*damn it*, I said it *again*) for that person. The same applies for our own selves of course, and that is what meditation is all about. Developing the ability to just *be* without expectation.

To take it further and to screw with your mind (and ego) even more, we are all connected so there is no "you" or "them" anyway. I'm an asshole, I know. *But it's true...* How do I know this? I know this because I have felt it in my heart and in my guts and balls. That truth has resonated through me loudly, like a monstrous, ridiculously loud fart on an old pew in an empty stone church. But in all seriousness, remember what I said about that compassionate bridge? *That's* where I connect with people and how *I* know we are all connected. Not because I'm some big deal guru. That ain't me folks, far from it.

Lets talk a little more about the idea of being strong and surrendering for just a second. I know I have touched on this before, but goddamn it, we are going here again and a little deeper this time! Put the air tanks on, we have gone down the path and are now at the edge of a huge, deep lake. We're jumping in and going deeper still folks.

Like I said before, for some men, especially *young* men, the idea of surrender, or giving in, submitting etc.. is unacceptable. I felt the same way as a young man and still sometimes struggle with it to this day. When faced with a crisis situation we sometimes struggle to hold on to our *stories*. We struggle to try to maintain the "reality" that we used to be comfortable in, or felt best defined us *before* the crisis. The problem lies in the fact that when we *define* ourselves by these stories, they also bind us.

I'm no Buddhist, but I do resonate with a lot of things in Buddhist practice. In Buddhism there is a term called *"being tied up without a rope"* and I believe that term applies here.

For example, if we are the happy go lucky kid who gets cancer and suddenly find ourselves filled with feelings of anger unlike anything we have ever felt, we may find ourselves unsure about how to proceed. We want to remain the "good" guy who is always happy when in this current "reality" we are a simmering vat of rage. Can you see how this might make things a little difficult? We are tied up without a rope. How do we untie that invisible rope? Drop it all, just be, and let the ego die along with the cancer cells. I know it sounds impossible and a little scary, but it is such a worthwhile practice to try to develop.

After all this time on earth and all these stories about our "selves" and our lives, most of us have never met "ourselves". If you are now sarcastically screaming, *"Because WE don't exist Asshole!"* you are on the right track. But if you are feeling freaked out, you are on the right track too as there is opportunity to grow in terms of exploring that fear. Remember what I said about fear while you are doing so.

When crisis hits, not only is our *physical* health challenged, so are our *stories*. It is not always as easy as; *take the medicine and move on.* So what do we do? Dive in and let go. Sit still and let it all happen. Let it all pass through you. We hate being still, calm and quiet. We like yelling and screaming and writing books trying to help people out. (Wink, wink.) We are human and we are messy and that is beautiful.

In short, *because I know you want to get an aspirin*, to truly be of service to others, you need to be able to be *fully* present. How to get there is a different journey for everyone. You just need to take that first curious step. It is time for a new story anyhow!

You will have time to do this in waiting rooms and at traffic lights. Meditation doesn't have to be sitting uncomfortably on a small pillow chanting and burning incense. Riding my motorcycle helped me meditate and go to some amazing places inside. Taking time daily to gently contemplate the things that scares us, hurt us, or makes us feel vulnerable is a fine practice to invest time in. Remember that it is called a meditation *practice* for a reason too.

Allowing someone to submit me in Jiu-Jitsu for *his or her* benefit helps me kill *my* ego. Consequently the more my *ego* died on the mats the better I got at Jiu-Jitsu. Their "victory" becomes mine. Besides, resistance on the mats will only result in broken bones and unconsciousness. Break habits and old thinking patterns, not bones. Be conscious of releasing your ego and soar, don't be *rendered* unconscious by your stubbornness and ignorance of not knowing when its time to submit. Get out of your own way.

Jiu-Jitsu is life...

We are all connected and we are all one bitches!

Again, I'm still rowing that boat baby. I'm still learning and *practicing* fully dropping the oars and letting the tides take me too. I'm not a master of any sort in *anything* and I will remain a white belt in life forever. Besides, being in a shit storm is the perfect, beautiful day to row that particular boat in.

When you spend enough time in those gooey, tender parts of yourself, after a while it becomes less uncomfortable.

Spend enough time in the shadowy parts of yourself and those places eventually lose that weird feeling and you lose the fear of those places. Suddenly, you are able to successfully navigate situations that were once uncomfortable. Instead of feeling confined by your mind and your life you may now feel a sense of *space*. You can breathe. You become deepened and hollowed out in a good way, no longer wanting to fill that space with anxiety and worrisome thoughts.

You become able and *willing* to step into the breach with someone else and spend time there *with* them. One day it is going to be you sitting beside the hospital bed and not laying in it. You will become the bedside Buddha.

When that day comes, I hope that you are well prepared. Being a caregiver can be tiring and brutal. You are sometimes left feeling helpless, afraid and frustrated. Wait, this is sounding familiar isn't it? Yes, being the caregiver can oftentimes be as shitty and frustrating as being the patient. We have talked about this before. Not everyone feels comfortable in the caregiver role. Like we discussed in "How to be a Kick Ass Friend," you need to figure out what you are comfortable doing; what your boundaries are. Doing something because you think *that's what someone wants you to do* is not a good plan.

Asking what people need is a good place to start. Let them lead. That being said, there will be times when you need to act and do the thinking for the person in crisis as they will be too sick or overwhelmed to think for themselves. When you are in crisis, *not* having to make certain decisions is awesome when you are overwhelmed and exhausted. These are the times your intuition and gut feelings will come into play.

Sometimes figuring out what to do is as much about feeling out the situation using your intuition as it is listening with your ears.

There will be times when people will want to talk about what they are going through, and times they won't. Sometimes it is good just to be there with them in the same room doing nothing but spending time with them. We have a tendency to want to fix things, but sometimes we just need to be a witness and let things happen. Hopefully the time spent in crisis will have honed your intuition.

Getting a feel for the immediate situation and of the needs of those around you is extremely powerful anytime in life, but *especially* while in the trenches of crisis. Don't wait to be the bringer of light or whatever the hell we should call it. Even in the midst of your chaos, you can be the person who makes someone's day.

Regardless of whatever state of mind you may be in, always remember that you can be of service in some way. Your experience, your attitude, and your willingness to be there for someone in whatever capacity they need, in my humble opinion, is the highest gift we can give to ourselves and to others.

I believe that it is in those moments of selflessness that we get to experience and more importantly share the gifts in our own hearts. We get to connect with the best parts of ourselves and really experience our humanity. Connecting with another human being is what being alive is all about. Whether it was helping someone in crisis or pulling a car out of the ditch with my truck in the winter, nothing has ever made me feel better than when I get to help somebody in need. That may change when I'm rich, but for now it still stands. I joke, I joke.

I hope that you explore the ways in which you can help others in your life. I hope that if you are in a crisis-type situation, you realize the power and satisfaction you gain from being selfless. I know that sounds confusing to you hardcore zen dudes, but you know what I mean...

Whether it is having the courage to speak with or listen to someone else in your shoes, or risk exposing yourself emotionally to a stranger (without making it about you) or just smiling at someone who looks like they need it, take the time to *try*. You will be the better for it, I assure you.

People tend to think they need to be millionaires or philanthropists to make a difference in this world. They sometimes think that you need a big education or a certain type of job to make a difference in this world. That, my friends, is complete bullshit. All you need is beating in your chest right now.

As long as you have a heart, you can help. Kindness and compassion are free to offer someone if you aren't afraid to share them. There is a reason that so many people that volunteer are either retired or older. Yes, retired people get bored in their retirement and have more free time, but I really believe the older we get, we see what matters most in this world. To give of ourselves is incredibly satisfying. Being sick made me realize how we are all connected.

We are all a part of each other's trip here. Jimi Hendrix put it best in the song *Machine Gun* when he sang the line *we are all just families apart.* Maybe Bob Marley said it best with *One Love/People Get Ready.* I am sure you do, but if you don't know those artists, check out their work. They were very special souls making very special music.

This trip on earth isn't about you or me. It's about *us.*

A great band is nothing without a great audience to hear the music. A piece of art is nothing without the observer. A delicious piece of cake is nothing until it is eaten and enjoyed. *Don't you just want one now?*

We need each other to make life worth living, and when you are being of service, that point hits home.

This may seem like hippy-dippy love and peace crap to some, but believe me when I tell you that to me, it isn't. If I learned *one thing* while going through sickness and crisis, it's that without our compassion and our humanity we are *fucked* as a species.

It is up to us to take the steps to put developing compassion for ourselves, our planet and each other, at the *forefront* of our greatest accomplishments here on earth. In the hopefully near future, aliens should cruise by in their spacecraft and be like:

"Wow, look at those humans!! They really turned their shit around didn't they? Look at all that compassion! It's fueling the whole planet! I think its safe to land there now..."

Sigh.

Maybe someday.

Like I said in the introduction, it seems like our technology is overriding our humanity right now. While there are many ways technology can enhance our humanity, the best piece of gear we have ever had or will ever have is sitting in your chest right now, beating away and keeping you alive. People go bananas over the latest cell phones, computers and technology in general. Imagine the world we could have if we could get as excited about our own heart's capabilities?

Your heart will guide you if you let it. I learned this in waiting rooms, treatment rooms and in the many places where I took the time to sit and reflect on my life.

Your heart is like a store. Open it up each morning and let people into it. Yes, some of them will try and steal from you; some of them will try and tell you your "goods" are no good at all. Some will try to tell you how to run your business. Some will be suppliers to your store, or be a part of your business for a little while, and some will be loyal to your brand till you close the doors for good.

There will be spills in the aisles that you need to clean up, and you may need the help of others to clean up the big messes. Renovations may be needed, or you may choose not to expand. There will be days when the store is full and days when the store sits empty. Remember to do your inventory each day, and remember to be a good boss.

Remember to be nice to the customers who walk in, to the best of your abilities. Oh, you thought I was going to say the customer is always right? As nice as that is to say, it isn't true. Sometimes customers can be assholes, but hey, it's your store and you can do as you wish! Just remember that some business is not worth having.

As long as you have a heart, you can change *your* world. Whether you give away your time, your money, your skills, your compassion or you just hold someone's hand that needs it, you will always be the richer in spirit for it.

Yes, being a multi-millionaire would let you do a lot of things and a lot of good, but don't let the lack of funds in your bank account stop you from being of service. What you have in the bank will *never* be more important or of more value than the currency of compassion.

Give it away, every single day.

If all you had to your name was a *single* penny in your pocket, you might think you were pretty broke.

But what if *that* was the last penny on earth and you ran into a man who was one penny shy of being a millionaire?

What would that rare penny be worth now?

Be a rare penny and make somebody who needs you feel like a millionaire by giving of yourself. Money will *never* be able to buy the way it feels inside when you do that.

I would bet my last penny on it.

18

INSIGHTS ON DRIVING THE MEAT SUIT AND EARTH SUIT INSIGHTS

"This body is not a home but an inn, and that only briefly."
SENECA

WATCHING THE MOVIE Avatar was an incredible experience for me. Not just for the special effects or the great story and message the movie delivered, either. Avatar blew me away because I realized I was watching a perfect example of what it is to be a soul riding around in a meat suit.

In the movie, the way that the humans became part of their avatar really hit me hard. I remember sitting in the theatre thinking, *"Holy shit, this is what I am talking about!"* The idea of riding around in this organic machine in order to experience earth has been something I have been thinking about since I had my first panic attack. We sometimes identify with our bodies so much as being "us" that we forget we are anything else but flesh and bone with blood and chemicals rushing through it. I know this to be true because I have experienced my soul wanting to get the hell out of my body.

Before your eyes roll, hear me out. What if a panic attack was just your soul throwing up? You drink too much booze and you puke. You take on too much of life, too much emotional, chemical stimulation and you have a panic attack. Would that make it easier to handle? In my mind the answer was and still is yes. Whether its whiskey or intense feelings I am "experiencing," I believe the body processes them both the same way. Too much booze, and the body screams,

"This is dangerous for me and the idiot driving me."

Next stop, Pukesville! Blllaaaaaggghhhhh… and now *we* are driving the porcelain bus.

Same thing with an anxiety or a panic attack—too much thinking, obsessing, worrying and stress and the body says, *"This moron's gonna fry his head with all this shit, time to blow the breaker,"* and then AAAAHHHHHHHHHH !!! You have an anxiety attack. What happens after an anxiety attack? You may feel a lesser degree of fear. You've blow your emotions out.

Yes, you are left trembling, vulnerable and terrified. But when you do see these events as *"breaker blowouts,"* it helps, because you start to be more aware of how you treat yourself. The experience can become less terrifying and more understandable and more importantly, manageable. For example, after a few really terrible hangovers, you should hopefully learn how to limit your drinking habits. After a few panic attacks, you hopefully learn how to regulate the intense emotional energy going on inside you to avoid blowing the breaker. I know I am oversimplifying a complex situation, but you get my drift? Okay, maybe it can be a genetic disorder or a chemical imbalance, but that's not as much fun now is it? I believe that my theory can also apply and be helpful.

It's not as crazy as it seems, right?

Get in and take a ride with me for a second, but don't touch the radio.

If you can see your body as an avatar—and not get all freaked out by the idea that you are a soul or a focused, conscious energy riding around in a body, you can make better choices. You can treat your body like a car. It makes things simple. Trouble is, a lot of people treat their bodies like rental cars, myself included. They "drive" them like they stole them. They push them way too hard, they put the cheap fuel in them, they bang them up without much care and they take them for granted and respond to any challenge about their behavior with a terse, *"It's mine, I paid for it! I will do what I want with it!"* Especially smokers. I really hate smoking.... You were given your body. It was a gift, along with your life, from other people. We don't own anything in this world save for our attitudes and memories.

Anyway, in the movie Avatar, there is a line that says:

"All energy is borrowed and one day you have to give it back."

I love that line. It makes so much sense to me. I hope I get to keep enough energy to endlessly travel the universe as a beam of light after I leave this body. I'm just sayin'.

So yeah, you didn't pay for your body, but you WILL pay for it if you neglect it. Guaranteed. Just look at people and their cars. Isn't it weird how the way they live their lives often reflects in the way they treat their cars? Think about it. I'm guilty of that one too, trust me. I'm lookin at my belly right now!

Shortly after I finished cancer treatment, I got a job at a cemetery working on the burial crew. One day while working at the cemetery I witnessed an older Italian woman and her adult, developmentally delayed son mourning at her husband's gravesite. These two would come every week. The mother was always really upset and the son was too. He seemed to be reacting to the fact that his mom was losing her shit.

On this particular day, I had been finishing a burial one row over from where the mom and son were. As usual, she was crying loudly and was in terrible distress. Her son was sitting on the grass rubbing it (the grass you sick pigs...) and crying. She caught me watching and called me over. The woman apologized for bothering me and told me what had happened to her husband. Heart attack, unexpected, and gone too soon. This was a familiar and sad story. She then asked me where his head would be, pointing to the grave. I pointed to the general area. She then asked me:

"How long does it take to... to...?" She gestured with her hands around her face. She was asking me about decomposition. The woman was clearly torturing herself thinking about this, and I in turn was thinking a thousand miles an hour trying to come up with something to help and comfort her besides the usual *"I'm sorry for your loss."*

It was at that point that the meat suit/earth suit/spacesuit revelation came back to me, hitting me like a ton of bricks. I asked the woman if I could speak freely as myself and not as a representative of the cemetery as we weren't supposed to talk to any "customers," just send them to the main office if they had questions and concerns. I told her my personal belief regarding death and the body. It went something like this:

Me: "Maria, (We will call her that) when they send astronauts to the moon, what are the astronauts wearing?"

Maria: "They are wearing the.... spacesuits?"

Me: "Yes, that's correct. Why did they wear spacesuits?"

Maria: "So they can...(hand gesture around the mouth) breathe and live on the moon?"

Me: "You got it. Now Maria tell me, when the astronauts are finished with the mission on the moon and they come home, what do they do with the suits?"

Maria: "I don't know, put in museum?"

Me: (In my head) "Shit good point, they do put them in museums sometimes and people come visit them... Dammit!" I recovered and said, "Sometimes yes, but Maria let me ask you this, do you think the astronauts or their friends and family come to the museum and cry looking at the spacesuits thinking about the moon mission?"

Maria: (looking confused but knowing I am close to a point) "Well, no, I don't think so"

Me: "Of course not, the spacesuit was part of the mission, when the mission was over the astronauts took them off and went back home. Maria, these (pointing to our bodies) are OUR earth suits. (A slight glimmer appeared in her eye, the light bulbs visibly going on in her head.)
"And this (waving my arms around, gesturing towards our surroundings) is our moon. We need these suits to live here on earth. And when we are finished with our mission, where do our suits go?"

Maria looked down at her husband's grave.

Me: "That's right; we put the earth suits in the ground, back in the earth. Maria, I believe that all that is buried here in the ground is your husband's earth suit."

Maria got it. She lowered her head, nodded and started to cry. She was in a *huge* amount of pain, but I hoped I had given her a different perspective that might offer her some relief.

I asked her what kind of support she had and told her about grief counseling. I also told her she shouldn't come back to the cemetery for a while. I encouraged her to take a break and give her son a break, too. Maria thanked me and gave me a strong hug. I only made a little better than minimum wage back then to bury the dead, but that day I felt like I had done something special. It was a good day in the bone yard.

In my opinion, we are driving meat suits here.

I believe we are spiritual creatures having human experiences here on earth. These bodies of ours are our earth rovers that we need to experience and explore earth in. When we are finished the mission, we don't need them.

Beep Beep--Heavy Shit Alert!

When I think of myself as a spiritual being or a beam of light riding around in this lower vibrational meat suit, it just makes perfect sense to me. Imagine driving a car and it starts running badly. Do you pull over and put sugar in the tank? No! You find out what's wrong and fix it to get it running well again. Or you don't and you let it just get worse and worse and let it break down. Then you cry out "Why? How did this happen?"

We take mechanics courses to learn how to fix our cars. We should have no problem taking energy courses to fix our bodies. Look at all the cash we put into our bodies, food, fake boobs, tanning, tattoos, hairstyles, clothing—all this money and time invested in something that we are going to lose someday. I'm not saying never do these things; have fun with your "car." Soup it up! But for god's sake put some time into the light machine that runs the meat suit! You can have the most beautiful car in the world but if you only put sugar in the tank, it's not going anywhere.

Like I have mentioned before, many times in the past, during extremely high anxiety events, I would feel my soul trying to get the hell out of my body. I can't describe that feeling any better than how my doctor explained what taking a bone marrow sample would feel like.

He said it would feel like I was being sucked "inside out." And when he pulled the syringe full of marrow out of my hipbone, that's *exactly* what it felt like.

So when I say that my soul felt like it was trying to leave my body, the best I could say is that it felt like "I" or what I perceive as "me" was trying to get out of my body. Sometimes I felt like I was hovering up and to the right over my body, watching from that perspective. It was a very uncomfortable feeling, to say the least. So after I had many of these incidents, I started to think about it. What was going on? Why did I feel this way?

Anxiety is described in the American Heritage Dictionary as:

"A state of apprehension, uncertainty, and fear resulting from the anticipation of a realistic or fantasized threatening event or situation, often impairing physical and psychological functioning."

I am sure there are many scientific reasons for why we feel anxiety. I believe that anxiety is one of the body's survival systems. Strong feelings of anxiety may sometimes be the body's way of telling you something is really wrong. Why do we have "gut" reactions? When they are so strong that they make us sick, what does that mean? What are they there for? Like a back-up warning sensor on a vehicle, maybe anxiety and those types of feelings are built into the body to keep us from backing over the cliff.

It's weird—we see each other with our eyes but only really "see" each other with our hearts. Some of us *never* "see" each other. We identify so much with our physical body that it can cause big problems within ourselves, because our bodies are constantly changing. Our world is constantly changing. Fluidity and non-attachment to, but respect for, the body is key. Rigidity is death. In death, the body becomes rigid. The only real good place for rigidity is in the bedroom, and only in specific parts at that, if I may go ahead and insert that image into your minds. Make it bigger than it is, please! Thank you.

When experiencing crisis, it can be very scary and unnerving to feel trapped in our bodies with our sickness. Like I have mentioned before, I used to have horrible, crippling anxiety—until I realized that "I" was not my body. As freaky as that concept seems, it really helped me when I adopted that mindset.

For instance, when I would be lying on a bed in a room with doctors doing weird alien autopsy type shit to me, I would try to remove myself mentally from the situation. The whole *"I can't believe this is happening to me"* panicked feeling from deep inside would start to build and take over. I would feel trapped and it became really hard to stay calm. When your body is being fucked with medically, you need to stay calm. But it is really hard to stay calm when you are being fucked with medically, right? Therein lies the problem.

Solution? Yup, time to do some deep breathing and crazy-ass visualization. Do the one where you put yourself in a chair watching what is happening to your body. You see it like a movie, becoming both the observer *and* all the characters. You can see yourself as an entity of glowing white light that takes the body right out of it. I went a little out there just now, I know. But mess around with the idea!

Staying calm in those conditions is not the easiest of tasks. Yes, we can distract ourselves with our smart phones, texting and all that stuff, but learning how to calm down sans technology will benefit you for the rest of your life. Especially when the grid goes down! Besides, you can't use your phone when they are working on you.

That is why the whole breathing thing is essential—take control of your body, relax it through breathing techniques and try to go somewhere else in your mind. Keep at it!

I'm gonna go on a bit of a side road here, partly to break up this heavy vibe and partly just to be an asshole and stir things up a bit. I'm going to tell you about an observation I've made.

I find it funny that people who would describe themselves as spiritual tend to be cat owners and atheists or non-spiritual people tend to be dog owners. Before you get all upset and whiny, just hear me out for a second. Remember, I'm having fun here.

Cats are the kind of creatures that don't need you. A cat lover knows that you can't force a cat to do anything. You can train a cat to do some things, but they are going to march to the beat of their own drummer. Cats come for love when THEY want it. If you try to demand love and affection from them, they simply walk away from you if they don't feel like it. Cats are frustrating to dog owners because they don't do what they are "supposed" to do.

Cat owners know this and usually like the fact that cats are independent and not so clingy. Cat owners don't need the constant reassurance from their pet that they are loved or that they are "the boss". Cat owners understand that you can't go demanding and controlling love (or life) all the time. They know that when the cat comes for a little petting or cuddle to enjoy and relish the moment, because it is not going to be forever.

Dog owners seem to be constantly trying to control the dog's behavior. They appear to love the fact that they can leave for five minutes and the dog will be a confused mess that erupts with joy when they come back. It could be argued that dog owners need as much reassurance that they are loved as the dogs do!

Wait! Stop typing that email full of hate and anger and just keep reading.

Dogs are predictable in their behavior and are somewhat steady creatures. That is likely very comforting to a dog owner. What seems to be important to the dog owner is the sense of being in control, of being the "boss." They run around with fanny packs filled with treats, whistling and clicking and giving treats to the dog, who just wants to run, chase squirrels, freak out and lick its own balls.

Dog owners take courses on how to train the animal. Sit! Lie down! STAY!

Do as I say. I am in control. That is fearful, distrustful behavior, in my opinion. The following could be the message that lies beneath the dog owner's actions.

"I will control this animal as I want to control my own life. I enjoy the predictability of this situation and it makes me feel powerful and safe. I feel better the more this animal submits to my will and listens to my commands."

Dog owners don't want to have faith. They want to *be* Gods. (Spell dog backwards while we're at it.)

This applies more to city dogs and owners, though. Country dogs seem to know the routines and fall into their roles on the farm. Of course, they have real jobs and responsibilities on the farm and some are not really pets. Regardless, this is just a theory of mine, and I sit here laughing as I think of you dog lovers, fuming and clicking your clickers and blowing your whistles at me. *Relax!*

I'm just trying to have a little fun with you. I love both species. Now sit down and calm yourselves... GOOD BOY!! Here's some ice cream...

Are you a cat person or a dog person? Do you trust and cherish life and love as it comes in natural waves or do you try to control and make demands of it? A cat person knows that you may or may not receive love and affection when you need it. It sucks to want to pet a cat and it slinks away under the table, just eluding your grasp, with that "you bore me" look on its face. Interestingly, the more you trust and ignore a cat, the more it will come and rub on you.

Chase and crave love, and it remains just outside our grasp. But having trust, knowing that love will come and go about your day, and love finds you.

Rubbing up against your leg, purring madly, perhaps?

I once heard that you could learn a lot about life from a cat. They always stretch as soon as they get up, they are very clean, they always get the rest they need and can be both playful and very serious. They rarely just give their love and affection away. They are excellent hunters and can survive on their own, but they also make a great companion.

Cats will always let you know where you stand. Yes, I'm a cat man. No, you in the back, I'm not a pussy; I'm a cat man. Like I said before, I love dogs too, but in my heart, I'm a cat man.

Now before I get millions of emails from angry dog owners I will make the argument for why dogs are great too.

Dogs are loyal, steadfast and will love you unconditionally. They will always be there for you and make you feel like you are their whole world. If you pour your heart out to a dog it will look at you the whole time, trying to decipher your message. Really, they are just listening for the words "food" or "walk."

Dogs are great to keep you exercised and busy; you can also meet other dog owners and strike up conversations when taking them for walks. The neediness of dogs may serve a person who feels they are not loved or needed by anyone. Dogs can be trained for jobs that help people and protect people. Also, many prisons have had great success with programs that allow prisoners to rehabilitate dogs. Interacting and training the dogs allow the prisoners to feel their own love, compassion and humanity as well as a sense of connection and accomplishment. See, hardcore dog lovers? I'm not such a bad guy after all! No emails please unless they are praising me....

So how does all this dog, cat stuff relate to crisis?

Well, like I wrote a little while back, *trusting* and *knowing* that relief, health or love will come to you from yourself and others will take you farther than *demanding* and *trying to force or control* those same things. These are two different approaches, two different energies. One is subtle and confident; the other is more harsh, more fearful and impatient.

If you are diagnosed with a disease or are experiencing crisis, try both approaches. See how each one feels. Which is your natural response? Do you trust that the right thing is going to happen or are you going to will what you want to happen into existence?

These are two different energetic approaches that affect us two different ways. What are the underlying messages?

The first is a message that states: *"I come from a place of love and trust."* The second is *"I come from a place of fear."* When you operate in the energy of trust, you know it will come to you, whatever "it" is. When you try to will something to happen, you are approaching the situation from a lack of confidence, or a place of doubt or distrust in my opinion.

Where do you want to come from energetically speaking?

You may think that only while in a state of crisis you need to develop a sense of trust in yourself and the process of life, but it isn't so. You had to learn to walk, to swallow (easy now) and to run. Maybe you had to learn how to ride a bicycle. You had to learn to trust the people around you when you were a kid. We spend our whole lives learning to trust our selves and the world outside of ourselves.

Some of us come from a "prove me wrong" place.

In this place, we reluctantly "trust" someone or something, but secretly believe that the person or thing will eventually screw up, confirming our *true* belief. This was never trust to begin with. It is hard to describe what trust feels like. It isn't quite like confidence or happiness; I think it is more like being at peace. Ultimately, I believe what we are all seeking is a sense of peace and contentment. Crisis is a great place to start the process.

I have seen people come to this place of peace and contentment near the end of their cancer experience. It sucks that they had to experience physical death to do so, but that doesn't mean it is the only way. Many people also meet their death without having reached this state, unfortunately. Just as it's not a given that going through crisis will lead you to inner peace and greater insight, it's also not a given that you need to experience crisis to gain those same things.

Being in crisis does offer you an opportunity for massive growth and understanding, should you decide to embrace the experience with this attitude. Even if you aren't the patient!

The biggest hurdle is developing that sense of trust. When I was in cancer treatment, I would have many thoughts about the mind-body connection. I remember thinking that the body had its own mind and my soul had its own mind. Two separate consciousness's in one body. Would that explain the constant fear?

Mentally I could process things and come to some kind of decision about it, but then the body would react differently. For instance, if you walk up to a busy street and stand on the sidewalk and think, "I'm going to walk into traffic," and try to convince yourself that this is what you are going to do, you may feel your body tell you:

"Whoa! I don't think so son!"

If you go so far as to physically try to take a step off the curb, you may feel a huge surge of fear or panic rise up in your body and a sense of physical resistance. The mind is "saying" one thing, the body the other. Yeah, yeah, science guy, I know it's probably the brain doing both but you get what I mean.

Well, now we are sitting in the waiting room again. We are about to go in for some god-awful procedure and the mental rationalization begins: *"Its cool, it will be okay, don't worry about it."* Then you feel the body saying *"Lets get the hell out of here!"* You may feel both the mind and the body start to freak out on you. Then it's like a three-way conversation going on. Now a part of you is trying to convince the body and another part of your consciousness that things are okay when the body doesn't believe it. I know this sounds crazy, but I remember it happening to me!

If your body is a horse, you must lead it to water. Sometimes a cowboy has to lead his horse somewhere the horse doesn't want to go, but with a gentle nudge and a soothing voice, he gets the horse to go there. Be a good cowboy and lead your horse through the difficult terrain. The cowboy knows the limits of his horse better than the horse does sometimes.

Holy shit, how many comparisons can I make? Horses? cars??

Anyway.

Maybe these things are happening because you are actually lacking something. You are thirsty because you need water. You are anxious because you aren't coming from a place of love and trust. Yes, your chemicals might be messed up too, I know!

When you are coming from a place of fear, you are going to be anxious and freaked out. It isn't easy at first to come from a place of love or trust. People tend to think it is, but it isn't. It is way easier to come from a place of fear. But you will hurt more inside coming from a place of fear. Maybe even more than the outside discomfort you may feel when you come from a place of love.

For instance, let's say you are dating someone and you feel the relationship is more harmful than good. You need to stop seeing that person. You could break up with the person, knowing that this may cause OUTSIDE stress and anxiety in the form of hurting the other's feelings and perhaps being judged by family, friends and peers.

But INSIDE you'll know that breaking up is the right thing for YOU. So you are willing to endure and experience the external bullshit and the internal feelings of discomfort and perhaps anxiety in order to achieve the internal peace you are looking for, which are no doubt deeper more "true" feelings than those surface feelings of fear and perhaps embarrassment brought on by the breakup.

Trust is a funny thing. Just like when you are thirsty and there is a glass of water in front of you, you *know* that when you drink that water, your thirst will be quenched. You know it because you have experienced that before. Developing that trust is key. It involves little leaps of faith on your part—putting the fear aside and trying a different approach. The positive results we may experience as a result of those leaps of faith will build our sense of trust in our selves and in the universe.

So when riding around in YOUR Avatar, remember to treat it as well as you can, be aware and listen to it, watch out for dogs and cats, and trust love. Simple right?

Oh, and I know I went on and on about cats and dogs and the way they are different. Well, the truth is, if you died at home and no one found you for a while, those same cats and dogs would eventually eat your body to survive.

Another lesson to learn from them I suppose.

Love those furry bastards!

19

HITTING THE G SPOT (GRATITUDE, DUDES. GRATITUDE)

"He is a wise man who does not grieve for the things which he has not, but rejoices for those which he has." - Epictetus

HOPEFULLY AFTER A while, the screaming stops inside. After a while you settle down and get into a groove and you begin to find your way in this new life of treatment. After the initial gut wrenching, anxiety-filled days of detection, testing and diagnosis, you begin treatment. After a few weeks of that, you may start to feel burnt out emotionally and physically.

You may sometimes feel empty or a sensation of having an emotional void inside after the crazy battles you have gone through. This might feel very disturbing. We automatically want to fill that void with something, and we usually go for the first emotion that comes up which is usually a negative or fearful one. I hope this isn't the case for you, but lets just run with this.

I remember waking up everyday during my pre-cancer "lost my mind" period and immediately doing a body scan with my mind to see what I was feeling. If I didn't feel any crippling anxiety upon awakening, my mind made sure it was there seconds later. It was as if I needed to feel that anxiety to know it was there to be able to control it. If I didn't feel that anxiety, I was very uneasy and would basically wait for it to hit me, so to create it myself was a lot easier than to wait for it to come "get" me. I know it's twisted, but that's just the way it was.

The thing about going through cancer treatment (or mental illness) is that you sometimes feel like a burden. You feel like a waste of flesh, like a pain in everyone's ass. Then you start beating yourself up and that leads to the whole "why me" questions, and the pity party starts, and soon enough you are a giant quivering pile of shit crying in the corner. No damn good, sir.

It is at this point that you may want to switch mental gears and start thinking about gratitude. I know, I know, I used to hate when people would tell me that too. Is it ironic the word grateful has the word grate in it? I think not. Because applied in the wrong context or used at the wrong time, the word can certainly grate upon a person's last damn nerve.

For the record, I am not talking about the type of gratitude that happens when the pregnancy test comes back negative or the word APPROVED pops up on the debit machine screen at the store when you aren't sure of what's in the account. I'm also not talking about the type of gratitude your mom wanted you to feel for the plate of vegetables you didn't want to eat. You know, the food the African children would have been grateful to have? *You ungrateful little shit! Eat your goddamn vegetables!* My parenting book, "A Bachelors Guide to Marriage and Parenting" is coming out next year.

ANYWAY!!

The type of gratitude I am talking about here is the long haul, knock-you-on-your ass, done-the-work, core-deep, and bottom-of-your-heart and from-the-balls type of gratitude.

During treatment, well-intentioned people would come up and say:

"Think about how lucky you are to be alive!"

Blam!! I would blow their heads off with a shotgun in my mind's eye.

"Think of all the lessons you are learning!"

Swoosh, chop! Massive, frothy, arcing, fountain of deep, rich, dark blood from the neck as the battle-axe takes the head clean off the body.

Although both of these statements are annoying to hear, *and this book is full of them, I know!* It is very important to remember that they are true. It is just that being told these things at what is probably the wrong time or by the wrong person in the wrong way, really pisses you off. I know the rush of anger that overcomes you when people are trying to cheer you up with stuff like this. Unless someone is blatantly trying to piss you off, they really are just trying to help. So don't cut their heads off, just say:

"Thanks for the kind words, but I must go now."

Fatigue and the grind of treatment will sometimes wear you down to a point where you are *very* irritable. People are going to try to cheer you up in all kinds of ways. People will try to drop knowledge and wisdom on you and try to make you feel better. There was a reason I spent so much time alone when I was going through treatment. I just didn't want to deal with people. I didn't want to feel their fear or desperation. Remember that a lot of the vibes you are feeling from people are often-times their own issues surfacing that they are attempting to make sense of. We always make it about ourselves; you and I both know it! Crisis situations bring up a lot of feelings in people and it takes experience and skill to know how to navigate those waters.

Yes people, I know it is hard not to take out your big bag of shit and throw it on the table and show it to the person in crisis. "Hey! Look! I've got a big bag of shit too!" Then this well-intentioned person starts with the spiritual shit and next thing you know you are wishing they would just go away. You may already be feeling terrible and don't want to feel worse, so it is totally cool to just excuse yourself, tell them its time to check your fellatio ratio (or some other medical term) and walk away from the people that are upsetting you.

In my experience, the real gratitude came later on, post-treatment. Yes, I felt incredibly happy and grateful on the last day of treatment when I walked out of the treatment room. Well, to be truthful, I walked into a corner and cried. Yes, it's true. I knew that there were no guarantees that the cancer wouldn't come back, but for the moment I was grateful that the treatment part was over. So when did the gratitude really kick in? I'm not sure, but I remember different instances when it would hit me.

Not long ago (18 years after treatment remember), I was watching a movie with my lady. The film had a powerful message about how we are all connected and we are here to help each other through our lives. After a particularly moving scene, I started feeling these very intense feelings from deep inside me start to push their way up. She noticed right away that something was wrong, and asked me if I was okay. At that point I thought that it was a good time to go to the bathroom and let these feelings out.

But problem number one is that my apartment was old, shitty and small and no matter where you were in it, you can hear everything. (Stop thinking about my girl using the can, you sick bastard.) So as I contemplated what to do and where, my body decided for me—I just replied "No" and buried my head in her lap like a big sad dog. These huge sobs rose up out of me and I said, "*fuck it*" and just let it out. To her credit, she just rubbed my back and let me do my thing. She didn't say a word. When I could speak again I told her that I was overwhelmed by feelings of deep gratitude.

I was just so fucking happy to be alive.

Did I have good credit? Nope. Great career? Nope.

I just felt an incredible sense of gratitude. For whatever reason, that scene in the movie just dug into me and knocked something loose. My lady was then, and is now, super cool and was just happy that I wasn't afraid to show my heart to her in that way. It was a great moment. Now, if I cried after sex, she would probably punch me, but *that* would be understandable.

Gratitude, to me, is an emotional signpost or reward that signals you've done some good work inside and are moving in the right direction. Is there a wrong emotional direction you ask? Well, staying stuck in emotional states that leave you feeling horrible for years are not the right direction in my opinion. But hey, shit ain't easy sometimes. I have been there baby. Still visit from time to time too!

To feel gratitude is a gift, and when it comes, it is beautiful and powerful. I wasn't able to feel gratitude until I had worked through all the anger and frustration and craziness I was feeling.

It doesn't hurt to take a moment to try to be grateful for something in your current situation. But it can also take some time to work things out. Don't push yourself too hard or feel bad for feeling angry or for *not* feeling grateful. It will come with time and digestion. Like a satisfying bowel movement, you can't *force* it.

What you *can* do is make lists of things you are grateful for. Start simple, being able to move, to see, to hear, the obvious stuff. Then you can expand into *all kinds* of areas. Take a potato for instance. Go get a potato and hold it in your hand. Look at that thing and think about all the steps that were involved getting that single potato to you. How many people were involved? The field that was cleared to grow the potato, the sun, the rain, the farmer, his equipment, and the people that built and serviced the equipment, the fuel in the vehicles, the farmer's workers, the trucks, the drivers, and the people who *built* the trucks. You can break it down endlessly.

All those things had to happen and all those people had to do all kinds of things to simply put that one potato in your hand. I say the following with love:

There is never a shortage of things to be grateful for if you pull your head outta your ass long enough to take the time to think about them.

Right? You could then write letters of gratitude to those people in your life who are a blessing to you. You could *do things* for the people who are taking care of you right now. You could write a letter to your *future* self-telling them how you are going to learn from all of this consequently setting *their* lives up for greatness.

And *then*, you could write a letter from your future self-thanking you for everything you did in the *present* moment that set you up for greatness. I mentioned letters, but you could do something as simple as give them a hug and say thank you. Hugging is an awesome way to connect with another human being that we don't do enough of. We need to hug more, to look each other in the eyes more and say thank you more. Laugh at me and call me all the names you want, but when you get a hug from me, you will remember it and *love* it. I bet you can do the same for others.

Taking the time to be conscious of what you are grateful for is a life-enhancing endeavor that is forward moving and life affirming. Feeling like shit and complaining about what you *don't* have only buries you in more self-pity. Work out your miseries, but move into gratitude to help you pull out of the muck and get unstuck.

Sometimes I think of gratitude as living deep in the well of our hearts. It is always there, but it is just buried really deep down under all this other shit; all the fear, all the sadness and the day-to-day bullshit that we feel is worth our attention. Gratitude sits down there in the deep parts of our hearts waiting for its turn to burst forth and shine and rock the fucking Kasbah. I think sometimes gratitude gets a little frustrated and throws up a flare to remind us it is there, waiting to be expressed through you. I'll give you an example of this.

I remember driving home from treatment one day and seeing a man in his late 20's early 30's walking along the side of the road. He was a working guy, still in his work clothes, and he looked like he had just come home. He had his young son with him and he was holding his hand, beaming at him as the tiny toddler stumbled along like the little drunks they always remind me of.

There they were, both looking so happy as they walked down that road. I suddenly had an explosion of emotion in my chest looking in the rear-view mirror at them. With that explosion came feelings of deep gratitude for simply being alive and the realization or more like a profound sense of *remembering* that love is the ultimate human expression. Love is what we are here to do.

Now remember I was feeling emotionally numb a lot of the time, yet this just leapt out, from *deep* inside me. My eyes filled with tears and I smiled, hoping to get the chance to someday feel what I thought that man was feeling at that moment. The feeling lasted for all of a minute, but a minute in heaven carries you a long way when you are spending your days in hell.

I didn't *force* that moment. I didn't plan it. It just happened. Somehow this reminds me of the time I got a message from a band member whose house we rehearsed at, saying the toilet was broken and to please schedule our bowel movements to happen before we came over. I laughed so hard thinking about all of us penciling in a good dump before rehearsal. I know what he meant, but I just thought:

"Well that would be nice, but I can't program my ass like a VCR."

Come to think of it, I could never program a VCR either. For you younger people, a VCR was a machine that played VIDEO CASSETTES. They were frustrating to use sometimes, and when you did get the time right on them, the damn thing would be flashing 12:00 days later it seemed. You needed to know the timing of the eject button too, and when to cough to cover the mechanical sounds when ejecting the adult film you stole from your buddy. It was a skill the youth of today will never have to learn. It's a shame. In life, timing is everything. I6t really is.

Gratitude is not something that you can call on at will anyway. You don't just snap your fingers and gratitude comes running like a well-trained dog. Maybe some of you can, but not this kid, not all the time anyway. I'm working on it!

Just like in my experience with the man and his child, it seems like gratitude just kind of shows up unexpectedly. Gratitude seems to be the emotional gold that you get to have after you have sifted through the shit.

In my experience, when you have sorted out the emotions, absorbed the experience, it seems *that* is when gratitude comes to town. That being said, even in our *worst* moments, we always have the option to try to be grateful for something or someone. It just sometimes takes a little effort to remind us of that. We all know that it is easier to remind *ourselves* to make a little room for gratitude, *especially* when we are down and out or angry, than it is to hear someone else telling us we should be grateful right?

We need to make room for gratitude. It is hard to do that when we are so full of our ego driven bullshit though. When we work at weeding our heart's garden, the beautiful *"floris gratitudis"* grows. Holy shit that was cheesy, but I kinda liked the imagery.

If they handed out emotional degrees in life, I'm pretty sure a master's degree might feel like gratitude does when it hits you really hard! But like finding the real G spot, you can't rush or force the process. You gotta go with the flow, ask for help sometimes and trust that it takes time to get a great "result." If you try to force or rush it, it just becomes awkward and frustrating for everyone involved. Trust me on that one.

Now go eat your goddamn vegetables or go to your room!

—∞∞∞—

20

BRING YOUR I.D.—
INTUITION, DREAMS AND
OTHER FREAKY SHIT

*"The most beautiful and profound emotion we can expe-
rience is the sensation of the mystical"*
ALBERT EINSTEIN

"Dreams are the royal road to the unconscious."
SIGMUND FREUD

"The only real valuable thing is intuition"
ALBERT EINSTEIN

AS YOU SPEND more time within yourself and become more accustomed
to what's going on in there, you may find that your intuition or "gut
feelings" become stronger. Plus, the treatment may give you superpow-
ers. The radiation treatment allowed me to see through walls and have
erections that glowed. Okay, that's not true, but since we are in this dark

room together, and I have a boner, what do you say we put it to good use?

ANOTHER GREAT LINE!!!!

Use it, it's all-good. But seriously folks, when I was in treatment, I found myself becoming more and more "open" to people's energy. I started to really feel things and have powerful dreams. My intuition started getting really strong and I started to pay attention to it. Before I tell you about some of the freaky shit that happened during treatment, I must admit that I have had weird intuition based experiences happen to me all my life.

So I've written about losing my mind and thinking that I was possessed by demons, so I am sure you are going to raise an eyebrow when I tell you that I have always heard voices. Well, I have heard voices and had feelings that gave me information, which has been helpful to me. For instance, at this exact moment, I am feeling that you are thinking I'm out of my fucking mind. That is both incorrect and not very nice. I have always had a very strong intuition about things and felt it was something to be developed and not be afraid of.

I have also found out the hard way that when I don't "listen" to those gut feelings, things usually go *very* badly for me.

I remember sitting in my living room when I was a young crazy man, back before I snapped at work, and a friend came over with a drug that rhymes with "acid". It was the microdot version of the drug and he was crushing it and cutting it into lines on the coffee table, asking me if I wanted to get high with him. At that time I was stressed out at work, partying too much, depressed and starting to get anxiety attacks while high. You really shouldn't take a powerful hallucinogenic when you are in a bad place emotionally. Not unless you are with a shaman or someone who can guide you so you don't lose your proverbial shit.

For the record, drugs can fuck you up and ruin your lives kiddies, be warned. If you do go out and try drugs and get messed up, don't blame me or this book or your parents or anyone else. I'm just saying. It is a choice you make. Remember that. Now read on about my awesome decision making abilities back in the day.

Back to the crushed acid on the coffee table.

I was trying to quit partying at this point and get my shit together. I was very anxious and screwed up. At that time I would dream of chaotic, post-apocalyptic, violent, crazy shit and it was not very fun. It was like there was a war in my head at night, so trying to just stop all substances at once probably wasn't very smart. Anyway, staring at the lines on the table, I came up with the bright idea that I would flip a quarter to see if "God" wanted me to get high or not. I decided that if it landed heads, "God" wanted me to get high. If it landed tales, "God" didn't want me to get high.

So I flip the quarter in the air and it lands on the carpet.

Heads.

At this point my *guts* start screaming at me to NOT do the line on the table.

Everything inside me, my guts, my cells, my heart, all of it is screaming at me to not do this. I even think I hear one of my ancient Scottish highlander warrior ancestors yelling at me:

"Don yu do tha', yu fukin bastard!" (Picture Mel Gibson in Braveheart, or Sean Connery in anything yelling that..)

I ignore it all, the feelings, the voices, the churning guts and I say, looking at the quarter:

"Well! I guess God wants me to get high, then!"

Sigh.

So, I bend down and snort up the line and immediately feel something inside me *get up and leave*. It was literally like a bunch of your friends just got up and left the room—I felt alone and I knew instantly that I had made a mistake. I started to chug vodka to try to knock myself out before the imminent bad trip started. I did *not* succeed.

The good news is, I did black out later on, but not before suffering through gut-wrenching anxiety and paranoia. In the end, I didn't remember much of the night so that was good, I suppose.

People, if you are flipping quarters to make decisions more complicated than who rides shotgun in the car (whoever yelled it first does, by the way), you may want to check your head or at the very least give it a hard shake. I'm no shrink, but that isn't a display of strong decision-making right there. The only good thing that happened that night was the whole super-strange feeling of my soul posse walking away. It was like they said:

"Fuck you, clown, you are on your own now, we're out of here".

Even in my messed-up mental state, I recognized that something had shifted inside me. I felt I had lost my guidance system. It sucked, but I paid attention after that. What's worse is one night while high, I wrote out this sort of map for myself entitled *"To Success or Failure."* Later on after all this crazy stuff had gone down, I found that map and realized that I had pretty much followed the course that led to failure. Nice work, dip-shit. The universe hands you a map and you follow the wrong path. Awesome.

Another time, I was sitting alone in the car, warming it up before I headed out to treatment. I was feeling pretty alone and miserable so I said out loud:

"Well boys, I am feeling pretty lonesome right about now so I could use some company. I don't mean people company either, I need you guys."

"The boys" were the name I gave to the invisible forces I felt in my life. After saying that (asking for help), I felt a difference in the energy in the car; it felt like it had filled up with people. I didn't feel alone anymore and it was comforting.

Now I know some of you are going to call bullshit on me and say that I am making this up. Fair enough. Given what I have already written, I might raise an eyebrow at this sort of thing, too. Maybe it could have been my imagination, or some kind of wishful thinking manifested in feelings. Whatever it was, it *comforted* me, so I'll take it. For the record, it is real to *me*, it helps *me*, and it makes *my* life better and harms no one. I am grateful to have those feelings and "voices" in my life.

There was also the time I was coming home from a gig in a town, a couple of hours away from home. We took two cars for that show because we had blown our van up coming home from an east coast tour the week before. The bass player, keyboard player and I were driving in a little Chevy cavalier and the drummer and other guitar player were farther up the highway towing our gear trailer. It was sometime after three in the morning and I was pretty tired. I was in the passenger seat with my arm out the window drifting off to sleep when I heard a voice tell me,

"You might want to put your arm inside the car and roll up the window in case you guys roll."

Without hesitating, I rolled up the window, put my hood up over my head, put the seat back, crossed my arms and legs and put my head on my chest.

The perfect crash position.

Next thing I know we are screeching across the highway towards a tree line. I think I was screaming at the driver and I felt like laughing for an instant as the tree line rapidly approached. At the time I co-owned a tree service and it occurred to me at that second that trees were ultimately going to kill me after I had killed so many of them. Yeah yeah, I'm a tree-hugger now. When you have taken out as many as me, you can judge. At least I can use a chainsaw.

As we left the road, I remember screaming out loud or maybe just willed inside my head:

"Protect me!"

It felt like every cell in my body had a mouth and had screamed it.

It was the most powerful one-time, LIMITED TIME intention-setting moment I think I had had up to that moment in my life. My whole being cried out for protection, and then something weird happened that I still couldn't explain if I tried.

James Brown showed up riding a unicorn that cried rainbow tears.

No, that didn't happen, but that would have been heavy though.

I remember hitting the ditch and then I remember hearing the sounds of the crash all around me. I felt like I was in a bubble and the car was moving *around* me. It felt like I was suspended in the air and the crash rotated all around me. Next thing I knew, I was standing beside the car, which was on its roof—a crumpled, smoking mess. I was talking to the guys that hit us and couldn't believe I was unhurt. I started feeling my teeth, my nuts, and my face—all over my body for damage or puncture wounds from the crash. I remembered that I wasn't alone in the car and looked for the boys. My keyboard player, a damn good buddy who was behind the wheel, was hanging out the passenger window, lying on his back and staring up at the stars.

I thought he was dead.

There was a lot of blood in his hair and around his head. I screamed his name and bent down to see if he was still alive. I thought his brains were coming out of his head, but it was the blood in his thick curly black hair that made it look that way. He just looked at me and quietly said,

"Duuuude, I think I dislocated my shoulder."

"You're alive!" I screamed and told him to be still or something, I don't remember. I looked around for my bass player, another close friend. I saw him sitting in the grass, away from the crash. He looked to be in complete shock. It was a really crazy situation; I was fighting shock too, and was still trying to piece it all together. I wasn't sure that it was even *real* at that time, to tell you the truth. It was kind of like when you get a cancer diagnosis but with more broken glass. It was eerily quiet and then suddenly more help began to arrive.

The first guy on the scene besides the guys that hit us was a long haul truck driver who was an ex-army medic and he got to work stabilizing the boys. God bless that man. The police arrived and took control of the scene. Soon the ambulances arrived and I listened to my buddy moaning for the hour-long drive to the trauma center in the town we had just left.

In the end, the driver shattered his right arm and ripped his scalp all to shit. *(He just gave me a framed picture of that head wound for my most recent birthday, that sick bastard. It is awesome, though.)*

My buddy in the backseat wrenched his back, had a head like a freaking beluga for a bit and had glass and gravel embedded in his hand, too. I got to the hospital and the nurse told me to go take my clothes off to look for any wounds. I went and removed my clothes shaking pieces of busted glass out of my hoodie and pants. I found no injuries. Nothing. Not even a red mark from the seat belt, no whiplash nor a sore muscle. Not even when the adrenaline wore off, and not even the next day.

I am six foot three inches tall and weighed 240 pounds at the time. I'm a big human. A cavalier is a small car. We found out from the guys who hit us that we did a single endo (car rolled end over end) when it hit the ditch and it rolled seven times after that. They were musicians too, apparently, and they hit us while trying to pass us in the fog. I couldn't believe I was absolutely *unhurt*. No one could. It freaks me out to this day but it also comforts me that I cried out for help and received it.

I guess you have to ask.

Tough break for my boys in the car with me—next time I'll yell out "protect *us*!" and we'll see what happens. That wasn't fun; I don't want to do that again anytime soon! I am glad no one was killed in either vehicle and we all came out of it alive.

So, if people want to laugh at me, or call me crazy for paying attention to my "voices," it's all good. I know there is some kind of energy in my life that guides me and helps me out when I get in trouble. How can I explain being in a car wreck and coming out unscathed while the two other passengers were smashed and needed to go to the hospital?

Maybe there is a scientific explanation for it, and I do believe science will explain a whole lot more of this crazy, weird stuff in the years to come, but in the end, if it protects me, *I'll take it*.

So if you feel this happening to you, go with it. Don't be freaked out if you feel like you can read people's minds and stuff like that. Don't confuse this with feelings of paranoia. If you are paranoid, that is different than what I am talking about. It's not that feeling when you are high on drugs and you think everyone knows you are high or that people are after you. This is a feeling that you are on another level or have more access to information, or can feel people's emotions in a *stronger* way. If you are worried at all about your mental health, seek help from a professional. Don't be proud. Just ask for help.

Don't be freaked out if you have really crazy dreams. Pay attention to them. I still dream like a maniac and often have some pretty remarkable experiences in my sleep. I have dreamt things that came true and I have had incredible moments where I have met up with friends and loved ones who have gone on before me. Yes, here comes another eye-rolling story.

When I was 27, one of my childhood friends, Eddie, succumbed to Cystic Fibrosis. Let it be known that Eddie was another angel in my life. He was a sarcastic, smart-assed angel, but an angel nonetheless. Eddie was a highly intelligent, very talented artist and a professional-level debater, or shit-disturber, as I like to call it. Eddie also had a heart of gold and a will and spirit to be humbled by. I grew up watching this guy struggle with his disease since we were in kindergarten together. Eddie was one hell of a resource to have when I went nuts and then went through the cancer experience, to say the least.

I remember Eddie's dad dropping him off at my place once (when Eddie was feeling well enough to leave his own house for a bit). I was suffering from agoraphobia and was too freaked out to leave the house at that time, so Eddie came over to hang out and see how I was doing. I remember him coming up the driveway with his oxygen and mask, walking all wobbly like a drunken old man. It used to break my heart. It was always good to see him though, regardless of the shape he was in. When he was all puffed up from the steroids or whatever the hell he was taking for his sickness, I told him he looked like one of those bloated dead bikers they would occasionally drag out of the river. He laughed his ass off and tell me he still had a bigger penis than me. That was Eddie.

Eddie was a true veteran in the world of crisis and used to tell me often that he hadn't known anything else in his life, so he couldn't be any other way *but* good at it. He used to tell me stories of all the heavy shit he was going through with his disease. When I started to get less paranoid and I could leave the house for a little bit at a time I would drive over to his place at night (he lived a block over) and we would just sit in my car in his driveway and talk. He had an oxygen hose that was long enough for him to do that. We would talk about life and death and girls and all kinds of stuff. We would talk about our dreams and what we wanted out of life.

At that time we both just wanted to be healthy. Eddie was on a waiting list for a double lung, and liver transplant. He spent his days waiting for that pager to go off. It was so refreshing to be around Eddie in those days. He wasn't going to be anything but brutally honest with me and I loved him for that. He would tease me about my situation and told me to try his on for size when I was feeling up to it. Coming from most other people, a comment like that would make me want to smash their faces in, but coming from Eddie, it was sobering. It always came from a place of love and I knew that.

I would be freaking out, feeling nuts, having panic attacks and thinking about blowing my head off and then I would see Eddie working his ass off to stay alive. It would crush me. (Don't compare, remember?) Eddie would joke about how *convenient* it would be for me to have an "accident" because my organs were a perfect fit for him. I loved that sick bastard. Eddie lost his mother to cancer before he died. I can't imagine the strength that that family needed to make it through every day during that period. Eddie was a good friend and a great human being who I think of often with great love and respect. Eddie never got his second chance at life and died at age 27. I miss him a lot.

Shortly after his death, I had a very powerful dream. Like a lot of people in this world that lose someone close to them, I was feeling guilty about not doing more for Eddie while he was still alive. I would think of him and feel horrible and pissed off that he was not able to get his new parts and ride off into the sunset. It really upset me to think of him.

So one night I had this incredible dream. I dreamt that I was in this white place. It was just light, really. Really bright light. I was standing there and Eddie walked up to me out of this super bright light. He looked *fantastic*. He was wearing an outfit that he really liked in life and had his favorite hat on and he looked really strong. I remember how it felt to see him like that, with no tubes or any medical shit hanging off of him. I was filled with love for him and felt elated at being able to see him again. I was crying in my dream and telling him how sorry I was. I was apologizing to him and he was laughing at me. He told me that he is better than good, not to worry about him and to live my life. I kept telling him I love him and he kept laughing and sending me love. I felt it coming from him.

I woke up crying, feeling relieved and grateful to have had this dream. I realized instantly that I was dreaming, but I still felt a strong "afterglow" of the dream. It hit me *hard*. As I started to calm down and get my shit together, I realized that there was something weird about Eddie's face. I then remembered that his eyes had been closed the whole time. I went back to sleep thinking that was strange, but I passed out and slept well for the first time in a while.

Weeks later I ran into Eddie's brother John (another fine man whose compassion and dedication to his family humbles me to my core) in a bar. We both had had a couple and I decided to tell John about the dream. I told him about all of the feelings it brought up and how Eddie looked awesome and told me he was doing great. I then told John that there was something weird about Eddie's eyes in the dream, that he never opened them the whole time. When I said that, John's face changed, and he told me something that would blow my mind and make me pay even more attention to my dreams forever.

John looked at me and said:

"Pete, the only things that were good enough to donate from Eddie's body were his eyes."

Yeah, Goosebumps for day's man....

I didn't know that information until that moment. So I had a few more drinks and thought about *that* for a bit.

I have to say that it would *really* piss Eddie off if I didn't mention that people should really sign their organ donation cards, or tell their loved ones that they want their parts donated. Better yet, put it in writing that should they meet an untimely end, they would like their organs harvested and donated. We don't need them after we bail out of the body and to bury them or cremate them is a selfish act. People, if you can save lives through your death *that* is pretty amazing. It might be the best thing you have ever done! Wait, that came out wrong.

So, for my man Eddie, *have some guts and donate your organs.* I thank you, Eddie thanks you and his family thanks you.

That being said, if you get my penis, I am truly sorry.

The last freaky experience I had was not long ago. While doing a tree removal I had been hit by a large limb that nearly killed me and busted me up pretty good too. I had multiple injuries and one of them was a shattered collarbone. Seven months after the accident my doctor finally agreed to do surgery to put in a plate and 11 screws to fix the broken collarbone.

A few days before the surgery I was writing in my journal about how I would like some powerful insights while I was in surgery. I know it seems insane to be asking the universe for insights especially during surgery but that's how I roll. I figured my monkey brain would be shut down by the anesthetic allowing the higher parts of myself access to the infinite. Or at least I *hoped* I would get *some* sort of information. I wasn't specific about what I wanted to know; I just said something to the effect of:

"Alright Universe, I'm going in for surgery and it would be really cool to give me some insights while I'm under. I am grateful for anything that will help others and myself. Thank you in advance for the download."

Then I let it go, thinking that if something comes, fantastic. If nothing comes, that's cool too. I had no expectations; I had just made a request.

So the day of the surgery arrives and I head into the hospital to get er' done. I get processed and next thing I know I am on the table and I am going under. As anyone who has had surgery where you are put under anesthetic knows, its freaky how one second you are on the table and then it is hours later and you are waking up in a recovery room. It seems like seconds have gone by.

Before I woke up, I found myself once again in some dream state in a place that felt very real to me. I was looking at myself floating in the air in front of me wrapped in what can only be described as shit. Yes, I was in some sort of shit cocoon. I heard or *felt* a voice say,

"So that's what you are feeling, that is the heaviness, the depression and the fear all wrapped up around you. You created it and you can release yourself from it."

Then the observing *I* felt what that shit cocoon felt like. I felt the weight of my existence, my fear, my anger, and all these less than awesome emotions. It felt slow and heavy. It felt terrible. Then I hear the narrator say:

"Now you are going to feel what it is like when you are free of all this."

What followed were some of the most *incredible* sensations I have ever felt. I was light and sound, I was pure awareness and I felt a belonging and a sense of being home like I have never felt in my entire life. Everything *earth* related was meaningless and I felt completely at peace. I felt like everything was me and I was everything. I felt clean and fast, like I could be anywhere and everywhere all at once. I didn't have a body, I *was* the universe and "I" was limitless and not an "I" at all.

It was an incredible place and words don't do it justice. The prevailing insight I was "feeling" and the message I was receiving was that there is nothing to fear, to go back and love and live without fear. Even now, words feel like big blocks of wood falling out of my mouth when trying to describe what that place was like. I opened my eyes at the height of this incredible experience and I realized I was *not* dead.

I immediately started sobbing. The nurse came over and asked me what hurt and what was wrong. I told her I just saw the afterlife or something like it and *I was devastated to have come back*. I felt that being back in this place, this "reality" felt *slow* and *heavy* and *unreal*. I absolutely felt like I had left my *true* nature and I was now back in the insane asylum. I was a prisoner that got a taste of freedom and now I was back in the cell. It was just devastating to be "back".

I felt the resonance of that place for three days and had insights about people around me that reduced me to tears. My poor girlfriend must of thought I was cracking up. I looked at her and could feel all her pain, *including* the pain *I* had contributed to her life. I wept in her truck trying to describe what that place was like to her. I wrote down what I remembered and I gave thanks for yet another cosmic ass kicking. That was of the most powerful experiences in my life, one of *many* up to this point. Once again, I asked, I received.

Death hasn't scared me for a long time given my life experiences and the amount of time I have dedicated to thinking about it, but *that* experience just sealed the fucking deal. I know I sound crazy and many people have always thought of me that way, but I wouldn't trade my experiences for anything. Life is incredible but I am looking forward to the adventure of death. I say that with the utmost respect for life, but I can look anyone in the eye and honestly tell him or her if *that* is what we have to look forward to, there is absolutely *nothing* to fear. I now understand when people say that there are things worse than death. I believe in my heart that there is nothing to fear.

Pretty crazy story right? I know. You can call bullshit on me all day long, come up with theories about what caused that experience and shoot it full of holes, but *here's the thing*.

I don't care.

Whether you think I'm nuts or making this up *won't bother me a bit*. I share these experiences in the hopes that some of them may help other people. That's it. I am nothing but grateful for these types of experiences, even if people think I'm crazy for sharing them.

Freaky shit? Absolutely. But I'll take it all day long.

So pay attention to your dreams. Dreams are very interesting to me and have been a source of wonder since I started to pay attention to them. Right before the cancer diagnosis, I had the classic *"naked running through the forest being chased by an unseen force or creature"* dream. It was scary as hell. I was running from this thing, this monster that I couldn't see, just behind me. I was bare-assed-naked and running as fast as I could through dark, terrifying woods. The path led me to the banks of this murky river and I ran to the edge of its shore. I skidded to a halt and turned to face whatever horror was chasing me, and that was the exact moment I woke up, covered in sweat-soaked sheets. Okay, so that dream wasn't very awe-inspiring, but it let me know something was definitely up.

Near the end of treatment, I had another archetypal dream where I was climbing a mountain. I remember looking up and sensing that I was almost at the top. I looked up and saw myself reaching down to help me. I grabbed my own hand and pulled myself up to the top. I felt real elation and I screamed my lungs out in triumph. I woke up feeling great and crying tears of joy. I knew I was going to be all right. Pay attention to those dreams and keep that journal close by at night. If you have powerful dreams, or any dreams at all, record them. If anything, it's funny to read about them years later. And sometimes you gain useful information.

Dreaming is just one of the ways we can connect with what's going on inside of us. I believe that crisis allows us access to parts of our higher selves or our consciousness that we wouldn't normally have access to under normal circumstances. Just spending a lot of time being quiet and not speaking can bear some pretty powerful fruit, in my opinion and experience.

Really intense stuff sometimes yes, but really cool—and comforting once you get used to it. Consider it a bonus if your consciousness starts to expand and these things start to happen. Relax, take notes. It is normal and natural. If you just yelled, "there is no normal!" you are starting to get it.

I found the whole process of writing, being quiet and reflecting on what was going on inside (and all around me) gave me more depth and perspective. I shut my mouth more, listened more and tried to be more present. I felt shitty physically and still felt like my head was like a radio station just a hair out of tune; I could think, but my thoughts still had a lot of static around them. The thoughts in my head and the feelings in my guts didn't always sync up. I would often default to the guts during those days and it seemed to serve me well for the most part. Sometimes you will be too tired, in too much pain, or just not in the mood to talk. Quiet is good sometimes. Quiet is where you can start to hear and feel the inner voice that is always there trying to help your ass out. If you feel it isn't, ask for it. It can't hurt now, can it?

Life is a mystery and we don't know *jack shit* about a whole lot in this world. There is a world inside that is there to be explored and to help guide us. Sometimes it takes a beating from life to quiet us down enough to hear it. In the end, it doesn't hurt to explore all these different aspects inside of ourselves. It can be fun and exciting, scary and powerful. Remember: *there is nothing to be afraid of inside you.*

Now, in the closet however...?

—⚬⚬⚬—

21

LET THEM GO

THIS CHAPTER IS for the friends and family of someone who is on their
way out.

As shitty and painful as it is to face, sometimes—well, every time—
we are going to have to deal with the fact that people in our lives that we
love are going to die, unless we go first. If you are dealing with someone
you love who is on their way out, I have a few things to say that I hope
will be of help to you.

First of all, I want to say that you are only in this difficult place
because you chose to love someone. That is awesome. I know it doesn't
feel awesome right about now, but it is, and this is why.

You chose to love someone with all your heart. Even when it got
shitty, you stayed in there with them till what now looks like the end of

their physical existence. That is a decision you will never regret. I have said it before—that choice alone makes you a rare gem. Its not that others are assholes for not stepping up, because it isn't an easy place to step up to, as I am sure you now understand. I have tried and failed to do so in my own experience. I didn't have the emotional fortitude at the time to go the whole way. I wasn't there yet. You may be saying that you had to, or are making some kind of excuse right about now, trying to push off the fact that you are awesome.

Don't.

Take a minute to give yourself a hug. You know, like we did in class when we were kids and pretended we were making out with someone in the corner. Or was I the only idiot who did that? Regardless, take a minute to say good fucking job for hanging in there with your friend or loved one.

Second of all, this last part of the journey is tough because you really need to stop seeing that person with your eyes. This is the time to really focus on sending those powerful, loving vibes out with your heart. We know how physically devastating cancer can be. It can reduce people's bodies down to almost nothing, aging them beyond their years. I won't go into details because it is unnecessary. What will happen to them physically will happen to them and you may witness some disturbing transformations. It is for that reason that you gotta go into heart mode and use your eyes to send love *into* them.

If you can, at the very least hold their hands, touch them; don't make them feel like a horrible monster. I know it is hard to see loved ones that way. It fucking sucks, but again, you will never, ever regret it. This is still an opportunity to experience love. It is an opportunity to push beyond what you may think you can handle and be selfless. Always remember that you are witnessing the shutting down of an *organic* system and that the *essence* of your loved one has nothing to do with this. You are witnessing the degradation of a *container*. I know it is hard to really embrace that and it seems like a cold way of looking at it but it is simply my way of looking at things. If it rings true and helps you, great.

I find that hanging onto the body of the person is just an exercise in futility and will always lead to more suffering. The closer someone gets to the end of the physical experience, the harder it is to deal with if we are so focused on the body. It is why it feels so weird to look at a person's body in a casket. Something is missing. We know it instinctively.

When we look at pictures of people, where do our eyes go? To their eyes. It's no secret that the eyes are the windows to the soul; so look there and *blast* them with love. The heart is the place where we know each other intimately. That is where I choose to focus my energies and awareness in the end. It just makes sense to me. I hope it does for you too.

In the closing days, your loved one may need massive amounts of pain medication. They may scream and may do or say disturbing things. Again, focus on the love, focus on being present and know that this is all related to the breaking down of the body and perhaps the mind. I know it is hard to watch and to hear. I know. But it is part of it and it will not last forever. You may start secretly hoping they leave sooner than later. Don't feel guilty for that. It is a normal feeling to have. It isn't selfish. No one wants to see anyone suffer, and it is merciful when someone in pain is finally released from the body.

I hope they leave quickly and without pain, but be prepared for anything—the best way to do that is to stay in the moment and simply do whatever needs doing. Remember that your kindness and your love will be felt, no matter what state your loved one may be in. I truly believe that. Coming from a place of love is the strongest position you can come from. Stay in it. If the person wants to talk, talk. Ask what they need, allow them to express themselves even if what they have to say is hard for you to hear. One of the most powerful things you can do is to simply be present with your loved one. Don't try to fix them, or pretend things aren't as bad as they seem or bullshit them. Just be there. Let them lead.

You can do it.

You have come a long way to get to this point and I hope you realize that. I hope you aren't beating yourself up and criticizing yourself for how you have handled this experience. Believe me, if you are committed to living, loving and sharing your heart, you will get *many* more chances to do this.

As tough as it is to go through, a long sickness does offer more of an opportunity to say good-bye to the person you love. Sudden death robs us of that powerful opportunity; so don't let yours go to waste. Dying people are often very open to talking and may want to make things right. If you have a beef with that person, squash it. Your pride can't wrap its arms around you and warm your heart with its love. Neither can theirs.

Realize, perhaps for the first time in your lives, that this is the time to be real. It is time to heal. It is time to be honest and open. Most of all, it's time to be humble enough to reconcile and make room for peace in both your hearts, especially with the petty stuff. In the face of our physical death, "being right" really seems childish and meaningless. Yay! You were right! Make sure to put it in the eulogy.

On the other hand, there may be some serious issues that need to be resolved that may not have been talked about yet. I hope that if you don't work everything out, you are prepared to bury these issues with your friend or loved one. That is why it is important to try to work these things out while the person is still alive.

The finality of death leaves a huge hole in our hearts; all your pride and the sense of "being right" will not serve you in the days, months and years after that person's passing. The only sense you may have is the sense that a *tremendous* opportunity for both of you has died along with your loved one. That would be the biggest tragedy of the day, in my opinion. Step up to the challenge of being exposed and vulnerable.

I have always found death to be a powerful teacher.

Western culture has taught us to be fearful of death, to run from it, to protect ourselves from it and to hide our children from it. But like the explorers who headed off into the unknown in wooden ships ages ago, I truly believe death is yet another mystery to be explored. Perhaps we could do so with the same courage and curiosity demonstrated by those ancient explorers.

Everyone is terminal, and death exposes us all to our fears and weaknesses. Death also exposes us to the raw nature of human love and compassion. No matter how tragic the situation is, know that love, compassion and grace will come to those who are courageous enough to open themselves to it. It may take some time to feel these things. You may have a lot of anger towards the situation itself. But that anger will not serve you when your loved one is on their way out. As much as death makes us think about our lives and our problems, try to remember that you are there for *them*. Until they bust out of that meat cage, you are there for them.

So cry, talk, forgive, rub their feet, hold their hands and be present. This is a part of life. Hell, this *is* life! This experience is going to be whatever you want it to be, but remember that every waking moment is a future memory that you have one chance to create. How you act now creates the memories of tomorrow. How do you want to remember this moment?

That being said; don't try too hard.

Remember to breathe and let your heart lead. It knows what to do. Have the conversations that need to be had. Ask your loved one if there is anything they want or need. Do they need a letter written? Is there anything they want you to do? Sometimes all you have to do is be there and no words need to be spoken. Some of the most powerful moments in my life were in those situations where you are just sitting silently and sharing space with another human being. Sometimes we need to just *be* there. Maybe that's why we are called human *beings* and not human *doings*. We just haven't figured it out yet.

When it comes time for that person to go, don't be surprised if they decide to bail out when no one is in the room. I have seen this happen before. My uncle bailed out right after the nurses gave him a sponge bath (why not get one more, eh?) They left the room while we were still in the lounge. Only seconds after the nurses left, he started to go. His daughter came in and yelled to us that he was going. Don't be insulted or feel bad that you weren't there if they bail out when you weren't around. Don't feel like they "died alone."

For the record, I don't think we ever die "alone." I think that when we move into the next vibration there are plenty of others around to help us out of our skin suits. But that's just me. Maybe death feels as private as poopin' and no one really likes to do THAT with anyone around.

The point is, we don't know how these things work. We should simply be prepared to deal with any situation the best we can. Again, that would be to meet these situations with an open heart and an open mind. We don't know everything and are not in complete control, so give yourself a break.

Unless you open your wallet and have "Creator of the Universe" on your driver's license, you can only do so much. Even the little things are huge in my opinion. (I tell myself that every time I am naked.) Just being there, for one, is massive. By the way, your driver's license should say "Creator of *my* Universe." That would make more sense.

I hope that you become a more open and expanded human being, with a greater capacity to receive and give love through this experience. I hope you come to a place of love, understanding and peace quickly and without too much pain and suffering. It might take a while, but keep breathing, sending and receiving love and compassion to the best of your ability. Start with yourself.

I have a hard time with the word "heal" because it sounds too much like "heel." I don't believe in a god who punishes people and makes them sick in order to find grace through suffering. That is just fucked up. I would say I hope you heal quickly, but it sounds like I'm insinuating that you were "broken."

I don't like to think that way. I know it feels like your heart is broken, but if you are feeling *anything* in your heart at such a time, it is doing *exactly* what it was designed to do. So go with it, feel it and experience the full range of what it is to be a human being who gives a shit. If anything, your heart hurts because of the herculean effort of trying to *will* some-one into health. I *completely* understand.

I have been there. Making deals, begging, raging, screaming, all that good stuff. But in the end, worn out and exhausted, I came into the moment, surrendered myself to it and tried to muster up all my love and compassion. I got out of my own way and let my heart lead me. Was it awkward, frustrating and messy? Yes. But that is life, isn't it?

I hope you can do the same.

I hope you have a friend that is there for *you*. I hope you have the support *you* need. Whether you need professional help or just someone to listen to you at home, at work or in a bar, I really hope you find what you need. Know that you will never be forgotten and that your efforts were not in vain. Believe that with all your heart.

In the end I hope you let them go.

When it is time to leave the body, it is selfish to want them to stay in order for you to avoid the pain that we know death will bring. But remember—the pain is your love turned way up loud, and it takes a while to adjust to the volume.

Let them go.

I hope you help release them from the shackles of the physical body and of this life, helping them make the transition from here to the great mystery with love, dignity and compassion. We don't know each other, but I commend you for what you are doing.

For what it's worth, know that somewhere, a complete stranger is smiling, knowing that you are a fucking *superstar*.

22

A MAGNIFICENT DEPARTURE

*"Death most resembles a prophet who is without honor in his own
land or a poet who is a stranger among his own people."*
KHALIL GIBRAN

*"Die happily and look forward to taking up a new and better form.
Like the sun, only when you set in the west can you rise in the east."*
JELALUDDIN RUMI

THIS CHAPTER IS for those people who feel like their body isn't going to
make it and are starting to think about an exit strategy. There is no right
way to die, as there is no right way to live. There is only what works for
the individual. I don't write the following to put pressure on you, gloss
over the powerful, difficult experience you may be living or to try to tell
you how to die. This is the letter I am going to read to myself when my
day comes and I hope some of it resonates with you.

Even though I got a *taste* of what some would describe as the afterlife coming out of my last surgery which impacted me greatly, even to
this day, until *my* death occurs, I can only *wonder* what it will be like.

I don't know what you are facing, where you are in your experience or how you feel about all this stuff, but if your physical death is near, with great respect, love and compassion, I would like to say a few things to you. I might not know you, or what is in your heart, but this is what I hope for you, friend or not.

First of all, I hope you have found the light in your existence, especially when met with the fear and grief of those who love you and don't want to let you go. Speaking of light, I hope you burn bright and show others how to go out. I hope that when people look into your eyes, they are met with compassion and wisdom. I hope that when people come to say good-bye and comfort you, they are left feeling like it was they themselves who received comfort and a gift not only through your friendship and love, but in having the honor and privilege of bearing witness to a great exit.

I hope you have found some sort of peace within you. I hope you have found a way to let go of the anger; frustration, fear, disappointment and whatever else may make your exit hurtful to you and those who love you. I hope you have found a way to let love into your heart and your life and I hope you found a way to share it. I hope you have something that you can't put into words, but shines out of your eyes that gives you strength and comfort. Whatever that is, I hope it fills you and surrounds you and those you love.

I hope you have friends and family that are courageous and loving enough to let you go. I hope their love is given freely and often, without judgment or resentment. I hope that you laugh often and are open and optimistic about the next stage of this trip we call life.

For the record, I'm not sure that death is anything but a door to something else. I hope that you feel awe and wonder when confronted with this possibility, and I hope that you find inspiration and not fear in the fact that we don't know what happens once we leave our bodies.

I hope you don't feel a lot of pain and I hope that when it is time, you are not alone in any sense of the word. I hope that you have the courage to let people be with you when you go. I hope that you are removed from the human trappings of ego—may all of that shit burn away from you like fuel tanks falling off a rocket on its way into the vast universe....

I hope and wish for you that Lady Grace wraps herself around you like a cloak, calms you and prepares you to bust loose from here.

I hope you have prepared your place, whatever that means to you, wherever that is, but for sure in your heart and in your imagination and guts. I hope you have said what you have wanted to say to the people you wanted to say it to. If letters need to be written, or apologies need to be made to allow someone to forgive you, I hope they are done so from the heart and that they become the cherished gifts of love they deserve and are meant to be.

If thoughts of a future that no longer seems possible come over you, I hope that somehow, you find a way to focus on, and express in the here and now, the love in your heart that can never be taken away from you or those that it is meant to comfort and embrace.

Don't be surprised or embarrassed if people show up to see you off and if they sit beside your bed and cry. Receive this raw gift of love with an open heart. Share your own tears; tell those friends what they mean to you. Sometimes you will sit in silence with loved ones and just stare at each other without saying a word. Marinate in the simplicity and perfection of those moments.

I hope there is a window where you can see the sun rise and set everyday. Remember that what we perceive as a sunset is a sunrise somewhere else. I hope you realize you are one and the same and understand the simple message behind this beautiful act of nature.

We all know that the end can be unpleasant as the body enters its final stages of failure. Know that it is your *body* falling apart. I hope that when you enter this stage, you are far away from the meat suit and well on your way to whatever awaits. I want to say don't worry about this part, that you won't be there to see it and you will have already said your goodbyes, but it may take a while and you may feel physical pain. That being said, I hope you don't suffer greatly and have all the help and support you need.

I hope that if this happens, you will have someone or a *bunch* of people who are committed to seeing you through the veil. I hope they are there when it gets hard to bear, and there when you turn to light and pure energy and streak across the universe like the beautiful, incredible miracle that you are.

Speaking of failure, I hope you have realized that you have not "lost" anything but your physical vessel. I hope you realize the futility of beating yourself up with angry thoughts. I hope you don't blame yourself or spend whatever time you have left with your heart wrapped in the chains of anger, fear and regret. Most of all, I hope you forgive yourself and anyone in your life that may need it. Realize the gift you will be giving someone and what a *powerful* position you are in. Forgive and let go of all those life-draining negative energies. They will no longer serve you, if they ever really did.

I hope that you realize and take comfort in the fact that by living you have made an impact on people's lives. You have *no idea* that what you have said and done in this life hasn't set wheels in motion for events that may change the world. Even in your physical death, you have the opportunity to change people forever. Through your actions now, you can influence someone's opinion about life and how to live it and leave it. That is a one-time opportunity my friend, unless you are Buddhist so they say...

Speaking of religion, if you are religious, I hope that you are strong in your faith and have the support that you need. If you aren't religious but are suddenly worried about God or judgment or any of that stuff, don't be. I'm pretty sure if there is an energy called "God," that it has a sense of humor. Let's face it; "God" has a lot more to answer for than *you* do, don't you think?

If you are afraid, remember this. While discussing death, a wise person once asked me what I was thinking just before being *born* into this life. He asked me if I was scared then, or nervous or excited. I told him with a laugh, I didn't remember what I was feeling. He told me laughing, not to worry about death then either. Something to ponder.

I hope that people come to the celebration of your life and gather together to share stories, laugh, cry and really send your meat suit off right. I hope that the food is as good as the lies and stories that are being told about you, and I hope your friends linger for a long time after the formalities are finished, remembering you, loving you and connecting with each other through your magnificent departure.

Congratulations—you are now myth and legend. You no longer need a body, as you will be forever carried in the hearts of those who knew and loved you. Yes, they will miss your physical presence, but their grief is their love turned up real loud and eventually they will realize that you are only a memory away. The love that they feel remains real and is the best part of you that they get to keep until it is their turn to go.

I hope you know how much people love you and I hope you weren't afraid to love them back. Love is energy and energy cannot be destroyed. Wherever you go, I hope you are fucking kicking ass and burning bright.

I might not have known you, but I wish these things for you. If you don't feel the same, that's cool. I hope you find the way to bust loose that works for you.

From the bottom of my heart I sincerely hope you get what you need.

My unmet friend, if one day we do meet somewhere far from here, don't be afraid to say hello, introduce yourself, and I'll buy you a cosmic beer.

23

Aftermath—Is the Party Over? Or has it Just Begun?

"Change is inevitable, growth is optional"
Author unknown.

Good, bad or ugly, everything must end.

This includes your treatment, my friend. One day, believe it or not, you won't be thinking about the crazy shit that's going on right now. One day you will go for a whole hour and not think once about cancer or mental illness or whatever crisis has brought you to this book.

Then that hour will stretch to two, then three, and then it will be a day that goes by without thoughts of sickness or crisis. Then, as sure as shit don't taste like sugar, it will be weeks and then months that you don't think about this madness. Eventually you will notice on the calendar that you have missed your anniversary of the final day of treatment. This will make you smile.

One day your physical scars will seem like they were there forever. But until then, enjoy the ladies asking about them and the awesome cancer veteran sex my friends. You have earned it! But before all that happens, like anything else worth doing in this world, you gotta put the time in, put the work in to create and get *used to* your new life.

You may need to grieve your old life and that's cool. That may happen at the beginning of the whole crisis experience and may continue throughout it. Letting go of what you once were, what you wanted to be, and accepting what simply is *now* can be difficult. In my experience, time spent letting go of expectations frees us up to simply experience the moment, which in turn enhances our awareness. When that happens, its pretty cool. It does take work and I am doing it everyday even years later, but sick or not, this particular practice won't hurt you. Give it a try.

Hopefully you will have taken advantage of the hard-earned advice I have given you in this book and are now a journaling, meditating, expressive, healthy, and happy martial arts-loving freak. Or whatever makes you happy. I hope that at least you are on your way to a new kind of living that doesn't suck as bad as the old one might have. Either way, you aren't getting your money back.

In my case, the first step of my post-treatment life was kind of set up while I was still in treatment. During treatment, I used to go to the cemetery where my mom's best friend was buried. I would visit her grave and talk and just spend a little time there. It was a really peaceful place. One day while driving home from the cemetery after doing my morning radiation treatment, I felt like I was going to vomit. I pulled over and threw up all over the street. It happened very fast. I was sitting on the street with my back against the old station wagon and I felt like a bag of broken assholes. I was bent out of shape, exhausted and worn out. Sorry for the visual, but I was feeling that bad.

So there I was, leaning on the wagon with big puke strings hanging off my chin, looking like a first-year college student after a party, or maybe just a Tuesday night. I looked to my left and realized that I had stopped in front of a new-age bookstore. It was attached to the back of some sort of church. To say this was a really strange place for a bookstore was an understatement. It was a residential neighborhood, with no other stores of any sort around at all.

So I stumbled into the store and the owner looked at me and immediately took me into a back room and told me to lie down. We made love for hours.

That's not true. Even if she had wanted to make love to my sorry ass, I wouldn't have been able to do it. I was in rough shape. She started doing Reiki on me (a form of Japanese energy work), to settle me down. She told me to rest for as long as I liked. She asked me what was going on and we talked awhile, till I passed out. When I woke up we spoke some more and she told me that one of her psychic friends was a mechanic who worked at the cemetery that I had just come from. Long story short, I ended up getting a job at that cemetery. Like I said before, it was the perfect place to work post-treatment. Going back to the wonderful woman who helped me out that day—Nancy, I will never forget your kindness. You are proof that angels walk among us.

I know I spoke about the cemetery briefly before, but I want to reiterate how important that job was in my re-entry to a "normal" life. Everyday I would bury dead people. (Burying live people is so much harder, what with all the kicking and screaming and the cries of, "I'm not dead yet!!") I would work alone most of the time and it was very peaceful. I had a lot of time to digest the past couple of years and I always had a little notebook with me to capture random thoughts or to write down lyrics and musical ideas. It was pretty difficult to wake up feeling sorry for myself when I buried people for a living. No matter how shitty I felt, I was on the sunny side of the shovel.

With every burial I was reminded of the preciousness of life and how fortunate I was to be here. I saw family members and friends mourning loved ones daily, in many different ways. Some screamed and wailed, others cried softly and silently. Some stood stoically, staring straight ahead while there were others who looked at their watches and around the cemetery with great indifference, waiting for the service to be over so they could leave. There were all kinds of mourners from different cultures, religions and walks of life.

My time spent working at the cemetery was when I first really thought about death and what it meant to me. The crazy thing was, I never really *allowed* myself to think about death during cancer treatment. It was never an option for me being the stubborn bastard that I am. However, I did think about suicide daily when I was out of my mind with panic attacks and crippling depression. It was comforting to know that I could make it stop if I wanted too, but disturbing to be having those thoughts at the same time. When the highlight of your day is the relief you feel when thinking that you can blow your head off, *you are in trouble.*

But when I was in cancer treatment, I never allowed those thoughts in my head. I wanted to change my life so badly that I focused hard on the future and being healthy. The cemetery was where I realized what I had been through and where it really hit home.

There I was in the calm of the cemetery, facing death every day in a new way. Working in the cemetery got me thinking about my own death and how I wanted it to be. I thought about what I wanted to do before that day came for me. That was the place that really allowed me to regain my focus and put things in perspective.

It felt great to use my body and feel its strength and vitality. It was so good to just stand there after a burial and see how beautiful the freshly laid sod looked and to know that I made someone's final resting place a beautiful thing. I took pride in my work and felt like I had the chance to reflect on what I had just been through in a place that would always remind me of what we all have coming to us.

I buried people from every age group and every walk of life. I realized that we all love; we all hurt when we lose someone and we all end up the same no matter the race, color or creed. While my friends were finishing college and university, I was once again being educated in a different way. My lessons came to me in feelings and insights that I would write in my little notebooks.

With every casket and every urn I buried, I would be aware of what was going on inside me. Initially, I felt a bit freaked out doing this work. I thought about what was inside the caskets. Doing this intimate work eventually allowed me to come to terms with many of the issues that I hadn't fully thought through in the past. Even with all the writing and journaling I had already done.

The cemetery is the last stop for the physical body. My hands were the last ones on those caskets and I am proud to say that I laid those stranger's bodies to rest with great respect and care. Like I said before, the cemetery was a place where I settled down and digested the cancer experience. It was where I did my graduate studies, if you will. The combination of solitude and hard work allowed me the time and reflection needed to start to put my experiences into perspective. I was then, and remain to this day, very grateful for that time in my life. It really was the perfect place to start re-integrating into normal society.

After the cemetery, I took a job as a parts driver at an auto supply store. I was playing in a couple of bands and writing my own music. I really didn't care about money at that time. I was just grateful to be out of the cancer clinic. After a couple of accidents (*I got cut off on the highway by a Dump truck with trailer carrying cement highway dividers; destroyed the car, lucky to be alive etc... then, a week later, the hood let go on the highway and smashed my windshield*), I decided it was time to move on. I worked as a doorman for a while in town and eventually, I got a job on a horse farm. The farm was beautiful and I lived in a small apartment connected to the main barn. If the horse in the stall on the opposite side of my kitchen kicked hard enough, my pans would rattle!

It was at this farm that I had an interesting post-cancer experience. Sometimes when you are receiving radiation treatment, depending on where the treatment area is on your body, the technicians will make a plastic mold of that body part to hold it in place and to ensure the treatment area is always the same. In my case, the mold was from my chin to just below my chest. They marked out the treatment area on the plastic mold and even circled my nipples in red. It was a nice touch. Then, lead blocking plates were created to stop the radiation from destroying healthy tissue and organs like the heart and lungs. These areas were also marked on the mold.

When I came in for treatment, I would lie down on the table and they would put this mold on me and screw it down onto the table to keep me in the exact same place every time. Then they would turn off the lights and line up the grids of red lights that shone down on me to make sure I was properly aligned in the target area. (*I wrote a song about radiation treatment called Red Grid Shines, never mentioning anything cancer related of course, sneaky bastard that I am, that was played on a bunch of radio stations across the country.*)

After my treatment was finished, I kept the mold and turned it into a piece of art. I had mounted it onto a canvas and wrote all over the mold and canvas what the whole cancer experience meant to me. One day after giving the horses their evening hay, I found myself sitting in my apartment staring at the artwork. Something came over me and I stood up, took it under my arm and walked out back behind the barn. I lay the piece down and went to get some gasoline. I then placed the piece in the burn barrel and poured gas on it. It was at this point that I got really anxious and realized that I didn't want to let this go.

I was really surprised by how badly I wanted to hold onto this piece of art. I told myself that in order to move forward in my life, I had to let go of this experience, even if I had to force it at first. With a strange fear and excitement, I lit a match and tossed it on the artwork, and with a "whoosh" it went up in flames.

I watched, as the words I had written were made bright by the flames and then burned away. The initial fear and hesitation I had towards destroying this piece melted away as fast as the flames consumed the mold. I was flooded with emotions, which surprised me as well. I realized how much I had been holding on to this experience and questioned why. I realized that I had allowed this cancer experience to really define me. I realized that I was so much more than just this experience and that any self-imposed definitions were only going to limit me.

So once again my eyes were opened and my heart let some fear go. Little by little, I was becoming more comfortable with this new version of me. As much as I had wanted to hold onto that piece of art as a trophy and as something that helped me figure out who I was, I knew it was best to let it go. It was nice to be warmed by the flames of my past. To be completely cheesy, I will say that I reminded myself that the brightness of the future depends on what you are willing to let go of and burn from your past. Let the flames from the wreckage of your past light your path to your next version of you or your next adventure. That's enough fromage for now. That was French. Google that shit!

The idea of "going back to normal" is such a powerful compulsion in the crisis experience. It can become an obsessive way of thinking. "*I just want to go back to normal*"—I can remember both thinking and saying that a million times.

Sometimes crisis feels like we are alone on a raft that is floating away from shore towards the open ocean. We keep looking back at the shore and freaking out, trying to figure out how to get back there. Eventually we get far out to sea and we can't see the land anymore. We can't see what's behind us and we can't see what's ahead of us. We don't even know where to start looking for land. Oh, and the waters are infested with sharks too.

If your old life was the shore you left, the crisis might be the time you spend out on the open ocean on that raft. Eventually you see land and you get a sense that you are "going to make it." When you do hit land, it might be different than the place you left. You might feel different from the time spent alone on the raft. Like the Tom Hanks character in the movie "Castaway," you too might experience some difficulty when you return to "normal" life. I'm sure astronauts have some mixed emotions when they return from space. That must be one hell of a trip.

The sooner you can cast the idea of what's normal out of your mind and vocabulary the better. It is completely "normal" to be freaking out at a cancer diagnosis. It is completely "normal" to want to kill yourself when you are so fucked in the head that it seems like a rational act. But don't do it, you bastards! It is completely "normal" to feel different or weird during and after crisis.

On the other hand, human beings are remarkably durable creatures. We can adapt to almost any environment and thrive. We can find and create meaning in any situation and we can call upon great internal resources when we need to. So we have *that* going for us.

I remember thinking about what normal was back when I was sick. I remember wanting to go back in time and "fix" things. I remember wanting to be normal so badly, it physically hurt (the tight chest, massive headaches and upset stomach from anxiety). Man, the time I wasted pining for normal. The scenery I missed because my head was shoved so far up my own ass.

I have gained a lot of insight from time spent thinking about things in a constructive, forward-moving way. Trying to somehow change what is happening by pining for the past is an entirely useless endeavor, but it is also a natural part of the healing process it seems. So what is the magic formula? How much time do we spend thinking about things, and when is it time to let it go? Well, that is for all of us to decide as individuals. You will know when you realize that you've stopped thinking about it.

My mom's friend Ann told me one time that I would one day forget that these days ever happened. Well maybe not forget them, but not be held captive by the raw insanity that I was currently experiencing. She was the one who told me to fake it till I made it, or until I forgot I was faking.

Ann is a legend in my mind, as well as in many other peoples. She was a force of nature and I was so grateful to have had her insight and experience, her fierce love and raw belief in life to draw upon in those days. People like that are like handrails on high towers in high winds. The situation would be a whole lot scarier without them. I really hope you have people like that around you during crisis and afterwards.

Even with people like Ann around, I still had a hard time believing that the crazy shit would ever end, especially in the days before I got diagnosed with cancer and felt out of my mind. At that time I wasn't sure I was going to make it. I thought countless times that if I had to live the rest of my life feeling that way, I was gonna have to find a way out. I'm glad I held on.

It isn't all rosy after treatment. At least in my case it wasn't. Shortly after cancer treatment, I was driving with my father somewhere and he suddenly pulled into the parking lot of a strip club (weird, right?) and started to rip into me about my situation. He was telling me to shake it off and that I was letting the experience be an albatross around my neck. He was really angry and I was shocked. Then I started to feel white heat filling my body and I started in on him, trying to defend myself. We both raged at each other, beating each other over the heads with our opinions and trying to "win." When my dad calmed down, he basically told me he couldn't handle the stress he felt my mother was under. I think that this eruption was also his way of letting his stress go. I told him that I was trying to get sorted out and that I was doing the best that I could. I felt like shit for putting my family through this experience and I am sure many people in crisis have felt the same way.

I don't blame my father for reacting the way he did. It was a rough year on him *to say the least*. First, his wife's best friend died whom he loved to bits. Then his son lost his mind, which was then followed by the death of his own mother, and *then* he watched his son go through cancer treatment. My dad went through all that craziness with his same steady demeanor. He got up, went to work, came home, and did the things he always did. Eventually I could see and feel the tension building up inside him and felt guilty for my contribution to it.

One day he came home from work with these great big steaks for dinner. He wanted to cheer us all up and it was a great gesture. I remember seeing his face fall when I told him I couldn't eat mine because my throat was sore from treatment. I had no saliva and couldn't taste food at the moment. I told him to enjoy his for the both of us.

My dad is a man who loves to laugh; he tried like hell to maintain a sense of normalcy in the house by just soldiering on in the face of despair and chaos. I can't imagine what it would be like to have all that shit happening to you all at once. I imagine he felt pretty helpless and frustrated. At that time, I wasn't going to engage in a touchy-feely conversation with my father about what we were experiencing as a family.

I avoided my family a lot because I felt like I was a source of pain and frustration to them. I didn't want to let them feel what I was feeling. I didn't want them to know how scared I was. I wanted to just push through it and get back to normal. I didn't realize that I was trying to get "back" to a town that had burned to the ground.

In retrospect, I have a huge amount of respect for my father and how he handled himself during that period. I learned a hell of a lot about being a good man from my father's actions. We didn't talk a whole lot back then, at least not about the deep shit. It was all too real and crazy to talk about right away. I did watch what he did, though. I learned to get up, go to work, tell the shitty jokes we've all heard before (with a few good zingers once in awhile, too), provide for your family and bring home a steak once in awhile, even if your kid can't eat it. Your kid is going to know what you were trying to do, and will love you for it. Come to think of it, I think he did go ahead and eat mine. That would have been funny and typical for my dad.

My sister told me that when she found out I had cancer, she went and started washing her hair for no reason other than she wanted to be busy. My father worked hard and maintained his routine. My mother tried to take on everyone's stress and make it all better. We all scrambled to keep our lives somewhat normal even though we knew they were never going to be normal again. I have so much respect for my family and how they handled themselves during that messed up period in my life. I will be for-ever grateful to have had them as my family. I have no doubt that without the strength and love of my family, I would have checked out long ago.

One of the reasons I wrote so much and spent time away from friends and family is that I needed to process what was going on inside without stressing people out. People handle stress differently. Some eat; some drink, some fight, some laugh and some become reclusive. There are many ways to handle stress; a lot of them are not good. My avoid-ance behavior didn't end with the treatment. In fact, I found that my post-treatment life was where I struggled the most.

After the intensity of treatment, with its pressure cooker-tense moments and the ups and downs that go along with it, I found "real life" to be a little, well, boring. I know, it's fucking crazy to think that way, but have you read this book? It's *me* talking here. The first thing I felt post-treatment was elation and euphoria; these feelings were pretty incredible. Then I settled down and realized that I had five years to wait before they could say I was officially "cured."

I would be going to the doctor every three months for tests for the first year, and then every 6 months for a few more years. The reminder was going to be there for me. I didn't just get to walk away clean, as it were. You are probably thinking *"whatever asshole, you got to walk away!"* I know it was a small price to pay for being alive and I was happy to pay it. The point is, the experience didn't feel "over" yet. Not to mention that I *still* wasn't right in the head at that point. Not even close.

The post-treatment phase brought a new kind of weirdness into my life. I didn't feel like my "old" self, not that I would have recognized him anyway. This new self was an interesting character, though. I was deeper, more in touch with myself and with life, but I was also as dark as I was light. I felt this intensity inside me and had this feeling like I had a gun to my head and a clock ticking. I also had this feeling that I had to do something really important with my life.

None of us ask to be born (well maybe we do, but for argument's sake let's pretend we don't), but when I got a legit second chance at life, I felt pressure. I had the stopwatch state of mind. *Tick tick, tick, let's go, motherfucker!!!! Do something with your life!* That sort of thing.

For a while I felt like I was playing catch-up with everyone. My friends all seemed to be on great paths in their lives and I felt far behind. Again, I realized I was ahead in a lot of ways as far as life experience was concerned, but I still felt behind. *Now* I realize that none of that shit matters. What matters to me now is being able to be right here. Right now. No matter what the circumstances in my life or the situation or position I may be in, I try to just be here without any expectations. It's a daily battle. I also realize that my health both physical and mental is most important to me. Everything else is secondary. I can handle anything as long as I have my head on straight and my health is good. I am sure that many bed-ridden millionaires would agree with me.

That being said, I still felt messed in the head after treatment. I still had issues with anxiety and depression, but was just gutting it out on my own. I was digesting the cancer experience and trying to figure out what to do with my life like any other young person. So, post-treatment, I still found it weird or difficult to be around people. I felt like I should be feeling great, happy and grateful, but the truth was I wasn't. My feelings were conflicted to say the least. Part of me was like: *"Come on man! Let it go! Let's have some fun for god's sakes!"* and the other part of me went on chewing and digesting and grinding away at all these messed up feelings.

Even when I did go out, I felt out of place. I would be in a bar with people my own age and they would be dancing, drinking and trying to get laid. I would be standing there watching it all, feeling like a complete fucking psycho and an outsider. I felt it was such a waste of time to be doing this shit. I felt like an 85-year-old man in a 22-year-old's body.

I also remember thinking I wish everyone could *get* and *survive* cancer; maybe we wouldn't be such a mess as a people. But then I realized we all react differently to things, and who's to say the cancer experience wouldn't turn some people into worse versions of themselves. I thought a lot of crazy shit.

Still do, in case you haven't noticed.

I also felt like I couldn't connect with my peers. I preferred my own company or playing music and writing. I started to go to open stage nights at bars and I started to go to jams, trying to connect with musicians and to lose (and find) myself in the music.

I had always been a drummer; I had only played guitar at home in my bedroom during treatment. I started to play guitar and sing at these jams and it was terrifying. The great thing about that was I had found a place to express myself, as well as people who appreciated the emotion that I was putting out there. Once again, music had brought me to a place where I could get my shit together.

When your treatment is over, you will be going back for tests, like I mentioned before. For me, those tests were blood work and X-rays. I will never forget my first post-treatment check up. I was in the X-ray waiting room with one other person; a visibly distraught woman of about 35 or 40. She was dabbing at tears in her eyes and since we were alone and I'm not the kind of asshole who just reads a magazine and pretends nothing is happening, I asked her if she was all right. She really wanted to talk—she immediately told me that she was here to get some X-rays done because her cancer had returned after a 10-year remission. She told me she had Hodgkin's disease, the same cancer I had just finished treatment for, and I started laughing to cover the chill that ran over me and the fact that I felt like puking.

I told her that was what I had just finished treatment for and was back for my first post-treatment check up. The poor woman covered her mouth and was so upset that she had somehow "ruined" my visit or jinxed me. She apologized; I told her not to worry and laughed it off, though I was kind of freaked out, to be honest. Okay, I was very freaked out. I was thinking, "*What are the odds of that happening?*" followed by, "*Is this some kind of sign?*" I just asked her questions and got her talking until they called her name. I wished her luck and never saw her again. I hope she is kicking ass and living well.

A rough start to post-treatment life!

At another check-up, my doctor was a young East Indian dude who figured he would warm up his patients with humor. He stood there, stroking his chin and staring at my X-rays for a minute or so. He turned back to me and said in a thick accent,

"Well... you are going to die."

My mind went blank and I stared at him slack-jawed and dumbfounded. I am pretty sure it was only a few seconds before he finished his sentence, but it felt like an eternity. I managed to force a single word out of my suddenly bone dry mouth,

"WHAT?" I croaked.

Then he said, pointing at me,

"BUT NOT TODAY!" He half yelled and then laughed.

I just sat there for a few seconds, completely stunned.

Then I think I called him a motherfucker or something. Then we both started to laugh. I told him to maybe not try that one again on anyone else, or at least deliver the punch line quicker, but he was just so pleased with how it went down that he just laughed and slapped me on the shoulder and told me to go home and make babies.

That son of a bitch.

The thing about post-treatment is that it is *another* new world. I really hope that you don't have the mental bullshit that I had on top of it, because it really complicates things. But if you do, don't lose hope, just keep on doing the work and things will get better. All the techniques and strategies found in this book apply to post-treatment as well. In fact, the writing thing, the journaling habit, is an excellent tool to continue using throughout your life. At the very least, you can use your writing to see how far you have come. Also remember, nothing gives you experience like experience. Just show up willing, everyday.

I hope that you can sort out and make sense of any shitty or confusing feelings that you may have. I really hope you aren't messed up too badly—but be sure that if you are, know that it doesn't last forever. Please be as easy on yourself as I hope you were during treatment. Remember that the same rules apply for the post-treatment world as they do for the treatment world. *There are no rules.* There is no right way to "do" it. Above all, be kind to yourself and give yourself permission and time to get used to your new landscape, inside and out.

Your body might feel different and be physically different. It may be missing pieces, organs, or tissue and it might be scarred and screwed up in one way or another. If this is the case and you are having trouble with it, don't be a proud, stubborn asshole. Get help for it. I told you about how I had issues with my body post-treatment. Finally, I didn't care if people laughed at me or called me names.

God bless em' if they do.

Besides, MILLIONS of people have read this book; filled with all these twisted opinions I have and all these messed-up things about me, and I DON'T CARE! *(Did you like how I set that part up about selling lots of books? Right?? RIGHT??)*

Now if they found out about my little penis and made fun of me for it, THAT would hurt pretty badly. But they won't, so let's keep it between us. Is that a line? It would probably work better if you had a big penis. Example:

You: "Hey hot girl in bar, I have a big penis but it's a secret, so lets keep it between us"

Hot girl: "The secret?"

You: "No baby, my big penis"

BOOM!

Okay, so that was brutal and took us way off topic. But in the spirit of *"This is my book and I'll write it any way I please,"* let's explore this a bit.

You could use a variation of that joke using your battle-scarred body instead of your small penis. (*See how I turned that around on you there?*)

Let's try it.

You: "Hey hot girl in the bar, I have survived cancer but I don't think I could live another day if you don't tell me your name."

So cheesy, but so good....
Or version two:

You: "Hey darlin, I thought I survived cancer but I am obviously dead because you are an angel I want to have sex with when God isn't looking."

A bit creepy but if delivered correctly.... Right? Right?

Okay and we are back.

That shitty joke section back there is a great lead-in to what I want to bring up next.

What are you now?

I say this because I never felt comfortable using the term cancer survivor. I felt really awkward with it and even more awkward participating in survivor's events. I remember doing a survivors' walk and I felt so weird about people clapping and stuff. I wanted to hold up a picture of my friends and family and pictures of the doctors, nurses and strangers that helped me through my experience and say: "*Clap for these people, THEY are the ones who deserve the applause.*" Come to think of it, I also think we should give our mothers presents on our birthdays. What did I do? She did all the work. *Thanks for life mom, here is a nice card and a gift for you! Now let's eat some damn cake!!!*

Back to the cancer walks and all those kind of events.

I just felt so strange to be there and to define myself as a cancer survivor. I like the term cancer *veteran* myself, if you have to use a term at all. The word survivor just doesn't do it for me. But hey, that's just this guy. You do what feels right for you and it's all good.

Celebrate your experience or don't. Do what feels good; I like to celebrate life, period. Having had cancer is a part of it. Maybe I didn't get close enough to dying or maybe I didn't have the worst of cancer experiences but I got the message to say the least. (*Don't kid yourself; there are cancer experience "rankers" out there.*) Like I said before, I felt more like a mentally ill person who also had to deal with cancer. I definitely was more terrified of mental illness than I was of cancer. I understood cancer. The crazy I didn't understand.

Talking about those events made me think of a time I was asked to speak at a fundraising event. It was one of those 24-hour events where people run and walk to raise money. My band was playing there and the organizers knew I was a cancer VETERAN and had asked me to speak. There were three of us who were going to speak that night.

I was running late and hadn't prepared anything. When I did arrive, there was a woman on stage telling a horrific story about a massive tumor that she had removed and it was a devastating story to hear. The crowd looked horrified and was definitely feeling the heaviness of the story. So here I am thinking to myself, *"What am I going to say?"*

Well, the lady wrapped up her story and the MC asked for a moment of silence to remember those who had succumbed to cancer. So now the crowd of a couple thousand people were *totally* bummed out, some crying softly and it is my turn to speak next. Great. I took a breath and asked the universe for some inspiration.

So I got introduced and went up, not knowing what to say and made a joke about how weird it was to be sober in front of a microphone for once (to a smattering of laughs).

Then it hit me.

Lift them up.

I began with how it sucks that we have to do these events. It sucks that something like cancer exists, but that it is great that so many people care enough to take the time to come out to raise money and awareness and all that good stuff. I then told people that it is good to honor the dead, that it is great to be respectful and bow our heads and be silent in their memory. But then I told them I would like to have a moment of celebration.

I told them that on my command, I wanted them all to scream at the top of their lungs. I wanted them to scream as loud as they possibly could, not to worry about being embarrassed or looking foolish or any of that crap. I told them that on the count of three we were all going to scream to celebrate the lives our loved ones had lived. I told them we were going to honor them with our roaring voices and we were going to have a moment of awesome remembrance that they were going to hear and love wherever they were.

When I said, "Can you do that?" I got one hell of a resounding "YES!!!" from the crowd. I asked them again and I got an even louder "YES!!!!" When I counted it off, that crowd ROARED!!! I threw my head back and let it go myself as loud as I could. I kept it going, and looked around at these people, young and old, screaming their goddamn heads off. It was a powerful moment.

Then my band, Loudlove (is there any other kind?) rocked the shit outta those people, giving them the energy they needed to spend 24 hours doing good work.

It was a great night.

And a big breath in....

So post-treatment, your soul might feel a little beat-up from the journey but those are just growing pains. Besides, you are here and you are breathing and you get to live another minute, hour or day to figure this shit out. There is no doubt in my mind that if you have come this far, you have changed. Whether you realize it or not, you have been deepened. Maybe we feel scared or messed up because being "deepened" might seem like being in a big deep chasm that we feel very small in. Then we climb our way out slowly, moving towards that light. It isn't until we crawl out of that hole that we realize how far down and consequently how high up we have come.

Again, NO PRESSURE!!! To put it simply, hopefully you have a little more space inside that you don't re-fill with negative, ugly shit. If you do, consider it compost and plant some seeds of love and compassion in there! Here we *grow* again!

Take the time to let the whole experience find its place in you. There is no timetable for recovery, so don't go put a gun to your head and put all kinds of pressure on yourself. As the Buddhists, or someone say(s), "*Carry water, chop wood.*" Live your life, keep writing, keep observing, and keep opening your heart to life and its experiences. Scream, laugh, eat, and sleep. Do whatever you have to do. It is all good.

Remember that there is no shame in asking for help if you feel overwhelmed. The whole pride thing should be reserved for parades full of celebrating gay people in costumes and for crazy old men who obsess over their lawns and vacuum their driveways. If you feel overwhelmed and over your head, ask for help. Find help. Even if it is reading an awesome book like this to know you aren't alone, finding a support group that doesn't make you cringe, or finding professional help.

There are resources to help you—seek them out. There is this thing called the interweb that can give you plenty of info. Be careful that you don't freak yourself out, though. There is a lot of information that can make you paranoid regarding side effects and long term damage from treatment.

Talk to your doctor about side effects to watch out for before you are finished treatment. Again, don't freak yourself out; just see what your particular treatment may bring you as far as side effects, either short term or long term.

To wrap this chapter up, as usual, I believe nothing is written in stone anyway—shit is gonna happen and unless you have become an enlightened master of some sort and there is no "you" anymore, *you* will be there to deal with it. This I guarantee!

24

THE SUPERUNKNOWN—A FINAL STREAM OF CONSCIOUSNESS RANT.

"Security is mostly a superstition. It does not exist in nature, nor do the children of men as a whole experience it. Avoidance of danger is no safer in the long run than outright exposure. Life is either a daring adventure, or nothing."
HELEN KELLER

KNOW AS I write this, I am "looking in a mirror."

All we have is this moment. There is no wrong or right.

We are surrounded by opinion and are obsessed with results, and we know that both of these can be questioned and debated by our-selves and others until we are paralyzed with fear, doubt and/or indifference.

All we *truly* control is our attitude.

The only thing you need to be in this life, in my humble opinion, is willing.

Willing to fail, willing to try, willing to show up each day and give it another shot. Willing to fall on your face in front of a crowd, or by yourself. Willing to be wrong, willing to accept blame and praise. Willing to sit still and shut up and drop *everything*.

Even your will.

Is this easy? Hell no. I'm still trying to figure all this out.

The thing is, I'm willing. I'm game.

Most days.

Some days I give in to the ego and believe the lies I hear in my head about the frustrations of my heart. Some days I fall apart even if I am smiling on the outside. Shit happens, don't beat yourself up about it. Develop a kindness towards yourself and a sense of sympathy for your suffering. The other way is brutal and a waste of *precious* time.

Don't be quick to brand these experiences. It takes time to figure out whether things are truly bad or good. Speaking about the whole bad and good thing, there is an excellent old Chinese (I think) parable out there about a white horse that appears in a man's paddock one day and changes his life in many different ways. Google it, read it and take its lessons to heart. While you are Googling things, punch in Chief Tecumseh's words of wisdom. Print them out and put them on your wall.

The optimistic and experienced man can tell you that a mouthful of shit makes a mouthful of honey taste so much better. I have learned a lot from homeless people about success and life in general. The world isn't set up for anything but experience. We are *all* terminal. We are all going to die. What are you going to do today?

Change your life or don't. Who said we all had to be famous? Who said we all had to be beautiful? Who are "they" anyway, and why do we trust them so much let alone care about *their* opinions?

Where did the pressure come from? Where does it come from now? Who says we have to do anything? Make up your own country. Make up it's own rules. Burn all the flags and blow up the borders. Scream like a lunatic. Be bad be good, it's all just opinion and perspective. Laughing and crying feel good. Good friends and a warm embrace will sustain you. Tell the ones you love that you love them. Don't wait, and don't worry—help is on the way and it looks a lot like *you*.

Reach out and ask for help. Burn your ego. Take it in the backyard and make it dig a hole and tell it to get inside and shoot it in the head. Don't feel bad for doing that either, it'll be back. Don't hang your hopes on a single person, but try to be hopeful. If that "fails" just *be*.

Scream. Be quiet.

Things don't always go the way we want them too, dreams don't always come true, good people die young and loved ones of all ages will die on us as well. Realize you will *never* have it all together. You may get the perfect job, partner, house or whatever you are striving for and then someone you love will die, or something will happen that will challenge your notions of security and safety.

That is when you will be happy to have eaten this gigantic shit sandwich. Realizing that there is no true security within ourselves or in this world can make the world seem frightening or the most awesome place ever. You *know* this is true deep down inside and I hope you respond to any of these challenges with courage and compassion.

Choose the awesome angle.

Fluidity is your friend, rigidity, not so much. Accepting the imperfections of life and acknowledging the perfect chaotic mess of it all is the first step to freeing yourself, so they tell me... I see it though, and some days I even *live* it. Some moments I am free and it is *beautiful*. I hope you have many of these moments. I really do.

Let go.

You can't "save" everyone and you can't "save" the world but you can start with yourself and work from there. You can do big things, but remember that small things matter and can make a difference *and* have an impact too. Spend a night in a tent with a mosquito to be reminded of that.

Recognize where you are and what you have.... Don't listen to me. Listen to yourself.

Don't listen to yourself, go inside and *feel* your truth.

Also be ready for your "truth" to be challenged and be ready to let it go when it makes no sense to defend, or hold onto it any longer. When you do, laugh.

Hard.

The anger, frustration and disappointments are there for a reason. So are your love, passion and your will to go on and make things better. Meditate, copulate, and *give yourself a break*.

The problem with self-help books is that they leave you feeling like you failed if you get through them and still haven't realized the dream life. That is bullshit.

Life is a dream that we make up ourselves.

You are a creator. Create something.

I'm beginning to realize that life is whatever we want it to be.

Whether you think life sucks or life is beautiful doesn't really matter as you are going to be right either way.

If you feel like shit there is a reason for it. If you want to change, you can. But you have to find a way. I am not telling you THE way to get better; I am just giving you some examples of what worked for me, and what didn't. Venting feels good but it is best done in a journal as not everyone will want to hear it, or knows how to listen. There is a time and a place for everything. Find the passion. Find the inspiration.

I hope that the cancer or depression experience leaves you feeling like you are an *enhanced* version of yourself. But then again, maybe less is more.

Perhaps it smashed off the fear and armor enough to expose the real you that was hiding inside. Maybe it knocked the dirt off of the diamond.

You tender fucker, you.

I hope you can see your life as beautiful, no matter how ugly or messed up it might *seem* to be.

I hope that you experience love and genuine friendship, first with yourself and then with others. Regardless, send love out into the world. Just do it and don't care what "they" think. Send "them" love too.

I hope that you do better than I did.

There are those who say there is no cure for cancer. I would have to agree to a certain extent, as there are days when "it" still haunts me. You feel sick and its cancer. You get itchy and its cancer. It's all in how we *respond*. I would go further to say that regardless of what your experiences or challenges may have been; we are *all* marching towards our own extinctions. That thought can fill you with fear or set you free entirely. It's your choice friend.

Some of you are going to go on and live your lives like none of this happened. Some of you will think about it for the rest of your lives. Some of you will let it be an excuse and some of you will turn this experience into something powerful and meaningful. Some of you will do all the above, depending on the day.

Regardless of the path or paths you choose, I do hope that you *allow* yourself to feel the rawness and the tenderness of life, and of your heart and soul. I hope you don't *forget* those feelings. Ever. I hope your experience leads you to a place of tenderness and authenticity inside that changes you forever.

I hope that it sticks.

In any case, be prepared to be different.
Release all expectations of "how you *should* be."
Be present no matter what—let the emotions be seen, felt, acknowledged—and then let go. Be Zen. Seriously, check that stuff out. It makes so much sense... or be a complete animal, I am a combination of both. Do whatever gets you a few more miles down the road.

Enjoy your body to the best of its abilities and to the best of its limitations, if any. If it has limitations, see if there are any ways around them. If there doesn't seem to be any, be open to the possibility that you might not have seen them yet. You can also accept what *is* and focus on your strengths, on whatever gives you the butterflies. Remember the "you" that people feel comes from within. How your body feels or looks is not "you" anyway.

Your body is a rental that will have an effect on you and your life, as it is the meat machine you ride in, but your body isn't *you.*

The *real* "you" is invisible. Okay, some glimpses of the real you *can* be seen, but *you* are mostly felt.

It's the light in your eyes, the kindness and love that people *feel* when you look at them. It is the feeling that they have in your presence. It is the love and compassion, the wildness and the calm that you *radiate.* All of that comes from within, and *without being afraid to show people your whole, good, heart.*

Your fancy clothes, haircut, big muscles and tan may get you in the door, but it's how you feel to people and how you make them feel that will make them stay or make them want you to stay.

When you are on your deathbed what will you wish for? What are the memories you want to have? What do you want to feel or have felt?
Who do you want with you? Where are you in the world?
What did you do with your life?
Who did you do it with? What was your greatest regret?
What was your greatest triumph or achievement? Think about these things now.

Don't wait.

Speaking of being on your deathbed, If I had one piece of advice to give you on *my* death bed *which is wherever I am at all times*, it would be to really try to live your life without fear and to do so like you are dying, because guess what, like I said before, we are *all* dying and even though we don't like to think about that fact I say, think about it!

Look in a mirror directly into your own eyes and say these words:

"I am going to die. This is unavoidable. I accept this fact and I choose to live my life as a free human being. Free from fear, worry, doubt or pessimism. I refuse to die having lived an unfulfilling life. My life is a gift to be shared and experienced fully and I will not waste another second insulting the universe by thinking I am not up to the task of living an incredible life full of compassion, beauty, courage, gratitude and inspiration. I am here to create, inspire and celebrate the miracle of life. From this moment until my heart refuses to pound, I'm down. I will endeavor. I am here to express myself and to help others. This life is mine and I am here to shine, so help me Universe!"

Embrace the fact that you are going to die! Think about that fact everyday to slap the shit outta yourself and to *wake up*! I know there are no guarantees, and by now you should know too, so *live* people!

LIVE AS A *FREE* HUMAN BEING!

Coming through any crisis experience, especially one that nearly *kills* you should teach you that you have a limited time here to express yourself, to enjoy simple moments and also to do *amazing* things.

The crisis experience should teach you that life is an amazing, mind-blowing gift to be cherished and *used*. Go out there and live because as you know now,

Life can be taken away at any time.

ANY FREAKING TIME.

"But I am afraid I'll fail!!"

ANY FREAKING TIME.

"My parents won't approve!"

ANY FREAKING TIME.

"I'm scared!"

ANY FREAKING TIME.

Seize the fucking day by the shoulders, bend her head back and French kiss that gorgeous creature deeply, passionately and with lots of tongue. Do it! You won't regret it.

I gotta calm down.

But seriously.

Your love is your strength. Your compassion is your currency. Your heart is your guide and your guts will never lie to you. One day you will look back fondly on your treatment and insanity days and dare I say, at times even *miss* them.

You may even look back at your days of crisis like an old, tough teacher you once had that made your life hell. Now you realize they actually cared about you and had your best interests in mind.

Maybe not, but don't feel weird or guilty if you do.

Trust me though today is better.

Today is all we have.

This moment, *this* breath. *This* is not bullshit. It is the truth.

I'd put my wee nuts on the chopping block to defend that statement.

But for today, just be here in the illusion.

Show up.

Breathe.

Life is fucking *amazing* and better for having had *you* in it.

Now go hug the shit outta someone you love.

—⊗⊗⊗—

25

YOU ARE MY HEROES—
THE SERMON CONCLUDES

LIFE IS AN amazing journey. It is terrifying, exhilarating, frustrating, and a whole bunch of other words that end in the letters i-n-g. What makes life amazing differs for all of us, but what makes it worth living for me are my friends and family. I hope that after writing this book, launching the website and travelling the globe promoting this thing, I will increase the size of my friends and family.

I say this because I know I am going to meet many of you while I am out there promoting this book and celebrating life. I am going to hug the shit outta you and thank you for helping me write this book, and most of all finish it.

I know what you are thinking. You're thinking,

"What do you mean Pete? I didn't do anything but buy like a hundred copies for all my friends and family! I had nothing to do with the writing of this book!"

Well, my unmet friend; *that* is where you would be as wrong as wearing socks with sandals.

Writing this book has been a huge undertaking for me. First of all, when I'm not recovering from whatever the latest chaotic incident is in my life, I work full-time, have a healthy relationship that I don't want to mess up, play music in a band, have a Brazilian Jiu-Jitsu addiction to take care of, marry people as a lay wedding officiant, celebrate the end of people's lives as a funeral celebrant *and* I also have a part time job as an ass model.

Okay, so the ass model part is not true. I have an ass like a couple of kicked in sofa cushions. The rest however, really is true. Writing (and re-writing) this book has been a part of my life for over two years. I used to write early in the morning before work, but then switched to writing late into the night. It has been an obsession that I have been grinding away at with all my heart and soul. I also had a cat named Quinn constantly demanding petting and driving me nuts during the writing of this book, so a lot of this was written with one hand....

No, that isn't some cute sexual joke, *although I wouldn't put it past myself.*

It has been an emotional roller coaster that has caught me by surprise many, many times. Making yourself blush, cry, laugh or swear loudly alone in a room from your own writing is as much a reward as it is draining.

The writing of this book has kicked my ass and the promoting of it no doubt will do the same. I am hell-bent on making this thing the best it can be and spreading the word of the BTB as far as I can. In fact, if this book moved you, tell people about it. Spread the word. Lord knows I could use the help!

However.

None of this would have been possible if I didn't have you guys pushing me, too. No, I don't know you by name (*although I will have met a lot of you promoting this bastard, I have no doubt of that,*) but I *know* you are out there. I know this because *everyday* someone is getting that fucking diagnosis of cancer. *Everyday* someone's life is getting rocked harder than a canoe full of cokeheads. *Everyday* someone is fighting an invisible battle with a mental illness, and *everyday people are checking out from both.*

The thoughts of you out there battling, dealing with this shit kept bringing me back to the old laptop. Those thoughts helped me peck out another page or two. Day in, day out.

I was 21 when I lost my mind and then got cancer. Maybe you are a young buck yourself; sitting somewhere wondering what the fuck happened and what is going to happen next. I wrote this book for *you* man. You aren't alone in this experience. I—and a whole lot of people—have been where you are right now, at this second. Yes, you might feel alone and I talked about that, but there is an army of people who have gone before you and are with you now, in the flesh, and in the ether. I hope this book, the website that goes with it, and all the good shit that comes from both lifts you up, makes you laugh, gives you hope, some ideas, inspiration, strength or at least brightens your day a bit. I am with you, brother. I am with you with all my fucking heart. *Believe* that.

Maybe you are a mother or a father or a sister or a brother trying to figure out what the hell to do. If you have made it this far, you now have a clue as to what worked for me, but just take deep breaths, and keep going, keep loving, keep communication open (with yourself and your loved ones) and realize that you aren't alone either. Find the help you need, allow yourself some grace and be kind to yourself. Use all the love you have on your loved one and on yourself. Be love. Be fierce. Believe. I wrote this book for you too, to honor my own friends and family and to honor you and the heart you are no doubt showing, if you are where I think you are. I am with *you* too.

Maybe you are a friend or a partner reading this book, trying to understand the tough, scary, overwhelming situation you and your loved one may be in. Maybe you thought this would help, give you insights and some tools. I hope it did that and made you laugh and feel less alone, too. I wrote this for you. I wrote this for that purpose. I am with *you* too.

All of you were with me writing this book. The mere thought of you spurred my tired ass out of bed at five in the morning to write for a couple of hours before work, and kept me going till way past bedtime after work. The thought of all of you reading and enjoying this book made working when I was burnt out from writing all night that much easier. It made my day job suck less, and it gave me the will to do it all over again the next day.

When I got really tired or didn't feel like writing, I looked up at a picture my mom took of me when I came home after having the psychotic break at work and the insanity began. It is a ridiculous picture that my girlfriend framed for me and put in my writing nook. The picture is one of me holding a huge sunflower in my parent's backyard.

My mom took the picture. I am smiling a fake smile and my eyes look like two piss holes in a snow bank. I remember thinking how I wanted to just be gone. I wanted to just end myself somehow. Every time I looked at that picture, I got fired up to write, to finish this fucking thing. I wanted to finish it for that messed up, terrified kid in that ridiculous picture who doesn't have a clue as to how *bad* things are going to get.

I also knew that this book was a way to say goodbye to the chaos of the past and to let it rest. I knew if I wrote this book, passed on what I knew and put it out into the world, I would find that last bit of peace that I have been searching for.

I can honestly say that I have done that to a certain degree; I do feel like I have found a certain kind of peace in knowing that I have passed on what I experienced including things that worked for me as well as some things that didn't. Don't get me wrong, I'm still a crazy mother-fucker trying to find his way like the rest of you bastards, but there is peace there too, knowing this book, my heart and soul, is out there for people to embrace, reject or stomp on. Either way, I am happy with that. I am glad I did it. I will not go to my grave wondering if I should have done this. No sir! For that I am grateful. I hope one day you can feel a sense of peace too, if you don't already.

Get your ass to the website; join the tribe of lovers and lunatics who will make thebadtimesbible.com the best website in the world. I want to hear from you. I want to read about you and how you did the "impossible." I want to be inspired by you and I want you to inspire others. I want to learn even more about life and kicking ass from the stories you and others will tell me. I want to hear from your friends, your family and all those people that love you. I want them to tell me stories about the crazy shit you did during your own nightmare/amazing journey. I want to sit and cry from laughter and tears reading your stories and watching the videos you make.

Let's honor our loved ones, our lives, and ourselves.

Let's tell our stories and the stories of those passed on so we can all live-forever.

Let's build an army of those who have been there and let's raise our voices and our torches to light the path for those on their way towards where we now stand with open arms and hearts alike. Oh yes, the book was only the beginning.

Only the beginning my friends...!

In writing this book I honor my past, my family and my friends. This is certain. But again, in closing, I do this to honor you, the person in crisis, the one in the trenches, the one doing the work. I honor you and I scream for you, hoping you hear my voice in the dark, urging you forward, waving my torch like the fucking lunatic that I am, dancing around the fire and keeping your place for you.

I wish for you my friend, strength at all times, in mind, body and spirit.

Speaking of minds, may yours be clear to guide you when the situation is murky. I hope you have more love in your heart than fear, and more compassion in your soul than resentment. I hope that we do get to meet and I hear your tale, and that we laugh like the madmen we both can't deny being.

Do your best.
Really, *do your fucking best.*

This is your time to give birth to yourself, as sick as that image is; I *know* you know what I mean. Be a champion of spirit and surprise yourself with what you didn't even know you were capable of.

I believe in life with all my heart.
I believe in love with all my heart.
I believe in what I have written here in this book for you.
But if you need to remember one statement and one statement only,

Be present. Believe in yourself and listen to your heart, live with courage and compassion and the rest will take care of itself.

Oh yeah, and my dad wants you to remember, *"You can't get em pregnant if it's just spit."*

Now you got what you need. The fire awaits my friend. I'll see you there.

Afterword and Acknowledgements.

This book has been a gift monster holding a key to a prison that I built almost 20 years ago.

I have toyed with and have been tormented by, the idea of writing a book for many years now, and it wasn't until I was once again thrown into crisis a few years ago, that I actually got started writing with the intent to really *do this*.

You see I got myself into a situation that didn't exactly go my way. I tried my hand in a business venture that destroyed me financially and threw me into *another* type of deep, dark, hole.

After this particular event took place, not having a place of my own anymore I put my possessions into storage, stayed at my folks for a bit (in my nephews room, on a tiny bed surrounded by stuffed animals and toys which was quite pleasant actually,) and then was kindly offered a place to live by my sister and her husband. It was the computer room in their basement and I was happy to have it.

In my trusty old Subaru was a hockey bag filled with some clothes, my Jiu-Jitsu gi and some books. I also had an old laptop that a former girlfriend gave me. (Thank you Melina.) One day, feeling extremely frustrated, angry and freaked out by my situation, I went for a drive to the nearby train station. I used to like to journal there, watching people and watching the trains. Yes, by now you know I am a weirdo.

Behind the station was an industrial area with some buildings. One evening, I decided to go into that area and poke around. I drove up to a building and discovered there was an outdoor plug. I pulled ol' Subey up to it and plugged in the laptop. As I waited for the old girl to come to life, I closed my eyes and asked aloud:

"Well universe, I'm in the shit again. What do I do now?"

As clear as day I heard a response in my head that said:

"You have to write the Bad Times Bible."

So, without thinking I opened a word document and wrote the title at the top of the page.

And then I started writing.

Putting my story down felt scary and liberating at the same time. It was embarrassing and humiliating but I kept at it. I never had writers block as each writing session was a blur of insights, memories and revisions of old journals and tiny note pads I had kept for all these years. Something inside me had a lot to say, and I really felt like I was just there to move my three typing fingers as fast as I could and *get out of my own way*. There were times when *hours* would pass in what felt like 15 minutes. There were chapters that felt like something else wrote *through* me. For example, Chapter 22, A Magnificent Departure was written in one sitting and I don't remember writing most of it. It was a complete blur and an amazing experience. It was exhilarating and exhausting.

I reached out to an author whose work I really enjoyed in John C. Parkin. My *supremely* tolerant and understanding girlfriend Terri found John's first book, *"F**k It, the Ultimate Spiritual Way"* and bought it for me simply saying,

"You need to read this."

I owe her a debt of gratitude for being the link to John and for kicking my ass when I got scared of doing this. Terri was a sounding board on this thing and a solid partner throughout, leaving me alone when I "had the headphones on." Terri also blew me away with the grace she exhibited when she lost her own father to cancer just before the printing and release of this book. I was humbled by her strength and honored to have been part of that experience. Thank you mama for being awesome. Especially when I suck. I love you.

After reading John's book I sent him the first few chapters of *my* book, hoping for him to let me pick his brain. John liked where I was going and gave me his full support, telling me to finish the first draft and get back to him. John believed in what I was doing and had faith in me. Having his support was then and is now, reassuring and comforting. I felt that someone "got" what I was doing. *That* felt fantastic. It was another amazing green light experience for me. Thank you John for being an awesome mentor and an honest sounding board. Your involvement with this book was huge to me. I am grateful.

You sir, are the *cat's ass*.

Three drafts later I was ready to go and I wondered what to do next. I sent off some queries to agents and heard nothing back from any of them. I didn't expect to anyway, as I am a nobody with no real platform to speak of, just some freak writing a book. My guts (and John) were telling me to self publish and do it my own way the whole time. So I listened to my guts (and John) and here we are.

I never set out to be a writer and I don't consider myself a very good one. I only set out to tell a tale and put it out there for the benefit of others and to make that internal voice stop nagging me.

I found I really enjoy writing and will continue to do so but man alive, do I have *a lot* to learn.

I've been telling stories my whole life through music, art and just plain bullshitting with people. I love stories, in all shapes and sizes. That's all a life is anyway, just a bunch of stories wrapped up in meat. When the meat is gone, *we* get to keep the stories.

I can still remember being that crazed, terrified, 21 year old kid looking in libraries and bookstores for books that could keep me company and help explain what was happening to me without much luck. It makes me happy that I am putting my experience out there for others to either gain from, or laugh at. Either way, I am comforted by the thought of this book reaching out into the world and helping people. I can also see that 21-year-old version of me reading this and smiling. He approves and that makes me happy. He tells me to get my ass in shape and be more creative, but he approves.

Writing this book has been an incredibly powerful experience. In a way, it has challenged me to once again, look at all aspects of my life and life in general under intense scrutiny.

This book has made me see how far I have come, how far I have to go and how grateful I am for the people I get to share my life with. That being said there have been so many people who have helped me in my life that I would need another book just to thank them all.

To keep it simple, and to avoid naming someone who doesn't wish to be included in this mess of a book, (save for immediate family and those who were a crucial part of the experiences I speak of in this book of course) I will say this:

Thank you to Shannon Ross and Michele Castonguay for your editing skills. I know I either re wrote or ignored a lot of your advice but I am writing this here to not only show my gratitude for your hard work, but to also let *everyone* know that any mistakes in this book are MINE!

Thank you to Ben Dionne at GoFer Productions for all your help with all things video, and web related. You are a talented man with a beautiful soul that I am honored to work with and call a friend. Thank you for your hard work. This is just the beginning. Thank you Andrew (Drew) Grant for the brainstorming and for being the first "Tommy" ever!

Thank you to Dave Draves at Little Bullhorn for doing the audio book and for your patience. You sir, are a good friggin egg. But you know we need to do it again right?

Thank you Jeff Larose for your tech help on the final cover and twisted sense of humor. Thank you to Scott Doubt for your amazing Graphic design skills. You are a Jedi and a *great* dude.

Thank you to my friends who have *always* been there for me whenever I blow through the guardrails of life, and who remind me who I am when I forget, *and* who *definitely* let me know who I am *not* when I get outta line. Your love and support is a precious gift to me. That's right, I said *precious*. You know who you are. I love you guys.

Thank you to my sister Tori and her husband Mick, who have always been there in so many ways it just makes me feel embarrassed. You guys are amazing and I love you both very much. Finn is a lucky little dude to have you both as parents, and I am blessed to have him as my nephew. He is the best of us all.

A big thanks goes out to Bo for dragging me to certain clubs during treatment for "inspiration" and for keeping things light when shit was heavy. Powerful thanks to Cousin (Chris) for being a rock since we were kids and for being a *constant* source of support and encouragement regardless of the crazy shit I get myself into.

A huge thanks goes out to the hardest working S.O.B. the Almighty ever put breath into; Ernie M, CEO of the *mighty* Trees Company (Ottawa's *finest* Tree Service). Even though I am an absentee friend, (are you happy now Julie?) thank you for a lifetime of laughter and inappropriate, well, *everything*. Big thanks to Stephanie D. S. for making me laugh when I felt broken, even if it was (sometimes) at your broken English. You have a heart of gold. Thank you for being there. You guys have all been there forever and I love you all very much.

Thank you to the Loudlove crew for years of hard work and sacrifice and to those amazing Loudlovers who supported us in our run for glory. Hans, Emi, Dan, Sean, Switzer and Mike T. You are beautiful bastards. Thank you. I have nothing but love for you all.

A heartfelt thanks goes out to Scott Shaw for coming through when I was in trouble, and for getting me off of the garbage trucks. Thank you Tim Barton simply for being you. Okay, Tony M you too, you handsome devil. Thank you David Lochhead, Charlie Landreville and Scott Clarke. You know why... I am gonna get there so help me universe.

Thank you to OAMA for being a sacred place of salvation and to all my training partners who keep me humble and grounded. God bless BJJ, one of the greatest teachers I ever had.

Thank you to every doctor, (especially Dr. Cross, a fine, fine man.) every nurse, volunteer, stranger and health care provider who helped me through all my medical adventures.

Thank you to those fine people who reached out to me when I got smashed by a tree and invested in me in many ways. You are a part of this. Thank you. I won't forget what you did or let you down.

Supremely heartfelt thanks go out to the invisible forces that I don't yet understand but know are at work to keep me on track and moving forward. Your mystery keeps things interesting to say the least. Thank you.

To all of those souls I have known and loved who are now dancing in the ether, thank you for your gifts of love, guidance and friendship while you were here rocking the lower vibration party. I look forward to you all showing me around when I join the greatest show *off* earth.

Finally, to my parents, Pat and Trudy, who I am sure, are *horrified* and embarrassed by this book. (I had to do this and you will get over it.)

You are my heroes. You have never given up on me no matter what chaos I bring into your lives. I love you both with all my heart. Thank you for being the incredible, hilarious, insane and loving people you are. I know how rare it is in this world to *still* have both of your parents alive *and* together and believe me when I say that I don't take your efforts or examples of how to live lightly. Thank you for setting the bar so high and for everything you have ever done for me. Most of all, thank you for the gift of my life.

I am starting to *get it* now.